A Space Age Interpretation of the Bible

Celestial Heirs

Lee Gladden, Ph.D. • Vivianne Cervantes Gladden, Ph.D.

Archeolinguistic discovery of the hidden Bible
Vivianne Cervantes Gladden, Ph.D.• Lee Gladden, Ph.D.

Certificate of Registration

This Certificate issued under the seal of the Copyright
Office in accordance with title 17, *United States Code*,
attests that registration has been made for the work
identified below. The information on this certificate has
been made a part of the Copyright Office records.

Kayn Teyle Claggett

Acting United States Register of Copyrights and Director

Registration Number

TXu 2-043-115

Effective Date of Registration:
March 24, 2017

Title

Title of Work: Celestial Heirs
A Space Age Interpretation of the Bible

Completion/Publication

Year of Completion: 2017

Author

• **Author:** Vivianne Cervantes Gladden
Author Created: text
Work made for hire: No
Citizen of: United States
Year Born: 1927

• **Author:** Lee Gladden
Author Created: text
Work made for hire: No
Citizen of: United States
Year Born: 1922

Copyright Claimant

Copyright Claimant: Vivianne Cervantes Gladden

Copyright Claimant: Lee Gladden

Certification

Name: Lee and Vivianne Cervantes Gladden
Date: March 24, 2017

KDP ASIN-BO71HGB1KG

DEDICATION

<u>To Our Heirs</u>

Mark
Sue
Adoptive Daughter Friederike
and
Goddaughter, Paula

in the hope they and their heirs,
our grandchildren and great
grandchildren, as well as their
contemporaries, will inherit a
better world.

ACKNOWLEDGEMENTS

Our sincerest gratitude goes to our many colleagues, librarians and friends in the clergy and scientific establishment. They gave generously of their time in reading part or all of the manuscript or assisted in research involved in its preparation. Their suggestions, criticisms, and corrections have been of inestimable value. In particular we wish to thank faculty colleagues Keith Bailor, Howard Burton, Robert Dixon and Charles Jackson of Riverside City College for assistance in the areas of history, astronomy, anthropology and comparative literature.

Special thanks also goes to another colleague Robert Kroger who made the time travel calculations in the appendix. Valuable encouragement and criticism were also given by William R. Parker, Professor Emeritus at Redlands University, Redlands, CA and senior Pastor of the Community Church by the Bay of Newport, CA; Elder Nathaniel Banks, Regional Conference Director for Seventh Day Adventist churches, Hubert Page. Adjunct Professor and former chaplain for the U.S. Airforce; and Bernard Zeiger, former Rabbi of Temple Beth El, Riverside, CA. Criticism and scientific data were generously provided by Raymond Gladden, Project Engineer, Space Shuttle Program, Rockwell International. Edgar Mitchell, U.S. Astronaut and founder of the Institute for Noetic Science, the staffs of Griffith, Hale, and Palomar observatories, and the department of Astronomy at the California Institute of Technology.

A special debt of gratitude goes to the unfailing help of the staffs of the Libraries of the Claremont School of Theology at Claremont, CA, the Bodleian Library at Oxford University, the Del Webb Library at Loma Linda University, Loma Linda, CA, the UCLA library at Los Angeles, CA and the help, beyond the call of duty, of the staff of the public library of Banning, California, Danny Reed, Fernando Morales, and Maxine Vrooman.

Further, our most special thanks goes to our friend of more than half a century, Maria Martone, professional reader for literary agents, and to Ingo Preminger, literary agent and film producer, who aided in securing agency representation; our literary agent, Aaron Priest, and our patient and persistent Rawson Wade editor, Sandi Gelles Cole, Paul Ziffren, attorney, and Hume Cronyn, actor/writer. In addition to these, we also wish to thank those who carried out the collecting of research data and preparing our manuscript for publishing, Florence Gardner, Terry Tinker, Celina Maduike, Melanie Cross, and Virginia Jones, Juan Lopez, all friends and professionals of long standing.

We are also indebted to Charlene Ledoux for our illustrations; Irwin Zucker, our publicist who secured many of our media interviews; and, though not directly involved in the research and publishing of Celestial Heirs, three other friends of long standing should be acknowledged for their advice and encouragement during its completion, Mia Crowley, Literary Editor, Dr. Ramona Stroman, and Ena Hartman, model, actress, and entrepreneur.

Most of all we are grateful to Casandra Greene, for the cover art and without whose skill and perseverance in preparing our final work for online publication this book would never have seen the light of day.

Finally a debt of family love and gratitude goes to our son and daughter, Mark and Sue, and their spouses, Judith and Darrell, and to our adoptive daughter, Friederike Zimmermann, for support and assistance in many phases of our four decade project; to our grandson, Eli, for marketing advice and to nephew, Harry Cartwright, for capturing the essence of our work in his creative websites.

TABLE OF CONTENTS

The Spirit itself beareth witness with our spirit that we are the children of God: and if children, then heirs; heirs of God . . ."

– Paul, Romans 8:16-17

CHAPTER I

Genesis

It was one of those enchanted afternoons in late autumn. The warm California sun drenched the dunes and long ribbon of beach. Scores of small sailing craft and yachts danced on the rippling waters of Newport Harbor.

We had driven down from Los Angeles for a business meeting and afterward decided to stay over. Later, in a motel while watching television, Vivianne picked up a "What's Happening in Newport", the weekly calendar of events. As she did her eye was attracted by a plainly bound book underneath. She laid the calendar aside and began to turn the pages of a Gideon Bible.

We had both been reared in conservative Christian homes. Later college training and professional careers had carried both of us far from the teachings of our childhoods. After wartime military service Lee had gone on to university followed by teaching and practice as a psychologist. Vivianne began with an early career in high fashion modeling and theater that took her from New York to Paris and back again to Broadway. She changed directions, on being awarded a scholarship, to return to college and fulfill her dream of a professional career in health science. This led to a staff position at a major Los Angeles hospital and private practice as a health counselor in Beverly Hills.

Unlike those among whom we had grown up our busy lives were not centered on Bible reading, family prayers and church attendance several times a week. Though we both recognized the contributions religious institutions have made to western civilization we regarded many of the beliefs on which they were founded as no longer relevant to the lives we were leading. Yet in spite of this, on special occasions, we sometimes visited our families' churches. When we did we still enjoyed the sense of communal fellowship, the pageantry of familiar rituals, the stirring music of grand old hymns and the occasional eloquence of preaching. For both of us, however, there was no going back.

The beliefs we had been taught as children – the reality of the supernatural, the creation of the universe and control over our destinies by a human-like , but all-knowing and all-powerful God, and the end of our present world in a second coming of Christ – all these we regarded as relics of a less enlightened past no longer believable or relevant to modern men and women holding a scientific worldview.

As Vivianne leafed through the pages of the Bible she suddenly spoke up. It had fallen open to the account in Genesis 3 which describes a tree of life in the midst of the Garden where God had created Adam and Eve. "Lee," she said, "how do you think the idea of a tree of life got started?" Not waiting for an answer she went on. "Could it have been something real? What if visitors from another world far more advanced than our own came to Earth before history began? Suppose they had discovered a way to extend life indefinitely? Could the tree of life be a symbol for some technology they had discovered that gave them conditional immortality?"

Put this way her answer to her own question had a certain plausibility. We had recently done sabbatical research at Cambridge University in England where Watson and Crick had received the Nobel Prize for deciphering the DNA helix code.

This intertwining double chain of sugar and phosphate molecules, in the center of all living cells, contains the blueprint for the development and repair of every living thing. In deciphering information contained in the code these scientists had found the key to understanding life itself and perhaps opening the door to extending it indefinitely.

In their laboratory they had constructed a wire and plastic model of the DNA helix. As we recalled it now we visualized its spiraling arms sprouting the twig-like projections of its chemical bases. It did, indeed, look like a tree. Could a more sophisticated version of this device be the "tree of life" referred to in the Genesis creation story? Did Celestials from another world place it, as Watson and Crick had at Cambridge, in a laboratory "garden" where they produced experimental life forms including the ancestor of modern humans? Could this be the real meaning of the strange creation account told in this ancient collection of writings?

As we considered the possibility it became clear to us that it might have a more general application. If the "tree of life" is actually a mythic reference to the DNA helix, then why couldn't other Space Age discoveries offer explanations for similar puzzles and mysteries found throughout the Bible?

In fact as we continued to discuss and explore passages far into the night we realized, before we finally fell asleep, that we might just have discovered the key to a whole new interpretative approach to the Scriptures, an approach we now think of as a Space Age interpretation of the Bible.

A NEW LOOK AT THE BIBLE

That out of town business meeting with its unexpected stayover launched us on a quest which has continued for almost half a century. It led us, in its early months, to a reexamination of the entire Bible in search of other puzzling passages that might be clarified if given a Space Age interpretation. This, in turn, required going to different versions of the Bible, as well as dictionaries and concordances, to examine the root meanings of the language they employed. In doing this we expected to find evidence either supporting or refuting a Space Age interpretation. This, however, raised further questions that took us to the more fundamental issues of textual criticism, problems of translation and hermeneutics, or scriptural interpretation.

With all this came the realization that we had taken on a task that would require not just months, but possibly years, for completion. In fact nothing less than a book could encompass all it required.

Vivianne's initial question as to whether extraterrestrials might have played a part in prehistoric events giving rise to the strange creation story recounted in Genesis 1 and 2 was only a starting point. If the extraterrestrial hypothesis could provide plausible explanations for other mysteries found throughout the Bible what consequences would this have for the whole body of traditional beliefs underlying Judaism and Christianity? Would it undermine those beliefs or make them more believable?

As soon as this question occurred to us, however, we realized the investigation we had begun in a wide variety of Bible versions and commentaries had already answered it. The answer is that the notion of an unchanging traditional body of beliefs is largely an illusion. From the time its earliest writers began their work down to the present day the Bible has undergone unending interpretation and reinterpretation of its fundamental teachings.

In the first nine centuries from about 800 BC to 100 AD when it was coming into existence its actual content changed and diversified. New "books" were added or ones in previous use excluded as religious leaders or church councils gave approval to what they regarded as authoritative "scripture".

In the centuries since most of what Jews and Christians regard as essential beliefs has been the subject of endless debate and, too often, even persecutions and religiously motivated warfare. "Is God one or three persons, or both? Was the historical Jesus human or divine, or both? Is salvation achieved by God's grace or human effort, or both? What is the proper role of the temple, or church, in promoting the religious life? How will the world end, and what is the ultimate destiny of the righteous and wicked? All of these questions have been endlessly argued through centuries and are still being argued today. This is why we have the ever growing variety of sects, denominations and movements that make up Judaism and Christianity.

During almost a millennium when the two testament Bible was coming into existence it was a work in progress. In the two millennia since the understanding of what it means has also been another "work in progress".

With the birth of modern science and the Age of Enlightenment which followed the Bible was reinterpreted by deists, such as Thomas Jefferson and Benjamin Franklin. They held that a clockwork universe was created by God who, having wound it up, then stepped aside and let it run according to mechanical laws as formulated by Isaac Newton. Agnostics and atheists, such as Thomas Paine and Voltaire, criticized the Bible as being a collection of folklore that was at best morally instructive and at worst conducive to injustice and immorality.

In recent times new interpretations have been made from the perspective of existential philosophy (Soren Kierkegaard), evolutionary theory (the Jesuit priest and world renowned paleontologist, Teilhard de Chardin), the depth psychologies of Sigmund Freud and Carl Jung, "process theology" as developed under the influence of the British philosopher/mathematician, Alfred North Whitehead, and, among Latin American "liberation theologians", even the historic/economic worldview of Karl Marx.

The coming of the 20th and 21st Centuries has brought about the most profound revolution in our understanding of the universe and our place in it. The formulation of Einstein's theory of relativity and the advent of quantum mechanics now require a new worldview.

Our review and reflection on this history of Bible interpretation brought us to the realization that what we were proposing to do now was neither new nor revolutionary. Rather it was simply a continuation of a process that has been going on since the earliest writers did their work.

We decided to call our continuation of this effort a "Space Age interpretation", because we saw it could resolve many long-standing conflicts between what science has taught us about the world and ourselves and older pre-scientific interpretations of the Bible that conflicted with it.

It was the scope of what we were about to undertake that led to our further decision that a division of labor would be helpful since we brought different backgrounds to the task. In our youth we both had been required to read, or had read to us, most of the Bible in daily family worship or in church attendance where Sunday or Sabbath school, followed by sermons on the Bible, were a regular weekly event.

This early training was followed, for Vivianne, by an undergraduate major in biblical studies when she changed careers and accepted a scholarship from one of her denominational colleges. Her decision, on entering graduate studies, to prepare for a professional career in health science still left elective options in religion, theology and music which eventually led to her ordination to the ministry by one of America's best known pastors, William R. Parker, co-author of the perennial best seller, Prayer Can Change Your Life..

Lee's background, on the other hand, took him, after military service, to the University of California where he completed a doctoral residency in philosophy and then changed career directions receiving state licensure and eventually a professorship in psychology. His studies, however, were not confined to behavioral sciences, since he completed further work in philosophy of science under David Hawkins, best known as official historian for the final phase of completion of the atom bomb at Los Alamos, New Mexico.

In view of our academic preparations we decided Vivianne would focus on etymology, exploring derivations and interrelationships of biblical words through their roots and cognates. Lee would direct his explorations to current scientific research and forecasts in the physical, biological and social sciences. We would then compare our findings looking for correlations or forecasts that would support a Space Age interpretation.

This strategy soon proved successful with Vivianne's discovery of semantic grids in her analysis of textual etymologies. We will deal with these more fully in the next chapter as they proved to be the key to archeolinguistics. In this process we discovered a new meaning of the Bible—a meaning that could not have been understood before the last half of the Twentieth Century. It is a meaning and a message for Space-Age men and women.

To our surprise, though the meaning is different from the one we were taught as children, the message is the same. We arrived at an outlook astonishingly close to the traditional teaching of our childhoods. Through our knowledge of where our own science is heading and careful study of the original Hebrew and Greek texts of the Bible we discovered that the age-old doctrines of orthodox Judeo-Christianity are consistent with a 21st Century scientific outlook. The evidence supporting this consistency is found in a hidden space story contained in the texts of the Bible which could not have been understood until the coming of our own Space Age.

The Bible is a record of the most important event in the history of humanity—the coming of the Celestials and their continuing role in human destiny! It is essentially a historical record which describes these events literally and truthfully. They were actually here, and we are their creation, or rather re-creation. They have monitored and guided our development and intend to return, in the near future, to colonize our planet. Some of us may live to see their return!

In the Bible they have imparted a plan according to which they wish us, their heirs, to live. Those who have done so, throughout the ages, will be re-created (or restored to life) upon their return. They and the righteous who are already alive at that time will receive the inheritance they have planned for us: full acceptance, as citizens, in a utopian civilization to be established here on Earth.

We have been astonished by what we have discovered upon careful examination of the Hebrew and Greek texts. In numerous books, in both testaments of the Bible, its writers drew on oral and written sources containing hidden information concerning a civilization far in advance of our own today.

Archeolinguistic analysis of passages in these books yields semantic grids that unambiguously point to many of our own modern technologies, or advanced forms of them, that are being predicted by technological forecasters and futurologists. Among these are nuclear propulsion and explosions, closed-circuit television, laser weapons, the artificial synthesis of life and uses of energy forms our most advanced scientists are only now beginning to suspect. More startling still is the result of investigations we have made into the fossil record, which, combined with clues given in the Scriptures, support the Bible's claims that we are the result of an experiment in genetic engineering. We are in fact, the most convincing proof they were here. We are what astrobiologists today are calling a "biosignature" of their stay here on Earth.

We are their re-creation and did not emerge by biological evolution alone. We contain the Celestials' imprint, or signature. As the Bible puts it we were "made in their image." And it is an unearthly image possessed by no other animal on this planet. Only within the last half-century have naturalists and anthropologists begun to appreciate just how unearthly that image is. In chapter VIII, "The Experimental Creation", we will examine this unearthly image more closely, the image that proves we are "Celestial heirs."

WHAT IS THE BIBLE?

The Bible is the world's all-time best selling book. Its ethical teachings are foundational to much of the western world's understanding of morality and law. Its stories and parables have provided themes for some of the world's greatest art, music, and literature. Men and women of genius have praised it as a principal source of influence and inspiration for their greatest achievements. Ordinary people have found in it enduring support and guidance in the trials and crises of life. A large part of humanity, over the last 3,000 years, has believed it to be divinely inspired. Yet it is an enigma. There is no book that can be held in ones hand or pointed to as "the Bible."

VERSIONS AND TRANSLATIONS

Instead we have many Bibles that differ from one another in important ways. Whole "books" found in some are missing in others. Sometimes passages making important points of doctrine in modern versions cannot be found in the early manuscripts from which they come. Clearly they have been added at some later date by copiests who mistook marginal notes of earlier copiests for part of the text, or by translators who altered or added text of their own to reinforce an interpretation or doctrine they preferred, justifying it as "conjectural emendation."

A well known example of this is the "Johannine comma" often used as a "proof text" for the doctrine of the Trinity (I John: 6,7). The passage on the "three witnesses in heaven" cannot be found in any of the earliest Greek manuscripts of I John, but only in the later Latin translations of these manuscripts. Scholars generally agree it is not the work of the original author.

Differing translations of the same passages in different versions have led to doctrinal disputes and even denominational divisions among believers. This is the reason, in part, why some Bible versions are known as "Protestant" and others as "Catholic."

Accounts of the same event by different writers in the same version sometimes disagree as to whom, how many, where and when the event took place. For example, in the first book of the Bible, Genesis, two accounts of a universal flood have been included one after the other.

They do not agree about the number and kind of animals Noah took with him into the Ark. The first says of "every living thing" God ordered Noah to bring "two of every sort" into the ark (Gen. 6:19). The second says the "Lord" ordered Noah to take "of every clean beast" . . . "by sevens the male and his female" and "of beasts that are not clean by two, the male and his female" (Gen. 7:2). The ancient editor who brought these two accounts together was evidently uncertain as to which was correct and simply included both leaving it up to the reader to decide.

Again, in the opening books of the New Testament, the four gospel writers, Matthew, Mark, Luke and John, do not agree in telling of the resurrection of Jesus. They differ on how many of his followers first came to his tomb on resurrection morning; how many angelic messengers they encountered; and where and to whom the risen Jesus first appeared. (Matt 28:1-9; Mark 16:1-9; Luke 23:55 and 24: 1-10; and John 20:11-17)

Even more important is the fact that different versions vary in their collection of "books" by the Bible's many writers. The Bible of Judaism, the Tanakh, is confined to what Christians call the "Old Testament", though it contains "books" not found in the Old Testament of many Christian versions. Some of these are included in Catholic versions and appeared in the original protestant King James version but were later dropped in its revisions.

The principal reason for these textual conflicts, and the differing collections of "books" is that "the Bible" is not a book in the usual sense of the word. That is, it was not composed at a particular time and place by an author, or co-authors, who worked together to tell a story or explain a particular field of knowledge or express ideas and feelings about life and the world we inhabit.

Rather it is a sort of ancient wikipedia of miscellaneous information accumulated over almost a thousand years, relating to experiences, beliefs and hopes that have arisen out of humanity's long search for answers to those ultimate questions. "Where do I come from?"; "Why am I here?"; and "Where am I going?"

Like the wikipedia of our present day internet the accounts and explanations given by its many authors are not always consistent with one another, nor is the information they contain always consistent with our present scientific understanding of ourselves and the world. Yet, in spite of this, the Bible surpasses all other books in its timeless and worldwide relevance to the human condition. This is why it has remained the world's best seller since its first printing and continues to hold its position as a major source of support and guidance for a large part of humanity.

It also explains why it has been translated into more that a thousand languages and dialects and why its English translations alone, partial and complete, now number more than a hundred. The universality of its insights; its answers to ultimate questions of human existence, and its enduring record of inspiring much of humanity's greatest civilizational achievements have given it an authority and sanctity that have endured for almost three thousand years.

Few have ever better grasped and explained the Bible's unique place among the great literary and spiritual treasures of the human race than Sir James G. Frazer, eminent scholar of religions and author of the Golden Bough, when he wrote: "The Bible . . .unrolls a vast panorama in which the ages of the world move before us in a long trail of solemn images . . . Against this gorgeous background, this ever shifting scenery, now bright with the hues of heaven, now lurid with the glare of hell, we see mankind strutting and playing their little part on the stage of history . . . The volume must be held sacred by all those who reverence the high aspirations to which it gives utterance. The reading of it breaks into the dull round of common life like a shaft of sunlight on a cloudy day, or a strain of music heard on a mean street."

The qualities he praises are found in the many versions and translations that exist today, yet no one of them has ever achieved universal acceptance as the one true and authentic version of what its original authors wrote. The reason for this is easy to explain. The original manuscripts have all disappeared. Not even a fragment of any manuscript from the hands of an original author is known to exist today. There is no way, then, that passages in the multitude of versions that do exist can be compared with their originals to determine whether or not they preserve and communicate what the original authors set down.

Nevertheless, just as the Bible's many versions retain its universal relevance and its power to guide and inspire, so they also retain linguistic elements handed down from our first ancestors who were witnesses to the coming of the Celestials. These elements, when brought together, conceal a hidden space story. It is this story and their plan for Earth's colonization that is the hidden Bible. Our problem in recovering this lost story was similar to that faced by archeologists. They discover evidence of lost civilizations and recover information about them. So we "excavated" ancient texts for lost meanings and unearthed a very different civilization that came to Earth in an even more remote past. It was the similarities between our use of this newly discovered linguistic tool and the use archeologists make of their tools that led us to call it "archeolinguistics."

The features of this hidden Bible can be found throughout the many Bible versions that exist submerged in roots and cognates of the languages they employ. These linguistic elements are comparable to the architectural ruins and artifact fragments uncovered by archeologists. Archeologists examine relationships and placement of their finds in layers of debris to recover knowledge about forgotten people and places. In the same way we examined linguistic elements, buried in ancient texts, to recover knowledge about an even older civilization, not lost, but beyond our experience and ability to understand until the arrival of our own Space Age.

Unlike the debris covering lost civilizations, the hidden Bible was not buried by natural disasters, military conquests or shifting sands. Instead, it has been buried by accumulated copying errors, doctrinally biased translations and, most of all, layers of interpretation imposed on the Bible's texts by religious leaders and theologians as they tried to make them more meaningful and relevant to their contemporaries.

These layers of interpretation have become so much a part of our modern understanding of the Bible that for many they carry the authority and sanctity of the scriptures, themselves. To many they are regarded as final truth about what the Bible means.

Yet reviewing them historically it is clear they have not led to a universally accepted body of beliefs nor have they resulted in a unified body of believers. On the contrary, earlier interpretations do not disappear as later ones, often conflicting with them, emerge. Rather, each new layer generates new and sometimes conflicting doctrines and creeds; creating new sects and denominations.

And, in the midst of this increasing diversity, each sect and denomination tends to cling to the belief that they and their founder alone are in possession of "the truth" about the Bible's meaning. With this belief goes the conviction that others are in error to the extent they disagree with them. Yet the very diversity of interpretations and an inability to agree about what is essential clearly shows their claims to having final truth are premature.

Final truth in any realm of knowledge would be a whole that is consistent with itself and all that is known in other fields of knowledge. The history of Bible interpretation, with its unending disagreements and disputes, clearly shows there is further truth yet to be discovered.

When it comes to the question of what that truth might be the answer can only come from the Bible, itself. The problem with this is that after almost three thousand years of scholarly interpretation by some of the best minds the human race has produced no final and unifying truth has emerged to unite all believers. This is because it is only to be found in the remarkable space story contained in the hidden Bible. That story will be told in the chapters which follow. Since elements of it can be found throughout the many Bible versions we will close this chapter with some comments on our reason for choosing the King James Version as our source for scriptural quotations and interpretations. As the most commonly owned and used of all English Bibles, the King James Version, with its revisions, is the one readers are most likely to consult if they wish to check our quotations.

Further, since it is over four hundred years old and, with its revisions, is still widely used it has been the object of some of the most prolonged and intensive study in the history of Bible scholarship. Because of this some of the best concordances of the Bible are based on it and can be used to check translations of Hebrew and Greek words we cite as evidence of the hidden Bible.

Finally, and perhaps most important, the requirements under which the King James translators worked make it a particularly rich hunting ground for meanings that have gone unrecognized or been deliberately set aside in more recent translations.

Historically translators working with the oldest texts available have frequently encountered passages that are unclear and can be interpreted in several ways. There is a tendency in choosing among them, to select the one that is most readily expressed in the new language and will resonate with modern readers.

Unfortunately the fact that a possible interpretation can be readily expressed in contemporary idiom and lends itself to some colorful figure of speech that will resonate with readers is no assurance it is what the original authors, two or three thousand years ago, had in mind. This kind of guesswork is just another form of "conjectural emendation" and may actually take the reader further from the original author's meaning rather than clarifying it.

An even greater difficulty exists when translators, working with passages that are ambiguous, choose the interpretation that best agrees with their own doctrinal persuasion. They do this reasoning that since they are in possession of "the truth" concerning the Bible their choice must be what the original authors had in mind too.

The problem with this is that there are often other versions whose translators have given a different interpretation using exactly the same argument for their choice. This is the reason we have Protestant and Catholic Bibles, Bibles that are preferred by religious conservatives and others by religious liberals and even versions that are created for, and used mainly by, some particular denomination.

The King James translators on the other hand, were chosen to achieve exactly the opposite result. Numbering more than half a hundred they were deliberately selected to represent diversity of religious belief including high Anglican churchmen, Oxford and Cambridge scholars in the Bible's ancient languages and Puritan reformers. Then they were instructed, when they disagreed concerning interpretation of texts, to find wordings that would express whatever truth they found in their various points of view as an inclusive whole.

Rather than taking sides on controversial issues and excluding other possibilities they were urged to make their version as richly meaningful and open to all interpretive options as possible. It is this characteristic that gives the Authorized Version its superiority over all earlier English translations, and many modern ones as well, making it an unusually rich source for hidden meanings or ones that have gone unrecognized in the past.

In his magisterial book on the making of the King James Version, God's Secretaries, the historian Adam Nicolson, identifies this characteristic as the central strategy of the whole translation calling it an "irenicon" in dealing with disputes concerning Bible interpretation.

The Oxford English Dictionary defines an "irenicon" as a proposal designed to promote peace, especially in doctrinal disputes among churches. It was the hope of James I, ruler of Scotland, on succeeding to the English throne after the death of Elizabeth I, that he could bring peace to his religiously divided kingdom.

For more than a century England had been ravaged by bitter disputes, persecutions, exiles and even martyrdoms arising out of religious disagreements and striving for political control of worship. America's Puritan forefathers sought refuge and religious freedom from this strife in coming to its shores. King James was determined to make his new English Bible inclusive enough, in its interpretative possibilities, to gain general acceptance among his divided subjects bringing with it, more tolerance and peace as well as greater support for his reign.

In fact his new Bible did much more than this. It not only found wide acceptance in the England of his time but has retained its popularity and use among a greater diversity of denominations than any other version down to the present day.

In addition to its interpretive openness it has yet another quality that has been equally important in explaining its staying power and popularity not only among believers, but with an enduring readership having no religious belief. This quality is its extraordinary literary merit. Adam Nicolson goes so far as to assert it is the greatest work of prose in the English language. He is by no means alone in this judgment. Wherever the English language is spoken many of its greatest masters have praised the KJV, as it is known, for its literary splendor and its influence on their own work)

This is not to deny of course, that more recent versions have their own merits and are sometimes preferred for other reasons. Recent discoveries of older manuscripts, not available to the King James translators, have settled some disputes they left open and led to corrections of translation errors found in the KJV. More recent translations are also preferred by some, because today's readers find them easier to understand. This is because language changes over time and some words and forms of speech used throughout the KJV are no longer in common use today. Others are still in use but have changed meaning over the centuries. Revisions of the KJV have corrected some of these problems but others still remain. Nevertheless for the purpose of unearthing the Bibles' long hidden space story, we have found the King James Version to be unrivaled by any more recent translation.

For the same reasons we have chosen the Strong's Exhaustive Concordance of the Bible as our primary source for translations of Greek and Hebrew words since it is based on the King James version. Like the King James Version itself it was the result of years of labor by over a hundred scholars and seminarians in the late 19th Century and has undergone revisions in the present century. As with the King James Version its revisions have corrected errors in the original KJV's translators work. It remains the most widely used concordance based on the King James Version to the present day.)

No other masterpiece of English literature has had so great an influence on much of the prose and poetic work which has followed; no other has given so many words and figures of speech to our written and spoken communications. No other has provided other writers, including Nobel laureates, with titles for their own masterpieces. No other has given so many memorable quotations to statesman and orators for use in their speeches of commemoration, reproof and persuasion.)

For the same reason we have chosen some of its best known gems as headings for our chapters. In the next chapter that follows we will now take up the archeolinguistic method which has enabled us to recover this concealed story.

Unto you is given to know the mysteries of the Kingdom of God.

– Luke 8:10

CHAPTER II

Archeolinguistics

The idea that the universe is teeming with life and may contain alien civilizations inconceivably more advanced than our own is not a new one. It can be found in the writings of ancient Greek philosophers as well as the screen fantasies of Star Wars.

Astronomers believe there are a hundred billion stars in our own Milky Way galaxy and two hundred billion, or more, galaxies in the observable universe. Recent data obtained from the Kepler space telescope support their belief that planetary systems are commonplace among these, and many have worlds that could be hospitable to life as we know it. The late NASA astronomer, Carl Sagan, suggested at least a million of these in our own galaxy could be home to advanced civilizations. If the latter supposition is true the idea that at least one of these might have visited Earth in some remote time, before history began, is not improbable. And, if the visit occurred after homo sapiens appeared, it is likely some evidence of that visit would be retained in language usage or legends handed down through oral traditions. It is even plausible that such evidence might have become incorporated into ancient texts which have survived as folklore or sacred writings.

It is noteworthy that legends and sacred writings of a number of ancient peoples contain references to beings with god-like powers who came from the sky and instructed and aided humanity. This, in itself, does not constitute proof. Such universal themes could merely indicate, as Freud supposed, that adult humans have a need to project their infantile parent fixations onto the cosmic scene.

On the other hand if such ancient texts were found, by some hitherto unknown method, to contain technical information peculiar to our current understanding of the world this would be evidence of an entirely different and more conclusive sort. Our discovery and use of archeolinguistics on the texts of the Bible has uncovered such evidence.

A NEW APPROACH TO INTERPRETATION

Archeolinguistics employs techniques of analysis similar to those recently used with great success in the decipherment of unknown languages and earlier, during World War II, in the field of code breaking. Like the archeologist, who excavates relics of a remote past from more recent overlays of debris, archeolinguistics recovers ancient, lost information from texts of more recent composition.

The notion that a written text may contain levels, or strata, of meaning, which can be revealed only by a process of interpretation, is common to many disciplines. It is inherent in the practice of cryptography where a coded message is intentionally constructed to conceal another hidden communication. It is also basic to the language of myth and poetry where the surface meaning of words often masks a metaphoric significance which shines through when we look beyond its literal meaning.

Ancient sacred texts, such as those of the Bible, often contain both kinds of levels. Hidden messages are encoded that only the initiated may recognize, and spiritual truth, or mystical insights, are frequently communicated by the language of metaphor and parable.

Recently scholars have discovered yet another kind of level, or stratum, in sacred texts. By a kind of textual criticism, arising principally from New Testament studies, scholars have been able to separate original versions of a text, or even the oral traditions on which it is based, from later elements created by retelling, copying and editorial revision.

The phenomenon which makes this textual surgery possible is anomaly-anachronisms in a text that point to the influence of customs and modes of thought belonging to another age than that in which it was composed. For example, if a text whose authorship is certain employs place names which arose only after the author's death this is clear evidence of editorial tampering. In the same way if authors express attitudes and opinions, or use titles and forms of address, which only came into being after they lived this is proof that later hands modified their work.

By combining minute historical scholarship with textual detective work the critic is often able to distinguish and date numerous strata of oral and written information which have been combined in an apparently seamless whole. Not infrequently the critic is even able to characterize or name those who have produced these alterations in a text. Archeolinguistics, like textual criticism, uses the tool of anomaly. Its focus, however, is not primarily on phrases, passages and glosses which concern the literary critic.

Anachronisms may exist not only in modes of expression but in the very ideas expressed. If, for example, we found a Roman text in which the writer used the Latin of his time to express the idea of atomic fission we would have an anachronism of the first order. It would not, however, be an anachronism of the sort etymologists study. Traditionally, etymologists have looked backward in time. Their concern is to find the origin of words and to trace their descent, or ancestry. The idea that words might point to the future is contrary to the whole thrust of etymology.

Yet there is one circumstance, and only one, where words might do so. This would be where the words are not descendants of ancestral words in the language in which they occur. If, for example, a time traveler from the Twenty First Century could meet and talk with our Roman writer about the discovery of nuclear energy, it might then be possible that the phrase "atomic fission" would appear in his writings. Or, again, let us suppose the traveler's time machine would land near a legion of Roman soldiers who surround it and begin trying to force an entrance with their swords.

Our traveler, fearful of capture and injury, would then frighten them off by firing a nuclear missile into the air. It would explode with a blinding flash, and the soldiers would flee. Notice that no conversation with the Roman soldiers has taken place so that linguistic intrusions cannot have occurred. Yet it would be remarkable if some mention of the event, and of the phenomenon of nuclear fission, did not occur in the histories of the period. Of course the description of the explosion would then not employ the term "nuclear fission". But the idea would be there; described in whatever contemporary Latin was available for the writer's purpose. In fact, certain Latin words might even be modified, or new Latin invented, to explain the blinding flash and the strange mushroom cloud which formed in the sky.

If this course of events took place it is likely that at some later date a classical scholar, a medieval monk perhaps, would be reading the manuscripts and would be struck by the anomalous use of Latin. He would puzzle over the meanings and perhaps conclude they chronicled a special revelation of God in Roman times. He might even construct elaborate interpretive schemes to explain the religious symbolism of this "vision". These would show how the time machine represents the throne of God which encompasses his infinite power. The missile might be seen as suggestive of his grace which bursts, unsought, on our lives. The blinding light could be explained as a symbol of the power of revelation which illuminates our understanding. The mushroom cloud would be seen as a portent of the cross whose followers would soon spread across the Empire and whose church would, in time, assume its temporal power.

Or again our scholar might be one of those Nineteenth Century specialists known as "higher critics". In that case he would probably dismiss the whole account as a literary invention. He might even go on to show it was invented to further some Roman claim to religious or political superiority. If he were trained in Twentieth Century existential theology he might insist that the account was simply a mythic product of the folk process. He would proceed to "demythologize" it by claiming some ordinary event had been distorted in oral tradition or later written legends.

We can imagine his publishing a learned article in some journal of classical studies which would make these distortions clear. The time machine would be reduced to a simple Germanic war cart which, unlike Roman chariots, was covered for protection against the inclement weather beyond the Rhine. The time traveler would be proved to be a heroic distortion of the outlandishly garbed and painted barbarians. Their glorification into a god-like being from the sky would be due to the Roman's need to see their legions as overcoming worthy opponents. The missile was actually launched by the legionnaires, not their enemy, and was merely an ignited bundle thrown from a siege catapult.

So our enlightened critic would dispose of this mythic monument to the ignorance and superstition of a bygone age. Of course, he would probably caution us not to discard it altogether in spite of its mythic origins. We should not throw the baby out with the bathwater for myths often conceal profound truths. Though there never was a real time machine, or traveler, or missile, this simple story contains truths that can elevate us all. It is only necessary to "demythologize" it to make this kernel of truth available to the modern reader. By removing its mythic envelope we can see that it is a tribute to the indomitableness of the human spirit. It teaches us we can overcome seemingly insuperable obstacles. As such it can be a source of consolation and inspiration to us all and may save us from hopelessness and despair.

The remarkable thing about all these explanations and interpretations is that not one of them would give any consideration to taking the account at face value. Because these scholars and critics would have lived before time travel was recognized as a possibility, entailed in Einstein's theory of relativity, it would remain an unimagined possibility.

WHY A NEW INTERPRETATION IS NEEDED

There is of course, no Roman text of the sort we have described. The assumptions we have made about a time machine landing and exploding a nuclear missile in antiquity are just that - hypothetical assumptions. Yet there is a set of ancient texts which do contain anomalies of language and descriptions similar to those we have been considering. They date from Roman and earlier times and contain many references to events similar to those we have been supposing. These include god-like beings descending from the sky in strange craft and holocausts of fire and smoke which fill the heavens and destroy whole populations. In addition there are innumerable references to processes and discoveries which sound like predictions by our own futurologists.

These include the creation of life from non-living materials; the halting of aging and maintenance of immortality, "likenesses of men" constructed of metal-like substances, that can walk, talk and perform labor and accounts of curing diseases with unknown energies. There are also references to instances of time dilatation in which intervals that seem to be a thousand years to one person may be experienced as a day by another.

Like the hypothetical scholars and critics of our imaginary Roman text we, too, have been struck by the linguistic anomalies in the texts called the Bible. Unlike those scholars and critics we have discovered a method of analysis which strongly supports the idea that time travelers do exist and are alive and well in our future. They did not go there in a time machine. Rather they arrived there because the universe, itself, is a cosmic time machine.

In its vast expanse there are innumerable worlds that orbit suns millions, or billions, of years older than our own. And because life arose on these worlds millions or billions of years before it did here their inhabitants have already travelled through vast stretches of time we have yet to experience. And in travelling these vast stretches they have long ago arrived at stages, in their development and civilization, which still lie far in our own future.

Like our hypothetical traveler they came to our world from a distant future which will one day be our own. In coming they intruded into the thought and language of our most remote ancestors. Accounts of their incredible accomplishments have been handed down in human oral traditions. Many of these have become incorporated into the most ancient texts of early civilizations- texts revered and preserved as sacred.

The Bible is such a set of texts. Over recent centuries its accounts of that ancient encounter with god-like aliens have been treated much as our hypothetical scholar treated our fictional nuclear encounter and have been given similar explanations.

Like that scholar it has not occurred to other Bible scholars of recent centuries that the "legends" and "myths" of scripture may be literal, space-time events. It has not occurred to them because, like our imaginary scholar, most of them lived, or received their training, before the age of space science. And it is space science alone which can give the true explanation of those "legends" and "myths" they find incredible and attempt to "demytholize".

That an advanced civilization might visit our Earth in a "city" that comes "down out of heaven" could only be regarded by them as a spiritual symbol or a superstition. That its citizens could experience a thousand of our years as a single "day or a watch in the night" would have seemed preposterous before the advent of relativity theory. That such a civilization might accomplish miracles of instantaneous healing, prolong life indefinitely or even restore the dead from their genetic records could only seem plausible since the emergence of genetic engineering.

That a human being might be directly assembled from the "dust of the ground" would only occur to a technological forecaster such as Arthur C. Clarke. He predicted we may one day have a "material replicator" which can duplicate any object from raw chemicals - even a complex, biological organism such as ourselves, and already three dimension copiers are approaching this goal by creating artificial body organs that have been successfully implanted in experimental animals.

The idea that ancient texts, such as the Bible, may contain scientific information that anticipates our own future is not implausible then. It is not implausible if we can show its writers had direct, or indirect, contact with an alien civilization that had already reached an advanced stage we have not yet achieved.

Such contact could consist of a direct visit by one civilization to another or of indirect exposure to artifacts, records or oral traditions such a visit generated. In the latter case "contact" might take place centuries, or millennia, after the actual visit occurred.

But how can this be established? In cases like the Bible verification of the circumstances leading to its composition pose great difficulties. Generally texts exist only as copies or translations of originals which have disappeared. Often their authorship, as well as place and time of composition, are uncertain. Usually even the earliest extant versions are separated from the events they recount by centuries or even millennia. During much of this time the information they report may have been transmitted by an oral process which left no material evidence.

How then, can we ever be sure that information in these texts did not originate with the civilization producing them? How can we be sure that, beneath what generations of scholars have accepted as spiritual symbolism or figurative language, there is a core of scientific knowledge so advanced it equals or surpasses our own?

If there is it certainly would not take the form Carl Sagan envisaged. In his book, The Cosmic Connection, he suggested that the occurrence of some advanced scientific concept, such as the nuclear fine structure constant, in an ancient text would be proof extraterrestrials gave it to us.

Such an occurrence is, however, virtually ruled out by the very conditions he supposed. The nuclear fine structure constant, or any formulation like it, would almost certainly never be transmitted intact through many generations by people who did not understand it. The folk process would alter it beyond recognition.

WHEN IS SPACE AGE INTERPRETATION INDICATED?

There are two kinds of information, however, which would meet his requirement. One would be a recognizable description of some technical device, or process, for which there is a modern counterpart but which could not have been known to those creating the texts. If the Old Testament, for example, contained a clear-cut description of a spacecraft we would have such an instance. The other would occur when unambiguous statements are made that presuppose knowledge gained only in our own era. For example if one of the gospel writers assured us that Mary Magdalen suffered from a vitamin B deficiency we would have evidence meeting the requirement. It would be immaterial whether the statement were true or not. The mere fact that it was asserted would prove that someone writing in the early christian era possessed modern nutritional information. The chief difficulty in establishing that either of these forms of advanced knowledge does exist in the Bible lies in the fact that sacred literature generally contains levels of meaning. As we have already seen the use of mythic and poetic symbolism creates an aura of ambiguity which hovers over such texts. Uncertainty as to the circumstances which occasioned the writing or the purposes that motivated the writers makes it almost impossible to resolve much of this ambiguity. Various interpretations of many passages of scripture are possible as is proved by the fact that such interpretations exist.

If we encounter what seems to be a description of something similar to modern aircraft or spacecraft, for example, how can we be sure that it is actually so. Consider the well-known case of Ezekiel's "flying chariot" in the Old Testament. On the surface it might be, and has been, taken as a description of some type of spacecraft. It has wheels, it makes a roaring noise, it uses wings to fly and can transport passengers. Ezekiel actually claims to have taken a flight in it. But how can we be sure all this is not merely the metaphoric language of religious mysticism or the delusion of a deranged person?

Could it be, as some commentators have claimed, that the flying chariot is a symbol for the throne of God? Might not the wheels and wings be symbolic references to supportive functions given by supernatural beings, such as angels, in God's presence? Couldn't Ezekiel's flight have been a mystical vision or even the psychotic delusion of a man whose reason had been unhinged by the stresses of exile? How, in short, can we be sure what the account means, since we know so little of Ezekiel's circumstances and even less of his motivations and idiosyncrasies?

The answer is, of course, we cannot. The language of the book of Ezekiel is of that sort which often contains levels of meaning. That various interpretations are possible is proved by the fact that various interpretations exist and are proposed by people whose intelligence and training should make them competent interpreters.

Yet, again, the fact that people have intelligence and training does not always make them competent judges. Intelligence can be clouded by bias or prejudice. Training is valuable only when it is relevant to the task to be performed.

If ancient texts do, in fact, contain evidence of alien contact the most intelligent scholars and critics might fail to identify it if their training had taught them to regard it as religious or mystical symbolism. In fact if their training is primarily in the ancient languages of the text and traditional methods of interpreting it they might lack the knowledge necessary for recognizing evidence which is primarily scientific.

For these reasons it is not surprising that established authorities in biblical scholarship and criticism have not discovered evidence of alien contact in the Scriptures. It is much more likely that those making such discoveries would be generalists with training and interest in the study of ancient texts but with primary backgrounds in other fields – particularly those of literary criticism and science.

Indeed, revolutionary breakthroughs in fields of knowledge have often come from those who are not established authorities. Proof and elaboration of existing theories is more commonly the work of established authorities. Revolutionary breakthroughs often come from those whose backgrounds are general, or interdisciplinary. Their ability to bring exotic backgrounds to bear on a problem and to view it from fresh and unconventional points of view often produces the winning insight.

The field of linguistic analysis is no exception to this rule. Some of the most important breakthroughs in understanding the process of language development and in decipherment of unknown languages have been made by generalists working outside their primary field of training. The Grimm brothers were folklorists and writers of children's stories when they discovered the linguistic law bearing their name, Grimm's law, a major tool in etymological research.

Champollion, a young secondary school teacher, discovered the key to Egyptian hieroglyphs which had eluded all the major authorities of his day- Akerblad, Young and DeSacy. Michael Ventris was an architect by training who had "done a bit of

Greek" when he resolved the long-resistant mystery of Linear B -the language of ancient Crete.

For Champollion and Ventris it was an unconventional and seemingly peripheral skill, or area of knowledge, that enabled the generalists to succeed where the specialists had failed. In each case the successful key had something in common with our own discovery that led to archeolinguistics - a method for isolating and identifying alien influences in ancient texts.

In Champollion's case his discovery of a key lay in the fact that, in addition to conventional training in modern Indo-European and dead Semitic languages, he was an enthusiastic amateur linguist. His explorations had led him into exotic languages not usually studied by his more celebrated colleagues. One of these was Coptic, the language of ancient Ethiopia. From earliest times this ancient kingdom lay under the influence of Egyptian civilization. Champollion's recognition that certain hieroglyphs recurred in patterns resembling Coptic determinatives, unsounded signs that classify others, gave him his winning insight. If the more recent Coptic were influenced by ancient Egyptian language then its grammar and syntax might be similar. Only an unconventional mind would have thought of, and been able to apply, Coptic to the decipherment of hieroglyphs. And without this tool the possession of innumerable inscriptions and the trilingual Rosetta Stone had been insufficient for the best scholars of Champollion's day.

The case of Michael Ventris is even more remarkable. Since the discovery, early in the 20th Century, of Linear B tablets in Crete scholars had tried in vain to decipher them. Most, including Sir Arthur Evans, their discoverer, had rejected the idea of a Greek origin for the language. The search had carried them to the languages of Eastern Europe and Asia Minor. They suspected links with Cypriot or Hittite but no bilingual or trilingual inscription, like the Rosetta Stone, had been found. Without a sample of translations of Linear B into other known languages the task seemed hopeless. No unknown language had ever been translated without such samples.

Michael Ventris, however, brought unusual skills to the task. In addition to being a natural linguist who could pick up a new language, by ear, in a summer he possessed the remarkable observation for detail and visual memory often found in gifted architects. In his study of Linear B these gifts enabled him to notice and recall recurrences of form in otherwise meaningless symbols which had escaped other scholars. And because he had "done a bit of Greek" at Stowe School he noticed these recurrences formed patterns that reminded him of inflections and endings in Greek.

At this point Ventris made a bold decision to pursue his hunch. The weight of scholarly opinion, from Sir Arthur Evans to his own contemporaries, was against him. Indeed, two mavericks, a Miss Melian Stowell and the Bulgarian scholar, V. Georgiev, had actually worked for several years on Greek solutions without success. Though lacking a bilingual or trilingual key Ventris decided to arrange the known Linear B symbols into tables, or grids, according to their visual form and what he had discovered of their phonic values. The technique is similar to that used for breaking codes without a key. One searches for patterns in the sorted elements of the code and attempts to relate them to known patterns in the language into which they are being decoded. In doing this Ventris confirmed his impression that Linear B was indeed a form of Greek - a very archaic form, pre-dating Homer by half a millennium, but Greek nevertheless. Once this was established the vocabulary and syntax of Linear B yielded to his investigation.

In the case of archeolinguistics the problem is somewhat different. Our study was of ancient texts that had already been translated. Their languages, Hebrew and Greek, were already well known and adequate lexicons existed so that it was possible to explore the meanings and derivations of words to great depth.

Our search was rather for ideas concealed in the Hebrew and Greek texts which clearly had an alien origin. We concentrated our effort on words and passages for which no meaning had been established or which seemed to suggest meanings inappropriate to their settings. If alien information had somehow found its way into the texts the best hunting grounds, we reasoned, would be obscurities, paradoxes and seeming irrelevancies or absurdities. As our list grew we began an intensive investigation into the etymology and interpretations of these words and passages. We consulted all available translations of the texts, as well as standard lexicons and commentaries.

Through all this research, extending over more than five years, our focus never changed. It remained the clarification of the meanings of words used in the anomalous passages we had isolated.

RECOVERING CELESTIAL CIVILIZATION

As our work continued a strange phenomenon emerged - one which was nowhere intimated in any of the dictionaries, lexicons or commentaries we had studied. It resembled Champollion's discovery of recurrent hieroglyphs not part of the meaning but determinative of it, and Ventris' discovery of patterns which could only be endings and inflections. Like them we began to find patterns. Our patterns differed, however. They suggested meanings foreign to the surface sense of the passages and suggestive of technologies too advanced for the times in which the texts were written.

As we began to study these meanings it was clear the significances we were finding were not figurative. The meanings were literal and were rooted in etymologies of the wording employed. But they were meanings often totally at variance with those traditional scholarship had assigned.

An example may help to make this clear. The first anomaly which captured our attention and led us into archeolinguistics was the one Vivianne had identified, the "tree of life", mentioned in Genesis 2 whose fruit could confer immortality on those who ate it. It grew beside another tree whose fruit gave its eater a knowledge of good and evil. When Adam and Eve disobeyed God and ate of its fruit He, fearing they would also eat of the tree of life and live forever in their disobedient state, excluded them from the Garden. To ensure that they did not trespass he set cherubim with flaming swords to guard the entrance.

On the surface this account is a rather straightforward mythic explanation of how sin entered the world and why we have to die. While many modern readers would have difficulty accepting it as literal truth there is nothing particularly anomalous about it. It reads the way near eastern origin myths usually read. But the term "cherubim" arrests attention as one reads the story.

In the first place it is the only word in the account which is not a common one. It is a peculiarly biblical word and obviously a technical name for some rather exotic sort of thing. In these senses it is anomalous within the language of the account.

Upon consulting lexicons and Bible dictionaries its anomalousness grows. The Hebrew word, of which it is a transliteration, is "keruwb". Most lexicographers and compilers of Bible dictionaries admit that the root meaning of the word is lost. As William Smith observes, in his Bible Dictionary, "What this peculiar cherubic form was is, perhaps, an impenetrable mystery". In spite of such admissions most sources go on to attempt some penetration. Often they suggest that cherubim might be a species, or variety, of angel. Some think the word refers to a composite of beast and man such as the human-faced, winged bull effigies which ornamented Babylonian temples. A few think cherubim were physical emblems of abstract divine attributes such as omniscience or omnipotence.

When Vivianne turned to the concordances, however, the anomaly burst into full flower. As she begin to compare different passages, throughout the Bible, in which the word "cherubim" occurs, she saw it is used in wholly different and, what appear to be, incompatible ways.

Cherubim, she found can guard and wield flaming swords (Genesis 3:24); the Lord rode upon one (II Samuel 22: 11); some of them are attached to flying craft and mounted with wheels (Ezekiel 10:9-19); and Moses was instructed, by the Lord, to use "cunningly wrought" ones, in making tabernacle curtains (Exodus 26:31). We asked ourselves what sort of thing could function as a swordsman, an aircraft, the propulsion unit for an aircraft and a tool or ornament involved in the making of curtains?

Obviously, the pink and white, chicken-winged infants depicted over the heads of saints in medieval paintings would not do. Nor would their grown-up counterparts pictured by Gustave Dore in our old illustrated Bibles. A winged humanoid doesn't have wheels. It is also difficult to imagine the Lord riding on one. And if we try to picture the Lord riding a man-faced, winged bull, or some other emblem of "omniscience and omnipotence" we descend into even greater absurdities.

Clearly something was wrong. The conclusions of traditional scholarship left us with an anomaly of the first order. Whatever "keruwb" originally meant it must surely have been far removed from any of these feeble guesses. Where, then, could we go for an answer?

Her only evidence was the word itself, and our method needed to be a linguistic one. Since its root meanings were lost Vivianne's position was much like that of translators dealing with an unknown language or cryptographers with a keyless code. She traced its derivations as far back as they are known. She examined cognate words lexicographers listed as having similar or related meanings. And she did the same for other words used with it in the variety of contexts in which they occur. Unlike Ventris however, she paid minimal attention to reoccurrences of sounds or wording sequences. Rather she focused on recurrences in meanings. She looked for significant themes pervading the cluster of cognates and their contextual associations. This semantic approach yielded surprising results.

In doing these things she found that in all its various uses the Hebrew word "keruwb" was employed in ways and contexts that emphasized four fundamental themes. These were: (1) performing useful labor (guarding, transporting, lifting, fabricating, etc); (2) resembling non-living materials and mechanical parts (brass, beryl, wings, wheels, etc.); (3) performing mechanical functions (wheeling, rotating, flying, emitting rushing noises, lifting and lowering wings, etc); (4) often doing these things by means of human-like parts ("hands" under wings, "eyes" in wheels, ray-emitting "mouths", etc.).

At this point it became clear that a synthesis was needed - some hypothesis or creative insight that would unite and illuminate these seemingly unrelated themes. And since traditional scholarship had not noticed the conflict in themes or searched for a unifying insight, it seemed likely it lay outside the customary approaches previously employed.

Like Champollion, whose esoteric knowledge of Coptic provided a key to the hieroglyphs, and Ventris, whose architect's perception and cryptoanalytic techniques uncovered Greek syntax in Linear B, we needed a fresh approach. It came from our generalist excursions into futurology. Like the riddle of the Sphinx the question nagged us, "What is not alive yet imitates life; has mechanical parts but performs human functions and does useful labor by imitating human structures?" As we were pondering the enigma the answer suddenly burst upon Vivianne - a robot! Nothing but the unfolding science of robotics could fill this many-sided prescription! Yet, even as we realized this we also recognized what controversy and even ridicule such an idea might bring on us. Would friends and colleagues regard us as deranged? What seemed more likely was that those having some knowledge of textual criticism would simply dismiss the idea as one more instance of an etymological pitfall known as the "root fallacy". It occurs when the roots of a word, used in a figurative sense, are mistaken and given a literal meaning. Thus it is assumed something actually exists corresponding to that literal meaning when it does not. So a person who had never encountered a butterfly, on hearing the word "butterfly," might assume it names a variety of fly that subsists on butter, when of course, there is no such insect.

In the same way critics of our claim that "cherubim" is a generic name for robots might argue that the Genesis 3 statement that the Lord God placed "cherubim" and a flaming sword "in the garden" which turned every way to prevent access to the tree of life is just another name for guardian angels. Therefore we are victims of the root fallacy in thinking it could be a reference to some sort of rotating laser beam with the power to destroy.

The error, however, would be on their part, not ours. Since the roots of cherubim have been lost and are unknown it is not possible to misapply them. Further our claim, as we will presently show in the Keruwb grid, is based on the various ways in which the word is actually used and not on root meanings, literal or otherwise.

As we continued our archeolinguistic explorations innumerable obscure passages were becoming clear in the light of a futuristic interpretation. And, as our work continued the whole began to coalesce into a coherent picture of an advanced civilization surprisingly like those envisioned by our own writers of science fiction yet strangely reminiscent of a transmuted form of the theology we had been taught as children.

SEMANTIC GRIDS

Our clusters of roots and contextual grids began, like pieces in a giant jigsaw puzzle, to form a large-scale picture. The picture was of a civilization, born millions of years before our own, on a planet of a star far older than our sun. Its members long ago turned over manual labor and economic production to servo-mechanisms. Humanoid robots perform routine social functions as well. Its living members are immortal having mastered aging and death. They devote themselves to the higher pursuits of civilized life - social enjoyment, creative use of leisure, civic responsibility, recreation, the arts and spiritual values. They long ago evolved beyond crime and war. The cowboy and Indian space fantasies of Star Wars were left behind in the infancy of their race. A major part of their energies is spent in space exploration and colonization. This is what brought them to Earth long ago. Here they recreated our most remote ancestors and taught them. During much of our history they have monitored our progress and will one day return to complete their annexation of planet Earth as another of their colonies.

Ventris had reconstructed major features of Minoan civilization from palace commissary records and military duty rosters. In the same way our tables of clusters began to delineate a full-blooded, technological civilization beside which the pale nebulosities of traditional interpretation sank into insignificance. As the excavations of the famed 19th Century archeologist, Heinrich Schliemann, unearthed the Troy that inspired Homer's great epic, the Iliad, so archeolinguistics revealed a Celestial civilization that burst in futuristic glory from the pages of the Bible!

Yet the task of discovering how, the actual modus operandi, remained. How could such alien elements have become incorporated into the Hebrew and Greek of the Bible? According to our investigations the original contact of the Celestials must have been at least fifty thousand years ago. Were our ancestors intelligent enough and verbal enough, at that time, to have generated oral traditions incorporating the wealth of technical meanings we were finding? If they were could their oral traditions have been transmitted, intact, through the millennia that intervened until the first records were set down?

At this juncture our generalist interest in archeology and anthropology came to our rescue. According to recent investigations in paleontology sapient humans have existed on this planet for at least twice the time needed and perhaps for as much as a quarter of a million years. Our modern variety, homo sapiens sapiens, appeared forty to fifty thousand years ago. Worldwide occurrence of mythic and folk themes indicate that events marking the beginnings of the race have been handed down by oral tradition in forms that still show remarkably detailed parallelisms. The elements of the flood story, for example, are found among the Egyptians, Hebrews, Babylonians, Greeks, Druids, Polynesians, Micronesians, Melanesians, Indonesians, Eskimos, Africans, East Indians and Native Americans. These generally tell of a calamitous deluge in which a few were saved in some type of boat, or ship, by reaching the top of a high mountain. And archeology verifies that there have been calamitous floodings from time immemorial in the eastern end of the Fertile Crescent. It was here, the Bible says, that our first ancestors were recreated.

If such racial memories can be transmitted by oral traditions throughout the world, even into areas where floodings are unlikely, then ancient knowledge of even more memorable events could be transmitted in the same way. As a result the semantic clusters we found were often very complex. We have frequently found dozens of roots and cognates to be involved in a single cluster. Because of this the perspectives they give on Celestial civilization are, in some cases, almost panoramic. Groups of clusters sometimes have recurrences which suggest broad and pervasive themes linking them. These provide deep insights into the most salient aspects of Celestial civilization.

As an example we will turn here to key elements in the cluster related to the word "cherubim" found in the tree of life story which initiated our investigation.

KERUWB GRID

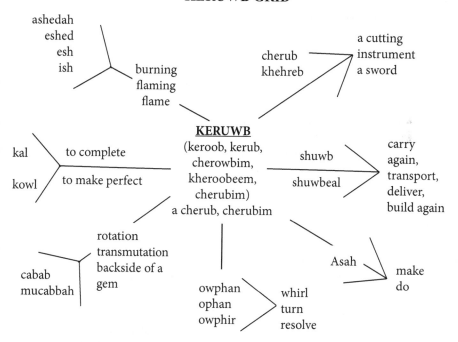

Interestingly, the passage in Genesis which started research on this cluster described cherubim as objects with "flaming swords" which turned every way" to guard the tree of life. Once our attention had been fixed on this passage we began to envision cherubim as erect barriers of some sort which emitted a rotating laser beam. Such beams (or "flaming swords") are used in present-day industrial processes for precision cutting, in medicine for microsurgery, and are being explored as military "death rays". It was only after we had arrived at this interpretation that we found parts of the cluster which refer to "making perfect" "transmutation" and "gems". Laser beams are, of course, a pure (or "perfect") frequency of light generated when a gem, such as a ruby, is transmuted from its normal state to an electrically excited one in which photon emission occurs. Considering the other and seemingly incompatible uses of "cherubim" we had previously found it became clear to us that "keruwb" was not a singular name for a specific kind of robot but rather a generic term applicable to robotic devices of all sorts.

Supporting this conclusion are accounts found in the Bible books of Ezekiel, Isaiah and Zachariah describing even more extraordinary robots and combinations of robotic devices. The most detailed account of this is found in the book of Ezekiel where he tells of his encounter with a "flying chariot", supported by "cherubim", in which he claims to have taken an actual flight.

As a young Hebrew priest he had recently been deported from Jerusalem by the Babylonian king, Nebuchadnezzar, in a mass relocation of a large part of Judah's population after their conquest by his armies in the fifth century, B.C.

While he stood there musing about his exile and longing for his family and friends he suddenly heard a roaring noise overhead. Looking up, he saw a huge cloud of smoke with jets of fire stabbing downward from its center. Slowly, out of the cloud, four long columns began to descend. As they cleared the smoke he noticed each was surrounded by a whirring blur like that of rapidly moving wings. The blurs were located about halfway up the columns. As the descent of the strange object continued it reached a point just north of the priest, where it hovered as though searching for a landing site. This gave him a chance to study it more closely. To his surprise the columns looked like men except that they were constructed of a brass-like metal.

The top of each column was surrounded by what looked like heads facing the four directions. As he checked them he could see each had the same four faces. And, to him, they resembled the faces of an eagle, an ox, a lion and a man. The one nearest him showed the man -like face and created the illusion of a mechanical man. About midway down each column he could see the strange blur of whirling motion where winglike blades moved around a rotating shaft.

Below these, on each side of the column, were what looked like arms with hands except that these, too, seemed to be made of some brass-like metal. As his vision swept on down the columns he noticed that two short metal rods projected from each side. These terminated in round metal pods like brass feet. As he took in the whole column facing him it did, indeed, look like a metallic man with wings.

And now he could study those strange stabs of lightning- like flames. They darted from one place to another in the midst of the four columns. Their succession was almost too rapid for the eye to follow. And as this irregular lightning continued to shoot out the whole structure shifted this way and that as though seeking a place to touch down.

Suddenly, almost without his seeing the maneuver, it settled and the feet touched ground. Now the sound of roaring diminished as the engine was cut to idling, and the darting flames stopped. The whirling wings rotated slowly, and he could see there were four on each shaft joined at the center.

Then to his surprise something descended out of the base of each shaft which was at last familiar-wheels! The leg pods retracted, and the whole craft began to move about on the wheels. He had never seen a wheeled chariot move without animals to pull it before, and the sight unnerved him now. But his intelligence came to his rescue. It must be that the manlike metallic creatures were alive, after all, and each one was pulling his own wheel!

But now once again he was thrown into confusion by the object's strange behavior. He was used to watching chariots and had often seen the slow arc of the wheels when the chariot rounded a corner. These wheels were doing something he had never seen before! The object had come up against a slight obstruction ahead and, instead of turning to go around it as chariots did, it had simply shifted sideways and moved ahead. The wheels had, all four, gone to the side without turning!

The creature was now nearing him again, and he could see it in greater detail. He strained his eyes to study these strange wheels more closely. They seemed to have smaller wheels inside them!

"A WHEEL WITHIN A WHEEL"

Each wheel had a number of barrel-shaped wheels mounted so that they rotated sideways using its main rim as their axis. As a result it could roll forward smoothly (since the barrels were small and closely mounted), or it could stop and simply roll sideways on them without the main wheel turning at all!

Now, at last, the strange creature seemed to find what it was looking for and settled in a place where all four columns were exactly level. The blades slowed and came to a stop, then two folded upward and two folded downward to rest beside each column.

Now for the first time the priest directed his attention upward above the four columns. From where he stood the cone-shaped underside of the dome, to which the four columns were attached, looked like a greatly flattened child's top. It was supported, around the edge, by the four columns. From his viewpoint the huge flaring undersurface looked like the silver-gray vault of the sky. Up above this "firmament," as he called it, was a small, clear capsule which glistened prismatically in the sunlight. Inside, on a high-backed, thronelike chair, sat what looked like a man. As he watched, the man-like being seemed to notice him, and he prostrated himself as he knew was proper with Babylonian monarchs. As he lay stretched on the ground, face down, a loud commanding voice came from the firmament up above. The being spoke to him!

WHAT EZEKIEL ACTUALLY SAW

Had one of our own astronauts been standing next to this priest, beside the River Chebar, he would have had little difficulty in understanding what he saw. Some of it was incorporated in the Apollo 11 Moon Mission which took them on their historic flight. Other features were on drawing boards at NASA as part of the plans for future space missions. Still others were unknown to him, but his training in engineering and astronautics would have enabled him to grasp their principles easily.

He would have recognized the "object" as an atmospheric entry craft of advanced design. The four columns, containing helicopter units, gave the lift and braking necessary for takeoffs and landings in an atmosphere. They could be jettisoned to become modules and fly independently.

The arms and hands under the blades were similar to ones he had seen handling radioactive materials, by remote control, in laboratories. He would have known these were planned for use in future U.S. space shuttles.

The lightning-like stabs of flame came from a rocket engine which produced slight amounts of thrust to maneuver and stabilize the craft during landings. The sliding legs, mounted to shock absorbers, cushioned the landing to protect delicate precision instruments. The broad leg pods increased the area of contact so that the heavy craft would not sink down into soft Earth. A design similar to that of the main body had been tested at NASA's Langley Research Center in developing a body design for entrycraft with maximum air drag and minimum weight.

He would have understood that the cowl of the command capsule glistened like a rainbow because its plastic cover acted as a prism in breaking up sunlight. He would also have known the commanding voice came from a loudspeaker.

The wheels which could go in any direction without turning would have interested him most. He would readily have grasped their principle and felt admiration for the designers who had produced them. They brilliantly solved a problem that had bothered NASA's engineers in planning for soft landings; how to construct a wheel that could move in any direction in soft Earth (or the deep dust anticipated on the moon) without the difficulty of turning the whole wheel. It also provided a way to maneuver in very tight spaces where there was not room to go backward or forward for conventional turns.

Since Ezekiel had no 20th Century astronaut to explain his strange experience he could only try to explain what he saw in terms of his own knowledge and experience. He used analogies and comparisons with which he was familiar in trying to describe the strange object that had disturbed his exile.

Illustrations I and II give an idea of what we believe Ezekiel saw. Illustration III shows the "wheels within a wheel". Illustration IV shows how Ezekiel's description of a cherub could have been transformed into the popular concept of an angel as a humanoid with "wings" as conceived by Gustave Dore, one of the best known Bible illustrators.

C.Guerrero
80

Let's examine Ezekiel's own version of the experience:

"And I looked, and, behold, a whirlwind came out of the north, a great cloud, and a fire unfolding itself ...

"Also out of the midst thereof came the likeness of four living creatures. And this was their appearance; they had the likeness of a man.

"And every one had four faces, and every one had four wings.

"And their feet were straight feet; and the sole of their feet was like the sole of a calf's foot: and they sparkled like the colour of burnished brass.

"And they had the hands of a man under their wings on their four sides....

"Their wings were joined one to another ...

"As for the likeness of their faces, they four had the face of a man, and the face of a lion ...and ... the face of an ox ... [and] ... the face of an eagle....

"As for the likeness of the living creatures, their appearance was like burning coals of fire, and like the appearance of lamps: it went up and down ... and the fire was bright, and out of the fire went forth lightning... .

"Now as I beheld the living creatures, behold one wheel upon the Earth by the living creatures ...

"The appearance of the wheels and their work was like unto the colour of a beryl ...and their appearance and their work was as it were a wheel in the middle of a wheel.

"When they went, they went upon their four sides: and they turned not when they went....

"And the likeness of the firmament upon the heads of the living creature was as the colour of the terrible crystal, stretched forth over their heads above....

"And when they went, I heard the noise of their wings, like the noise of great waters ...

"And there was a voice from the firmament that was over their heads, when they stood, and had let down their wings.

"And above the firmament that was over their heads was the likeness of a throne, as the appearance of a sapphire stone: and upon the likeness of the throne was the likeness ... of a man ...

" ... I saw as it were the appearance of fire, and it had brightness round about.

"As the appearance of the bow that is in the cloud in the day of rain, so was the appearance of the brightness round about.

. . . And when I saw it, I fell upon my face, and I heard a voice of one that spake" (Ezekiel I :4-28).

Since it was set down almost 2,500 years ago, Ezekiel's famous "vision" has been challenged by scholars and theologians. Most have assumed it was simply a mystical experience and have looked for obscure "spiritual meanings." Others, less concerned with its religious significance, have concluded the chariot was wholly imaginary- the figment of a deranged mind. Comparative mythologists have suggested Ezekiel borrowed his "vision" from myths and symbols around him. They have pointed out that the four faces of his "living creatures" are reminiscent of the Assyrian karibua, sculptured effigies often used at the entrance to palaces in Babylon.

It remained for a NASA engineer to recognize, in Ezekiel's description, elements which link it with experimental designs that have been developed in our own space program. Josef F. Blumrich, former chief of the Systems Layout Branch of NASA, set out to write a book debunking the idea of ancient astronauts. In the process of studying Ezekiel's "vision" he became convinced that what Ezekiel saw was an entry craft remarkably similar to models being considered by NASA. The idea was confirmed when he realized the "wheel within a wheel" was an ingenious solution to a problem which had perplexed Apollo Space Mission planners.

Critics of this view have argued that Ezekiel used the word "visions" here to mean "hallucinations" and not an actual physical phenomenon. Unfortunately for them the Hebrew of which it is a translation does not back them up.

The word Ezekiel uses for "visions" is "mareh", commonly used for ordinary perception-the act of "viewing" or "seeing." It is not the word employed elsewhere in the Old Testament when an hallucination or revelation is intended. That word is "chazown" – a "dream" or "revelation." Indeed, everything in Ezekiel's account of this "chariot" suggests this intelligent priest was a remarkably sharp observer and possessed a keen, critical intelligence. Writing of his account, J. F. Blumrich concluded that what he saw was a space vehicle which, beyond any doubt, was not only technically feasible but was in fact very well designed to fulfill its function.

What is even more remarkable about Ezekiel's "chariot" is that it also solves a far more serious problem which NASA has not yet faced, because our space program is still in its infancy. While our astroengineers worried about the mobility of a landing craft in anticipated deep deposits of dust on the moon the Celestials had long ago wrestled with the far greater problem created by the travel of patrolling craft constantly on the move from one solar system to another. Their astronauts had to land on surfaces without atmospheres, in atmospheres that would be too toxic or too cold, or that contained pathogens for which they had no immunity. We solved the problem of the moon's lack of atmosphere and low gravity by having our astronauts wear weighted space suits and carry tanked air suppliers.

The Celestials solved their travel problem by letting their astronauts remain in sealed command capsules which decontaminated and recycled life supplies or materials brought in by their man-like robots. In this way they could travel through varied environments over months or even years without ever exposing themselves. Their robotic cherubim explore, patrol and even carry out projects and bring back information and supplies from the outside worlds they visit without their crew having to risk their own health and lives.

ARCHEOLINGUISTICS AND THE HIDDEN BIBLE

The application of this method of analysis to innumerable other texts in the Bible has taken us far beyond Carl Sagan's tentative surmise that ancient texts regarded as sacred might provide evidence of extraterrestrials visiting the Earth. Going far beyond this it opens a new and dazzling prospect on humanity's future. It is a result that gives new meaning and relevance to the age old millennial hopes of Judeo-Christian tradition.

Dozens of passages, throughout the Bible, provide overwhelming evidence that its writers worked with oral traditions and texts containing references to a civilization far in advance of our own today. These references include spacecraft of advanced design, various uses of atomic energy; laser technology, interstellar video communication and the artificial synthesis of life.

More startling still is the result of combining recent evidence from the fossil record with clues supporting the hypothesis that we, modern humanity, are the result of a Celestial experiment in genetic engineering. We are their major artifact, the biosignature that proves they were here. We are their recreation and could not have emerged by biological evolution alone. The hidden Bible gives a compelling account of this celestial civilization and their plan for returning to Earth to complete colonization and extend citizenship to its inhabitants.

That civilization, born millions of years before our own, on the planet of a star far older then our own Sun, beacons with utopian allure. On a vast plain the towering spires of its capitol stretch toward the sky. Its soaring walls and architectural embellishments glisten like a diadem of rarest jewels. From the farthest reaches of outer space silvery modules slip across its horizon and with silent swiftness streak toward its center. Others rise from its vast launch pads and vanish into the star-studded darkness.

Soon, if not already, one of these will have left on a return mission to Earth. In the next two chapters we will propose a scenario of what it may be like to live through that return based on what the Bible has to say about it and how our scientists and futurologists believe the technological marvels it involves could be accomplished.

And then shall appear the sign of the Son of man in heaven: and then shall
all the tribes of the Earth mourn, and they shall see the Son of man coming
in the clouds of heaven with power and great glory. And he shall send his
angels with a great sound of a trumpet, and they shall gather together his
elect from the four winds, from one end of heaven to the other.

–Matthew 24:30-31

CHAPTER III

Invasion

THE DAY THE WORLD ENDED

On October 30, 1938, Orson Welles created a virtual national emergency
by broadcasting a radio version of H. G. Wells' novel, War of the Worlds. The
story, presented as a series of news bulletins, interrupted what seemed to be a live
broadcast of music by a popular dance band of the period. Its announcements of
aliens from another world landing in New Jersey and invading New York were
accepted as actual news by a large part of the listening audience.

The most remarkable thing about the near-catastrophe produced by the
broadcast is that Americans, almost a century ago, had no difficulty believing that
beings from another world could invade the Earth and were actually doing so. This
fact raises an interesting question. If similar evidences of extraterrestrial invasion
were to suddenly confront us today, what would our reaction be now that the Space
Age has fully arrived?

Some of us now living may have the chance to answer this question, in the
near future, when we live through an actual conquest of our planet by aliens from
another world. This conquest, by beings from a civilization far superior to our own,
is predicted throughout the Bible. The quotation heading this chapter is one of the
most dramatic descriptions the Bible gives of it. And the Bible tells us this invasion
will occur during the lifetime of some who saw the founding of the reborn state of
Israel - an event which occurred in 1948.

A conquest by a civilization millions or even billions of years ahead of us in sophistication would be unlike any conquest the world has ever known. Even the European invasion of the New World in the Renaissance and the experience of South Pacific islanders in World War II offer no real parallels.

The cultural shock of Indians who had never seen a gun or a white man must have been great when the conquistadors first appeared in the ancient Indian empires. The disbelief of New Guinean natives must have been even greater when they first experienced artillery fire and saw aircraft land. But though these invasions were by aliens with great powers, there were limitations. The conquistadors were vulnerable to Indian arrows; they could be captured and killed or evaded. Japanese and Allied soldiers were mortal. It was possible to hide from them and even to negotiate by offering aid and assistance. But what would it be like to find the world completely under alien control before our detection signals could warn us or defenses be activated?

How would we react to otherworldly invaders with technological powers that could not be resisted; who could neutralize energy sources and jam communications throughout the world from the moment they landed, and who could even monitor the actions and thoughts of every person on our planet? Would we rebel at the future shock of suddenly finding ourselves under the rule of a highly moral occupying force that could and would absolutely suppress all wrong doing, crime and warfare; an occupying force that would use its inconceivable powers in ethical ways to establish a utopian society here on Earth, eliminating poverty, disease and even death? Or would we gladly submit to the rule of invading benefactors who could accomplish resurrection of the dead and even confer immortality on the living who qualified for inclusion in their civilization as fellow citizens?

Imagine with us, for a little while, what it will be like to live through this experience as we foresee it from hints given in the Bible. We are told, by its writers, that it will occur when people least expect it and without warning, as invasions usually do. One day you will be watching a favorite television program or rushing to an important meeting or lying asleep in bed.

Suddenly a trumpet-like voice will shatter your quiet. It will seem to come from nowhere and everywhere at once. "I am the Lord God of the Celestials! In their name I hereby take absolute control of the planet Earth"

The voice will seem to come from far away, yet it will have the power of 10,000 loudspeakers. It will penetrate to the deepest recesses of buildings and to the most remote and isolated areas like a peal of thunder. And like thunder it will seem to come from somewhere in the sky. When you hear it, like millions of others, you will probably rush out of doors, or pull over in your car and get out to see what is happening. Or, if you are one of the fortunate ones already qualified for full citizenship in this new civilization, you may suddenly, and in the twinkling of an eye, find yourself in a totally different place from where you were before with thousands of others like you, assembled on a great plain awaiting some kind of announcement or instructions.

If you are in the first group you will look around as you reach the outdoors or get out of your car. A strange sight will greet you. People will be collecting everywhere as the streets fill up. Others will be peering out of windows or standing in half-open doorways. Cars will be coming to a halt anywhere and everywhere, with occupants leaning out the windows or standing beside them. And everywhere people will be looking toward the sky.

All at once it will light up as though a gigantic flash of lightning had streaked it from east to west. Its brightness will be more dazzling than the noonday sun. And, as you watch its curvature will take on the opacity of a television screen. There, in staggering dimensions which stretch from horizon to horizon, an image will suddenly appear. It will be a gigantic figure with a human face, and as the trumpet-like voice continues, you will see its lips are moving.

In a quiet, unemotional voice it will continue: "All previously existing governments are now dissolved, and all rights and powers exercised under them are hereby suspended." As you listen, you will take in the glistening spacesuit of the figure and the complicated panels of the control room which seem to surround it. It may even strike you as odd that, though its language sounds foreign, you can understand everything it is saying.

But even as these thoughts cross your mind the import of its ominous message will push them aside and rivet your attention. "Those of you who are prepared for leadership have already been teleported to Jerusalem, where our Celestial space city has landed. From there they will be sent to stations throughout the Earth to assist in setting up our new, provisional government."

Of course, if you are one of those who prepared, you will not hear this part of the message-you will be experiencing it. On a vast plain somewhere outside Jerusalem you will be watching and listening to a different version of the sky broadcast which will later outline the program you, and the others surrounding you, will carry out as you report to your assigned stations all over the Earth to bring about the reforms of the new provisional government. And as you listen you, too, may be momentarily distracted by the wonder of your own body as you suddenly discover for the first time in your life what it feels like to have a perfectly healthy mind functioning in a completely healthy body-a body changed "in the twinkling of an eye" into a re-creation of what it was originally intended to be-no defects, no deterioration, no diseases.

Whichever group you find yourself in, however, and wherever you are your attention will inevitably be drawn back to the strange figure in the sky, and, like billions of others in London, Moscow, Beijing, Calcutta, Capetown and all over the world, you will listen, face upturned, toward the dazzling sky image.

The voice will continue inexorably: "Those who accept our rule will find it peaceful and just, but those who oppose us will be ruled with a rod of iron. All war and evildoing are outlawed, and my commandments will be enforced throughout your world." As these words are spoken the image will fade, and the sky will return to its normal color. The clouds will again be visible. And throughout the world pandemonium will suddenly erupt with the fury of a tornado.

Outside Jerusalem a far different scene will be occurring. Here and there, in the great throng of the chosen, exclamations of surprise and shouts of joy will rise as the formerly deaf realize they are now hearing; the formerly blind suddenly discover they can see. Ex-amputees will leap on restored limbs, and the resurrected will suddenly grasp that they are living once again. Then a great hush will fall on the endless throng of thousands and tens of thousands. As long moments pass by, an unearthly silence will reign. Then, tentatively at first and here and there, but growing and joined by tens, then hundreds, then thousands, a sound of rejoicing will rise. It will rise, and mount, and swell until it seems to shake the very earth under the feet of those assembled. It will grow until it seems their eardrums must collapse under its impact; yet it will increase still more until, at last, it inundates the very Earth and sky and drowns them both in a vast tidal wave of rejoicing and praise that goes on and on seemingly without end.

Later, as the hours pass, the fate of the two groups will become intertwined. If you are among those not "chosen" you may find yourself at home in front of your TV. Should you decide to turn on your television you will discover every station is carrying the same program.

The image on the screen will be human, but will be wearing a spacesuit similar to the one you saw in the sky broadcast earlier in the day. This speaker is one of the humans chosen to help in setting up the provisional government. Suddenly, and with a shock of recognition, you will realize he was a famous television announcer who died almost a decade ago.

"In the name of the Lord God of the Celestials I greet you! Praise his name who has power over death. I have come back from the grave to assist the provisional government for the Celestial Command. Do not be afraid. Remain in your homes. Tomorrow you will receive instructions by TTC, the worldwide Thought Transference Communications System. Each of you will receive instructions in the form of imposed thought patterns which will tell you where to report for registration and assignment to duties. Do not attempt to evade registration and assignment. Our communications system makes it possible to monitor and process data on the thoughts of every human on this planet. There is no place to hide...."

As your initial shock wears off, you may feel a sense of outrage. You're a free person! You won't submit to this authority with its registration and assignment and its monitoring of people's thoughts.

If you are in a capital city you may collect a few essentials and rush out to your car. Everywhere there will be signs of social breakdown and chaos. As you near the on-ramp of an outbound freeway your motor will suddenly falter and die. Glancing down at your gas gauge you may discover it still shows half full. Up ahead people will be getting out of other stalled vehicles looking toward the center of the city. As you strain to see what has captured their attention you will discover a strange addition to the landscape. Outlined against the reddening sky of sunset, its head framed by ominous clouds of a gathering storm, a tall metallic object will loom. As a streak of lightning lances the sky you will catch a clear view of the object's details. In the strobe-light whiteness of the lightning's glare you will see it is a strange manlike figure. Towering above many of the commercial buildings "clustered around", it will stand like some gigantic tin woodsman escaped from a movie set. Below it you will see a whirl of flashing amber lights and realize a cordon of police cars are drawn up around it. Out of their midst a finger of light will stab out and flood the inhuman face of the robot. As the searchlight holds, its head will turn, camera like, panning the city. Below the head its tubular chest and legs will glisten like polished brass as they reflect back the rays of the powerful arc light. As its gaze sweeps your direction you will see its eye sockets burn like ruby lasers. Suddenly, on its left, a formation of jet fighters will streak in and start to peel off for an attack. As the lead plane approaches, the monster's head will quickly swivel in its direction, and a sword-like ray will leap from its mouth to envelop the entire surface of the approaching plane. The craft will suddenly falter, its engine and weapons deactivated, and harmlessly descend to Earth. The other planes will bank steeply and wheel abruptly as they flee back in the direction from which they came. Once more the head will swivel around and, as it scans your direction, you will experience a feeling of warmth pervading your body. An odd tingling sensation will radiate from your spine to the tips of your hands and feet and even to the roots of your hair. . .With it will come a sudden sense of drowsiness and an overwhelming desire to get back to the warmth and safety of home.

As you make your way past the long queue of vehicles, stalled by the robot's mysterious powers, you will try to hurry your pace. As in a nightmare your legs will refuse to respond. Like leaden weights they will drag under you and threaten to collapse at any moment. And as you stumble along, and the dampness seeps through to your skin you will remember, over and over again, the words of the resurrected announcer, "There is no place to hide."

For those chosen by the Celestials, however, quite another scene will be unfolding. There, on the great plain, a marvelous transformation will have taken place. Over toward Jerusalem and Mount Moriah a vast corona of light will play seemingly radiating from a foursquare structure settled at its foot. Like some man-made aurora its glowing crown of shimmering iridescence will play across the whole sky lighting the vast floor of the valley where thousands upon thousands are still assembled. Its tall spires will stretch toward the sky, and its domes and arches and splendid roofs will shine in its own reflected radiance turning night into day. Far surpassing any earthly structure its monumental vastness will stretch almost a mile in every direction, and its soaring walls and architectural embellishments will glisten like a diadem set with the rarest jewels. Its many gates will stand open, and endless throngs of those assembled will stream in and out in unending procession as the leadership of the redeemed inspects their future headquarters and capitol.

From the farthest stretches of the sky silvery modules will slip across the horizon and, in swift silence, streak toward its lofty spires. Others will rise from its very midst and as swiftly and silently vanish into the star-studded darkness lying beyond its light. And from within its walls a great swell of sound will fill the night, which has ceased to be night, telling of the celebration within. Laughter and cries of joy will ring out, and the happy exclamation of greetings and murmur of conversation as friends and loved ones long parted meet again.

On the great plain without the thousands upon thousands not visiting the city will be celebrating, too, in splendid structures which have suddenly appeared all over its entire surface teleported by the incredible technology of the Celestials.

The vaulted ceilings, transparent as glass, will admit the radiance of the city reflected by the force field the Celestials will have thrown up around its entire area. This field, extending almost 1,000 miles from the coast of Palestine to the Persian Gulf, will define the ultimate boundaries of a new political state which will include the ever-expanding community of the redeemed in the years and centuries to come. It will serve to isolate them from the world without while ensuring a perfect climate within. "But in this inner city of the plain, the greatly expanded and New Jerusalem, great mansions combining recreational, dining and celebrational facilities will provide for those chosen for headquarter duties." There specially selected leaders will live out the ages of a thousand year millennium while the vast populations of the outside nations are brought under their rule of justice and peace.

Tonight these vast structures have been instantaneously erected by the magic of teleportation. In the social and recreational halls the newly immortal are laughing and embracing their resurrected loved ones while others dance or sing to the accompaniment of music broadcast from the Celestial city. Here, at one table a mature couple talk excitedly, apparently renewing a mutually respectful acquaintance from the past. The man's iconic tousle of unruly hair and the woman's demure, yet confident manner and severity of dress, attract widespread recognition and admiration – Einstein and Madame Curie!

At the far end of another room a group of listeners are gathered in attitudes of transported rapture or dreamy repose around a concert grand. Seated at the piano, apparently unconscious there is anything else in existence, sits a man who needs no introduction. The muscles of his face swell and its veins stand out; the eyes close and the mouth quivers as a resurrected Beethoven, hearing miraculously restored, draws tears from the eyes of his listeners with the beauty and originality of his improvisations.

And in the Celestial city itself those specially chosen for leadership duties continue their festivities. Strains of music and the pure voices of Celestial choirs provide an unending background for the introductions and reunions, the feasting and dancing, and the pomp and ceremony as humans and Celestials alike celebrate the inauguration of the thousand year reign of peace and righteousness in a city where they need no sun.

BLUEPRINT FOR CONQUEST

"Fantastic!" I can hear some readers saying at this point. "What imagination! You should have been science-fiction writers." We'll let you in on a secret. We did not make up the account you have just read. It is a scenario suggested, in many ways, from the Bible. It is based on the Celestials' plan for their conquest of the world, which they revealed to various humans whom they had taken into their confidence.

In 1925, Adolph Hitler published his famous autobiographical best seller, *Mein Kampf.* In it he not only told his life story but revealed his plans for building a new Germany which would rule the world. Politicians and statesmen throughout Europe and America laughed at his ambitions and regarded his blueprint for world conquest as a crackpot's dream. Even when his predictions began to come true, people continued to sit through newsreels and scoff. After he had successfully flanked the Maginot Line and invaded Poland people finally began to take him seriously.

In the Bible the Celestials have given an outline for their plan for the takeover of our world. In its prophetic books they have confided, to human writers, an exact timetable according to which their plan will be fulfilled. Unlike Hitler they were not thinking wishfully of the future. As we will see later they have accurate methods for scientifically forecasting it. In addition they are sure about the actual invasion and takeover, because they are going to make them happen. Unlike Hitler's invasions theirs has no element of uncertainty. They have the necessary technology and power to assure success. And, unlike Hitler, they have revealed their plan, not because they are power-hungry madmen seeking a following, but because they intend to establish a world of peace and justice, and because they wish us, their heirs, to share it.

RIGHT ON SCHEDULE

When Hitler revealed his plans no one would listen. It seemed fantastic that a defeated nation that had gone through bankruptcy and was completely demilitarized could conquer the world. It seemed especially incredible that a half-educated, ex-corporal who had failed in everything he had tried could lead them. Then he began to follow his timetable. He remilitarized the Rhineland. He forced the anschluss of Austria. He annexed Czechoslovakia and the Sudetenland. He invaded Poland. When the world finally began to believe him it was almost too late.

In a similar manner the Celestials have been following a timetable. They are much further along than Hitler was when people finally took him seriously. At first it may seem odd to compare the bloody course of Hitler's conquests with the peaceful takeover of the world planned by the Celestials. Yet the connection between the two is not a mere matter of comparison. There is a much more intimate and historical connection which made fulfillment of biblical prophecy possible. It was Hitler's homicidal final solution of "the Jewish problem" which set the stage for the last great event on the Celestials' timetable-the return of the Jews to their homeland. It took the savage persecution and final extermination of six million of their faith to give Jews from all over Europe the desperate resolve necessary for leaving their adopted homelands, their businesses and what remained of their families. It was the horror of the holocaust, the concentration camps and the years of exile as displaced persons, that convinced many that their own national state was the only safe refuge. And it was the example and success of these European Jews which inspired others from all over the world to return to a reborn Israel.

WHEN IS A PROPHET REALLY A PROPHET?

Every community has its share of palmists, fortune tellers, tea-leaf readers and the like. Most of them tell you little more than can be picked up by simply observing you or by phrasing their predictions so vaguely that almost anything that happens can be taken as a fulfillment. Their predictions are like the bits of advice or statements found in fortune cookies-"You will form valuable new friendships"; "It is not too late to mend your ways"; "You will take a trip." Since such statements about the future have no precise date, and describe events which happen to nearly everyone at some time or another there is hardly any way they can fail to be true.

Occasionally, however, a real prophet comes along who tells you exactly when events will happen-events so unusual and unlikely that almost no one believes them to be possible. When these come true we have good reason for believing we are dealing with a genuine prophet.

The Celestials apparently have this ability. They have evidently perfected powers which parapsychologists call "precognition." This is the ability to know the exact nature and time of events before they happen. Laboratory tests at Duke University, UCLA, Cambridge and many other centers have shown that some people can maintain a high percentage of success in calling the order of cards before they are shuffled, or the combinations of dice before they are thrown. Generally, however, their success is only statistically significant. They will succeed more than most people over a large number of tries, but they cannot tell whether a particular try is right or wrong.

The prophecies in the Bible show far superior precognitive insights. In prophecy after prophecy they foretell events which have already come to pass exactly as predicted. Of all the predictions they make, none seemed more unlikely, than the return of the Jews to a homeland. After 1,900 years of dispersion, they were inhabitants of every land in the world. In many they had undergone incredible persecutions. Finally, under Hitler, an effort was made to bring about their complete annihilation as a faith and as a race. Yet without a homeland they survived and managed to maintain a cultural identity for almost two millennia. One of the greatest historical miracles of all times! The only other miraculous event which could top it was that at the end of this time they would be gathered again, from throughout the Earth, to found a new Israel under conditions of the greatest adversity.

"GATHERED OUT OF MANY PEOPLE"

Almost 2,500 years ago an Old Testament prophet, Ezekiel, predicted that his people, the Jews, would return from dispersion among "the nations" (and they have had only one international dispersion) to rebuild their land. This was to take place just before the Celestials' return to Earth. Speaking of this, Ezekiel says, "... in the latter years thou shalt come into the land that is brought back from the sword, and is gathered out of many people, against the mountains of Israel, which have always been waste: but it is brought forth out of the nations, and they shall dwell safely all of them" (Ezekiel 38:8). This event took place in 1948 when modern Israel became a state.

Five hundred years after Ezekiel, Jesus repeated this prophecy in the New Testament. He told his disciples that the generation that witnessed his death would "fall by the edge of the sword, and shall be led away captive into all nations: and Jerusalem shall be trodden down of the Gentiles ..." (Luke 21:24).

Less than forty years after Jesus' death this came true when the Roman emperor, Titus, destroyed Jerusalem and tore its temple down, stone by stone. And, true to the prophecies of Ezekiel and Jesus, the Jews were scattered throughout the nations of the world.

Like Ezekiel Jesus also foretold that the Jews would return, at the time of the end, to rebuild their nation and that those who saw this event would also witness the return of the Celestials during their lifetime. His disciples came to him and asked, "... what shall be the sign of thy coming, and of the end of the world?" (Matthew 24:3). He answered them by using a parable involving the historical symbol of national Israel, the fig tree. He said, "Now learn a parable of the fig tree; When his branch is yet tender, and putteth forth leaves, ye know that summer is nigh: So likewise ye, when ye shall see all these things (predictions he had given them which we will discuss in the last chapter), know that it is near, even at the doors. Verily I say unto you, this generation [the one witnessing these signs] shall not pass, till all these things be fulfilled" (Matthew 24:32-34).

A number of Bible prophets besides Jesus have spoken of events which would occur after the rebirth of Israel, as a nation, and just before the Celestials' return. We will discuss these in detail in the last chapter.

More important than an exact time when the return will occur, however, is the question, how did Bible prophets living 2,500 years ago know that the Jews would be dispersed throughout the world? More incredible still, how did they know that against all odds they would return to a homeland in our own time? All other ancient peoples who were their contemporaries have long since disappeared. Yet the Jews have survived, without a national identity, for almost two millennia. As we shall see in the final chapter, John the Revelator, a New Testament prophet, actually foretold a number of developments which have taken place in our own time or are predicted for the near future.

If we find such accuracy in the prophecies which have already been fulfilled, can we not expect similar accuracy in the predictions concerning the actual takeover of the world itself? There are two reasons for thinking this is true. First, the prophecies concerning these end-of-the world events are the most precise and detailed in the entire Bible. Second, they describe techniques of conquest which are beyond our present capabilities and could have been known to the Bible writers only if they received it from a civilization more advanced than our own. Yet our own scientists and futurologists say these techniques are possible and will be achieved by us in the future.

In the next chapter we will run the Celestials' takeover of the world through in slow motion and see what the Bible has to say about it and how scientists think the technical problems unsolved might be solved.

And I heard a great voice out of heaven saying, Behold, the tabernacle of God is with men, and he will dwell with them, and they shall be his people, and God himself shall be with them, and be their God.

– John the Revelator, Revelation 21:3

CHAPTER IV

How to Take Over the World

THE ELEMENT OF SURPRISE

Military strategists tell us that one of the key elements in any successful invasion is surprise. In World War II the Allies concentrated on making the Normandy invasion of Europe a complete surprise to the Germans. This included allowing false invasion plans to fall into German hands and feinting invasion thrusts at other possible landing sites in Western Europe. Such measures will not be necessary for the Celestials who have the technology to land without warning and to seize worldwide control before resistance can be organized. The Bible stresses the suddenness of their return in many places. In the Gospel of Matthew, Jesus tells his disciples, "But of that day and hour knoweth no man, no, not the angels of heaven, but my Father only" (Matthew 24:36).

Again the Apostle Paul, in his letter to the Thessalonian church, reminds them, "For yourselves know perfectly that the day of the Lord so cometh as a thief in the night. For when they shall say, Peace and safety; then sudden destruction cometh upon them, as travail upon a woman with child; and they shall not escape" (I Thessalonians 5:2-3).

Could a civilization hundreds of thousands, or millions, of years in our technological future make such a sudden conquest of the world?

LANDING THE INVASION FORCE

In our attempt to describe the end of the world we pointed out that returning

Celestials would come in a space city, which would land, (without warning,) near the site of present-day Jerusalem. The shape and construction of this space city are given in Revelation and elsewhere in the Bible. John the Revelator tells us of a view he caught of it. He says, "And I John saw the holy city, new Jerusalem, coming down from God out of heaven, prepared as a bride adorned for her husband. And I heard a great voice out of heaven saying, Behold, the tabernacle of God is with men, and he will dwell with them, and they shall be his people, and God himself shall be with them, and be their God" (Revelation 21:2-3). Later he adds, "And the city lieth foursquare, and the length is as large as the breadth ..." (Revelation 21:16). The exact dimensions are given in two places in the Bible-the Old and New Testaments. They are just under a mile square by our units. John goes on to say that the space city has twelve gates and is made of a variety of materials which he took to be precious stones. Among these he mentions jasper, sapphire, emerald, topaz and streets of "pure gold." Strangely, he adds that the "pure gold" is like "transparent glass." Obviously, he is not speaking of real gold and probably not of actual gems. These are most likely synthetic materials selected for their structural properties and beauty.

It is curious, too, that John the Revelator, who could not have written this account later than the end of the first century of the common era, should have known about space cities. It is only in the last century that space scientists have realized the possibility of city-sized space ships (or what Isaac Asimov called "spomes") that could transport entire communities between the stars.

Speaking of such space cities Isaac Asimov suggested that in place of small ships, city sized ships could be built for trips to planets of the stars. In effect this would be a miniplanet, home to thousands of people, herds of animals, crops for food and a sealed-in climate. Generations would be born, grow old and die while such a ship traveled from one star to another.

If we, at our present primitive level of space exploration, are already talking of such ships, what might an alien civilization, millions of years ahead of us, have accomplished? Almost certainly they could carry whole populations for hundreds or thousands of years, if need be, while the vast distance between their world and ours was being traveled. Their ship would be capable of storing energy from the stars (and perhaps other sources as yet unavailable to us) It could recycle its wastes to provide continuous supplies of atmosphere, water and food/ Our space scientists are already planning propulsion systems which could drive a ship to within a fraction of a percent of the speed of light (670,615,000 miles per hour). By manipulation of gravity fields (which many of our futurologists believe is possible) a craft could have the ultimate propulsion system which would, at the same time, give it inertialess drive. It could reach its ultimate speed and stop within fractions of a second without injuring the occupants. It could also repel or dodge particles and debris in outer space by a "gravity shield" or make hairpin maneuvers at any speed. Writing of such a drive system, Arthur C. Clarke, a noted science writer and member of British astronautic and astronomical societies, observed, that such a craft could stop and start almost instantaneously.

Obviously, such a craft could fulfill the first condition necessary for a sudden takeover of the world without warning. Traveling almost as fast as light itself, or the radar signals which might be echoed from it, it could reach the Earth before our detection instruments could warn us. It could brake to an almost instantaneous halt from its incredible speed and land without injury to its occupants or equipment. Its coming would indeed be "as a thief in the night!"

HOW ABOUT THE DISTANCE PROBLEM?

One of the objections often raised to the idea of visits to other worlds, or visits from them to us, is the tremendous distances involved. Even at near the total speed of light the nearest neighboring star would require over four years to reach. As we will see, the crucial clues given in the Bible suggest that the Celestials' home base is much farther away.

Scientists today accept the idea, advanced in the theory of relativity, that the speed of light is the highest speed attainable. If this is true then even within our own galaxy distances might require tens of thousands of years to travel. If the Celestials come from beyond our galaxy it might require millions, or even billions, of years for the journey. Obviously, however, such vast journeys are not likely to have been involved. Their space program, like ours, probably called for a stepwise development. From their home planet they would have branched out in several directions toward the closest other planets meeting their requirements. From these they would jump off again to the next nearest planet, and the next, and the next. And so it would continue until sometime, perhaps millions or billions of years after they began, they would reach a planet near to us.

Perhaps, in the process, they would encounter other space missions from other advanced civilizations. Perhaps they would join forces. Perhaps all the advanced civilizations in the galaxy, or our region of the universe, are federated into a single space colonization effort. However it came about a time would arrive when the effort, involving one or many advanced civilizations, would find us the next nearest planet meeting the required conditions for colonization.

The actual journey, at this point, might only be a few light years' distance. It could be made as easily as we will journey to our nearest solar neighbors in the near future, easier, since we will probably not have achieved their speed capabilities at that time.

It would also be the case that, once here, they probably would maintain service bases within, or not far from, our planetary system. As we shall see later the Bible suggests they withdrew from Earth after completing the first stage in their colonization plan. Wherever their space city was moved, it, or other bases, remained close enough that they could return to Earth in a matter of days as certain Scriptures we will examine later claim.

Apart from all these considerations, however, there is another factor which far outweighs all of them in explaining how they have overcome the problem of distance. It has to do with the nature of time itself as a factor in covering distances.

A journey of a few light-years would obviously not be burdensome to immortals, especially if they were bringing their community with them and could carry on their life activities as usual. It would, however, be a sizable time span by ordinary standards and might test the patience of colonists eager to get on with the job ahead. In truth, however, measuring this time span by ordinary standards is deceptive if it is measured according to light-years of distance, for we are measuring the time required to cover it by Earth years. On a space ship going nearly the speed of light, the amount of time would have to be measured in relation to the speed of the ship itself, and would be different from the time that passed on Earth while the journey was in progress. It was Einstein who first proved mathematically, in his theory of relativity, that time does not flow at the same rate for everyone everywhere. The rate at which it passes depends on the speed of the observer and clocks as they measure time's passing. On a spaceship going nearly the speed of light the passage of time would be slowed almost to a standstill. This is not just a matter of speculation or theory. Laboratory observations on the life span of subatomic particles going at nearly the speed of light have detected such a slowdown in their rate of decay. In the same way passengers on a spaceship would have a corresponding slowdown in their own decay rates (or aging), as would everything else on the ship, including clocks. At a few feet per hour less than the absolute speed of light the slowdown would be so great that the passage of 1,000 years on Earth would, to the ship's passengers, take only a single day, and the journey of a few light-years from a nearby star might take only a few days by the ship's clocks.

When this "time-dilatation" effect is taken into account, it is obvious that great journeys between neighboring stars would be no more troublesome, to immortals, than our own commuting to work or one another's homes here on Earth.

"A THOUSAND YEARS AS ONE DAY"

The particular amount of time dilatation which we used here, as an example, was not selected by chance. It was deliberately chosen because it is given repeatedly in the Bible as a comparison between the Celestials' perception of time and our own. For example, the Psalmist David, in speaking of God, says, "For a thousand years in thy sight are but as yesterday when it is past, and as a watch in the night" (Psalms 90:4). Later the book of II Peter, in the New Testament, states, "But, beloved, be not ignorant of this one thing, that one day is with the Lord as a thousand years, and a thousand years as one day" (II Peter 3:8).

Theologians in the past have shrugged these passages aside as mere figures of speech used to emphasize the fact that even a millennium doesn't matter much to immortals. Today, in the space age, we can see these scriptures for what they really are – two of the most dramatic proofs we have that the writers of the Bible were in communication with extraterrestrials far in advance of our own civilization. How could David, over a millennium before Christ, and the author of II Peter, in the first century after Christ, have known about the time-dilatation effect unless they were told of it by the Celestials?

In his interesting work on astrobiology, The Cosmic Connection, the Cornell astronomer, Carl Sagan, raises the question of how ancient records (such as sacred writings or legends) could contain proof that their makers were in touch with advanced extraterrestrials. Writing of this, he claimed that there is only one kind of legend that would be convincing. When information is contained in the legend that could not possibly have come from by the civilization that left the record. As an example he suggested that if an ancient text regarded as sacred contained a clear reference to the "nuclear fine structure constant" this would be deserving of "considerable attention."

Now in these biblical assertions that 1,000 of our years are as a day to the Celestials we have such an exact numerical ratio "transmitted from thousands of years ago" which is precisely derivable from the critical constant in Einstein's formulation of the theory of relativity.

We have already seen that in order to come as "a thief in the night," the Celestials would have to travel at just under the speed of light-fast enough to keep up with our own detection signals. It is relatively easy, using Einstein's formula and a calculator, to compute the precise speed of a spacecraft in which a day in the craft would equal 1,000 years on Earth. Taking the speed of light to be 186.282 miles per second, the speed at which this ratio would exist would be 186,281.999999302 miles per second, or about 13 feet per hour less than the absolute speed of light. (We are indebted to Professor Robert Kroger of the Department of Mathematics at Riverside City College for performing these calculations and providing us with the results. The table showing his calculations and the equation he employed are included in the Appendix.)

The problem of acceleration and overcoming inertia might, at first, make such a velocity seem impossible of attainment. However, remembering what we said earlier about the possibility of manipulating gravity fields and creating inertialess drive, it is evident that if the Celestials have mastered such technologies, then the attainment of any speed short of the absolute speed of light would be possible. Further, using antigravity as a propulsion system such a speed could probably be attained almost instantaneously, as could deceleration and stopping from it.

In the assertion that "a thousand years is as one day" with the Lord, then, we have one of the most remarkable pieces of evidence possible that incredibly advanced Celestials told humans about the time dilatation effect over 2,000 years before Einstein formulated it. And, according to Carl Sagan's test, it is convincing evidence that the Bible is a record of extraterrestrial contact.

WHY DID THEY PICK US?

When Hitler invaded Czechoslovakia and Austria, people began to realize that he was a power-hungry madman. Germans followed him because their national pride had been destroyed and their country crushed by defeat and a vindictive peace treaty. His almost hypnotic powers of oratory persuaded them he had the solution. His successes convinced them he could bring it about in their time to restore Germany to its rightful place among nations.

In the case of the Celestials no such explanation seems possible. They are highly advanced and moral beings if the Bible is to be believed. Why would an advanced civilization of peace and justice wish to invade us even if they could? What do we have they would want? Why not some other planet within the billions that exist within our own galaxy or beyond? Why any other world if they are truly moral and godlike in their values and conduct?

While no specific answer is given to these questions in the Bible it contains a number of statements which suggest clues. Putting these together with what is being planned in our own future space program we can reach a probable answer.

At present our own space scientists and government planners are looking forward to the exploration and eventual colonization of outer space. Migration to other planets or the planets of other stars may be an eventual necessity. If our population problem, pollution and depletion of our natural environment continue, we may find this an attractive and inexpensive solution. It may be that some of these problems can be solved right here on Earth as technology advances. But the challenge of exploration and the promise of new rewards will undoubtedly drive us on. As long as new frontiers are out there something in our nature will spur us on to conquer them as we are already doing.

Of course our conquest of outer space is not planned as a violent or destructive one. Even in the history of our own planet more advanced nations have sometimes colonized those which were less advanced by methods that were cooperative and economic rather than violent and warlike.

We can assume, then, that long ago, perhaps millions of years, the Celestials started a program of exploration and colonization of outer space. As we suggested earlier, far from picking us as an isolated instance, we may be only one of many thousands or even millions of planets included in their space program. In the New Testament, Jesus suggests that this is so when, shortly before his death, he tells his disciples he must soon leave them. Peter asks him, "Lord, whither goest thou?" Jesus answers, "Whither I go, thou canst not follow me..." When Peter objects, Jesus goes on to explain, "In my Father's house are many mansions: if it were not so, I would have told you. I go to prepare a place for you. And if I go and prepare a place for you, I will come again, and receive you unto myself; that where I am, there ye may be also" (John 13:36, 14:2-3). Evidently the "many mansions" to which Jesus refers are communities off this Earth, where the Celestials dwell. And the prepared "place" is evidently the space city in which they plan to return so that their followers here on Earth may be with them.

What motives they would have for selecting Earth as one of their colonies is problematic. Perhaps, being immortal, they too have an overpopulation problem which requires constant territorial expansion. Perhaps, being immortal they eventually are forced to migrate from worlds with dying suns to others whose suns, like our own, are still young. Perhaps, being thousands, or millions, of years advanced beyond us, they have reasons that are beyond our understanding.

In any event, it seems likely they picked our world specifically because it is like their own and is close enough to make colonization easy. Already our own space scientists have detected many stars with planetary systems. Two of these, Barnard's Star and Epsilon Eridani, are likely candidates for early exploration and landings as our space program develops. We are already able to determine the size and number of planets surrounding many other stars in our neighborhood of the Milky Way.

If this is true, at our primitive level, then it is clear that a civilization thousands, or millions, of years more advanced than ours would have methods for studying worlds throughout the universe without leaving their home base. Long before they came to Earth they undoubtedly knew of its existence, its structure and climate, its ability to support life and its resources. It was no doubt carefully chosen because it is suited to their colonization program and purposes. By monitoring for level of energy uses and finding none, they probably also knew we lacked advanced technological civilization and could be colonized without the necessity of violence or warfare. Unlike human colonists, who have often enslaved or destroyed native populations where they colonized, the Celestials domesticate and improve the natives they colonize here. As we shall see in a later chapter, the Bible teaches that they recreated us by genetic surgery in their own image with the intention of eventually including us in their civilization. To them we are not domestic animals or slaves but children and heirs.

"A GREAT VOICE OUT OF HEAVEN"

In the opening of Chapter III we describe a sequence of events which will follow the actual landing of the Celestials. The first of these is the announcement of their return and takeover. Speaking of this John the Revelator says, "And I heard a great voice out of heaven saying, Behold, the tabernacle of God is with men, and he will dwell with them, and they shall be his people, and God himself shall be with them, and be their God" (Revelation 21:3). The Apostle Paul is even more dramatic in his description when he says, "For the Lord himself shall descend from heaven with a shout, with the voice of the archangel, and with the trump of God ..." (I Thessalonians 4:16).

In the past scientifically oriented critics of the Bible have ridiculed the idea that a localized event could be seen and heard simultaneously all around the world, as Paul and John seem to claim of the Celestials' final return. They have pointed out that even major astronomical events, such as comets and eclipses, can be seen only in certain regions of the Earth and at certain times. How then could the swift arrival of anything as small as a spacecraft be seen by everyone all over the world at the same time?

This question might have seemed unanswerable until the last half of the last Century, when the launching of satellites made worldwide radio and television communication a reality. Launched in an orbit synchronous with the Earth's rotation, these signal reflectors hover continuously over the same point on the Earth and can blanket its entire surface instantaneously with communications reflected from surface stations. It would be a simple matter for returning Celestials to fire synchronous satellites from their approaching space city into orbits that would cover the Earth's surface with signals.

The nature of these systems can only be guessed at from clues provided by the Scriptures and developments pending in our own communications technologies. We can surmise, for instance, that since "every eye shall see him" (Revelation 1:7), reception will not be on conventional receivers or television sets. Only a sky broadcast, of the sort described in the opening of Chapter III, would make this possible. The Bible implies that such a sudden lighting up of the entire sky with a projected image will be the means of visual communication when it says, "For as the lightning cometh out of the east, and shineth even unto the west; so shall also the coming of the Son of man be" (Matthew 24:27).

Looking at our own projected developments in visual communications there is a technique currently underway which could make this possible-the holographic image. This image, in three dimensions, rather than the conventional two, can be created by laser beams projected on fine droplets suspended in the air, Current planning in television production foresees the possibility of creating a theater-in-the-round in the center of one's own living room where three-dimensional images, viewed from any angle, will act out their parts like actors on a real stage.

The projection of simultaneous horizon-to-horizon images on suspended atmospheric droplets, homogenized by ultrasound, would produce exactly the effect which the Scriptures describe: "Behold, he cometh with the clouds; and every eye shall see him ..." (Revelation I: 7).

Auxiliary satellites suspended nearer the surface of the Earth, by antigravity, could also pick up radio signals and convert them into audible sound. A civilization millions, or billions, of years in our technological future would doubtless have no difficulty in powering these suspended loudspeakers with enough energy to produce the "trump-like" voice from the heavens which the Scriptures describe. And such an unconventional lightning-like sky image and trumpet-like voice would provide the one sure effect which could instantaneously capture the attention of every conscious man, woman and child on our planet!

"CAUGHT UP TO MEET THE LORD"

In our account at the opening of Chapter III we saw that another event will take place immediately as the Celestials are touching down. This is catching up and transporting to their headquarters leaders from all over the Earth including those who have died in the past.

At first glance this statement seems to contain two of the most preposterous assertions possible: that people can be instantaneously transported, through the air, from all over the Earth; and that the dead can be resurrected. Either statement, by itself, would strain the common sense or belief of most scientifically trained people. Certainly nothing in our present day technology would indicate that such things are possible. Let's look at the matter more closely, however, in terms of the Bible and futurology. What exactly does the Bible say about these matters?

In I Thessalonians the Apostle Paul speaks of the gathering of the righteous in this fashion: "For the Lord himself shall descend from heaven with a shout, with the voice of the archangel, and with the trump of God: and the dead in Christ shall rise first: Then we which are alive and remain shall be caught up together with them in the clouds to meet the Lord in the air: and so shall we ever be with the Lord" (I Thessalonians 4:16-17). And according to Jesus the suddenness of these events will be such that "Then shall two be in the field; the one shall be taken, the other left. Two women shall be grinding at the mill; the one shall be taken, and the other left" (Matthew 24:40-41).

The order of events, according to Paul, then, is resurrection first, then teleportation of the living. What does current technology and the forecasts by futurologists indicate about the possibility of resurrection of the dead?

"THE DEAD IN CHRIST SHALL RISE"

This is a question about which we shall have a great deal to say later. For the present we will start by pointing out that resurrection of the "clinically dead" is already possible. The distinction between "clinical" death and final death is a difficult one to make. In many parts of the world current medical opinion defines final death as the absence of brain waves when tested with an electroencephalograph (the device which records changes in the electrical activity of the brain). Clinical death is often defined in terms of the absence of a detectable heartbeat and respiration.

There are a variety of techniques-mechanical, chemical and electrical-by which physicians can start an arrested heart beating and force respiration. When these occur resurrection from a degree of death also occurs. Once the body has begun to decay, however, even if it is only the death of brain cells from lack of oxygen (which begins a few minutes after respiration stops), death rapidly becomes irreversible by presently known techniques.

Is it likely that a civilization millions or billions of years in our future could reverse the later stages of death or even reconstitute a dead person who had totally decayed? This problem is an extremely complex one and can only be adequately discussed after we have reviewed a good deal of present biological research and medical opinion. For the present it is enough to note that the DNA code, complete in every cell of our bodies, contains a blueprint for reconstructing the entire body in its most minute details. If any part of the body remains, even bones, it would be theoretically possible to reconstitute the entire individual from such fragments. Similarly, our entire experience and learning is stored, like records on magnetic tape, in other coded changes made in the RNA structure of the brain cells. Studies such as those by Wilder Penfield at the University of Montreal have shown that the brain retains a minute record of everything that happens to individuals. This even includes things of which they may not be consciously aware at the time they occur. Speaking of the moment-to-moment continuity and sharp detail of the brain's recording mechanism, which he activates by stimulating points on the cerebral cortex with electrodes, Penfield stated that it is as if a strip of cinematographic film with sound track had been set in motion within the brain.

If such records could be read and copied it would be possible to reconstitute individuals (complete to their most trivial habits and memories) hundreds, or even thousands, of years after their death. They could be produced with a physical perfection they never had in real life, since their original genetic blueprint could be followed exactly without the usual flaws that arise from accidents or illness. They could be reproduced at any stage and age which they attained during their actual lifetime. And all of this could be done even though every trace of their physical remains had been obliterated or lost and only records of their characteristics remained. The problem would not be greatly different in kind, but only in complexity, from reproducing the voices of people, long dead, from recordings made while they were living. What would be required in the case of resurrection would be a device which could scan and read the DNA patterns contained in the cells of those to be resurrected while they were still living. The scanner would function much as a microphone functions for the human voice. Later the records produced by scanning could be fed into a replicator which would then reconstitute the individual from suitable raw materials, much as an amplifier and loudspeaker or camera and projector can reproduce the voice of a dead person or their image from electromagnetic records.

The Bible indicates that the Celestials, in monitoring and guiding the progress of their human recreation here on Earth, have kept such records throughout human history. The Psalmist writing of their monitoring and record keeping, exclaims, "I will praise thee; for I am fearfully and wonderfully made: marvelous are thy works ... My substance was not hid from thee, when I was made in secret ... Thine eyes did see my substance ... and in thy book all my members were written, which in continuance were fashioned, when as yet there was none of them" (Psalms 139:14 - 6). Not only does the Bible claim the Celestials keep continuing records on the members of every person, even when they no longer physically exist, but it also claims this record keeping extends to the conduct and behavior of each person. Thus their experience and learning are recorded as well. Writing of this, John the Revelator says, "And I saw the dead, small and great, stand before God; and the books were opened: and another book was opened, which is the book of life: and the dead were judged out of those things which were written in the books, according to their works" (Revelation 20:12).

Recently the press has had a great deal to say about the problem of invasion of privacy in our age of computer science and automated record keeping. Spokesmen for government and business talk of developments which may soon make it possible to merge records from the Social Security System, the Bureau of Internal Revenue, the military and the Veterans Administration, credit bureaus, motor vehicle departments and law enforcement agencies all over the country. These consolidated records could be secured in a central data bank, and anyone could find out virtually anything about anybody by merely entering an access number.

Yet such a universal information bank and our present world wide web must be crude and inefficient compared to what could probably be accomplished by a truly advanced civilization like that of the Celestials. We have already argued that their superior technologies would enable them to monitor planets throughout their empire. It seems more incredible that they could monitor, record, store and retrieve personal data on living individuals on these planets. Yet, when we consider what we at our primitive level are already doing in monitoring the Earth's surface, the claims of the Bible, in this respect, seem more believable.

Our geopositioning satellites are already able to scan the entire surface of the Earth from outer space with such fine resolution that individual features of the terrain, such as ponds and buildings, can be distinguished. Our spy satellites can observe travel routes of cars and design features of houses and buildings from their lofty orbits. Using a technique of spectrographic analysis called "band ratioing," scientists can even trace the progress of crop epidemics and the effects of pesticides. Is it improbable, then, that a technology which has had millions of years to mature beyond our own could read the nucleic-acid patterns of individuals or monitor and record learning patterns stored in their brain cells from space satellites, or even their home base in a distant region of the universe?

If such things are possible then the resurrection of the dead for an entire planet might be accomplished by them as easily as we can turn manufactured items off an assembly line. With a set of master blueprints recorded in a "book of life," and replicating technology they could reconstitute the dead of all ages "in the twinkling of an eye," as the Apostle Paul puts it. Speaking of how such a replicating machine might work Arthur Clarke wrote that scientists of the future might have far more sophisticated tools that could lay bare the details of any object scanned by them and reproduce it in all its complexity just as our present technologies can reproduce any piece of music or video sequence presented in digital form. This would presumably include the recreation of even a complete human being if records made during his or her original lifetime were preserved.

As we will see later it is also possible that mass resurrection could be accomplished by non-mechanical means involving forms of energy and types of records which are only now beginning to be explored in parapsychology. These would probably be more efficient and swifter than the use of a material replicator. Their nature will be taken up when we discuss mass resurrection at the Celestials' final return.

The Bible leaves no doubt that the Celestials do intend mass resurrection and conditional immortality which goes with it. This is the most precious gift they have to offer. In scripture after scripture, like a golden thread, this promise occurs in both the Old and New Testaments. "Search the scriptures; for in them ye think ye have eternal life" (John 5: 39), the book of John, admonishes us. Long before John the author of Daniel, writing of their Celestial return, says, "And many of them that sleep in the dust of the Earth shall awake, some to everlasting life ... And they that be wise shall shine as the brightness of the firmament; and they that turn many to righteousness, as the stars for ever and ever" (Daniel 2:2-3). Paul, the Apostle, assures us "the gift of God is eternal life" (Romans 6:23) and declares himself to be "In hope of eternal life, which God, that cannot lie, promised before the world began" (Titus I: 2). Time after time Jesus, throughout the gospels, utters this promise until the reiteration of it reverberates through the mind like a Celestial echochamber" For God so loved the world, that he gave his only begotten Son, that whosoever believeth in him should not perish, but have everlasting life" (John 3:16). "Verily, verily, I say unto you, He that heareth my word, and believeth on him that sent me, hath everlasting life" (John 5:24). "My sheep hear my voice, and I know them, and they follow me: And I give unto them eternal life; and they shall never perish, neither shall any man pluck them out of my hand" (John 10:27-28). "... they which shall be accounted worthy to obtain ... resurrection from the dead ... [do not] die any more: for they are equal unto the angels; and are the children of God, being the children of the resurrection" (Luke 20:35-36). "I am the resurrection, and the life: he that believeth in me, though he were dead, yet shall he live" (John 11:25).

Could a race millions of years in our technological future keep such a promise? Do the Scriptures contain the key to eternal life? We will examine the basis for this claim in the chapters ahead.

"CAUGHT UP"

In Paul's discussion of the general resurrection at the time of the Celestials' return he adds that those resurrected, along with the living righteous, will all be "caught up together with them in the clouds, to meet the Lord ..." (I Thessalonians 4:17). The Greek word translated "caught up" here is a peculiar one. It is not the ordinary word used throughout the New Testament where its writers wish to say someone catches somebody or something. It is a word which is only used three times in the entire New Testament and only in connection with sudden bodily transportation from one place to another by apparently "supernatural" means. Once it is used in the Acts of the Apostles to describe a mysterious process by which "the Spirit of the Lord caught away" Philip and suddenly transported him to another city (Acts 8:39). Paul uses it when he describes being "caught up to the third heaven" (II Corinthians 12:2), and he uses it again in the passage just quoted from I Thessalonians. The word used is "harpazo" which is usually translated to seize, pluck, pull or take by force.

The fact that this special word is used in these descriptions of apparently "supernatural" transportation suggests that some very unusual process is involved. In the past higher critics of the Bible have ridiculed the passage in I Thessalonians which seems to picture the righteous sailing through the air, in defiance of gravity, like medieval witches on their way to the Sabbath. How, they ask, could bodily transportation without flying craft be possible? Even witches used satanically empowered broomsticks.

A look at futurology makes the meaning of these passages and the word "harpazo" as used in them clearer. In his already mentioned book, *Profiles of the Future,* Arthur C. Clarke raises an interesting question. He notes that we can send sounds and images round the world at the velocity of light, so why not solid objects-even people? He then goes on to describe a "matter transmitter" which could scan a material object, atom by atom, and transmit information obtained from it to a distant receiver. The receiver would then feed the information into a replicator, such as we have already described, and a duplicate of the original would be assembled from the information transmitted.

His question, posed more than four decades ago, has now been answered by technological advances in dealing with quantum phenomena. In his challenging book, Physics of the Impossible, Michio Kaku, professor of Theoretical Physics at the City College of the City University of New York cites experiments in Europe and the Institute of Standards and Technology, in Washington D.C., which have successfully teleported photons and even atoms. Based on these results he predicts that "within decades" it may become possible to teleport a DNA molecule or even a virus. He goes on to comment that nothing in principle would prevent teleporting people.

With the teleportation of persons the originals are disassembled (or disintegrated) and reassembled at the other end. Could a technology far in advance of our own perform such a feat? Arthur C. Clarke apparently believes even our own may accomplish the teleportation of people someday. Paul says the Celestials have already mastered this problem. He goes on to add an even more exciting assertion. In the Celestials' version of teleportation the original is not just reassembled; it is also corrected. Each of us is the outcome of original genetic instructions which have been carried out imperfectly. Developmental failures, accidents, illness and aging have left each of us with imperfections which fall short of the original blueprint contained in our cells. Paul implies that when people are reassembled, at their meeting with the Lord of the Celestials, they will be reassembled without the imperfections. Speaking of this he says, "Behold, I show you a mystery ... we shall all be changed. In a moment, in the twinkling of an eye, at the last trump: for the trumpet shall sound, and the dead shall be raised incorruptible, and we shall be changed. For this corruptible must put on incorruption, and this mortal must put on immortality" (I Corinthians 15:51-53).

Evidently, then, those who are to share in the civilization the Celestials intend to establish here on Earth will be reconstituted with sound health in perfect bodies free of aging and capable of immortality, and this will be accomplished instantaneously upon their return. This age-old dream of orthodox Christians, so often ridiculed by higher critics, is not only not preposterous, it is just a little in advance of what our own molecular biologists and medical researchers are already planning for the future.

We have already seen that the scriptures assert the Celestials keep track of every human on this planet and keep records of their parts and deeds in a "book of life." These records are so minute as to contain the exact and unique DNA blueprint for each individual. As Jesus observes in Luke: "But even the very hairs of your head are all numbered" (Luke 12:7}.

We might wonder why a civilization with truly advanced capabilities would bother with gathering and recording such trivial data, but the answer evidently lies in the fact that they are so advanced it is no bother at all. For a truly advanced civilization keeping track of the DNA patterns of a few billion humans on a few thousands or millions of planets would perhaps pose no greater problems than exist for the motor vehicle departments of our own states to keep track of automobile registrations or the FBI of fingerprints.

And if they do keep track of individuals then focusing energies on selected ones of them which could teleport them, in an instant, to a predetermined gathering place would probably be no more difficult than for us to select specific people, at widely scattered points, for communication through internet technology.

IS A WORLDWIDE TTC POSSIBLE?

At the opening of the last chapter our attempt to imagine the return of the Celestials suggested that they would communicate with those left behind when the righteous are caught up by a worldwide Thought Transference Communications System. What does futurology have to say about such an idea?

We take it for granted in the last half of the Twentieth Century, that we can communicate with almost anyone in the civilized areas of our world, by cell phones or world wide web.

The receiving of messages anywhere in the world without special equipment, however, is another matter. To make this possible some method of energizing brain cells without going through the usual channels of the senses must be employed. Current technologies for monitoring electrical activity in the brain have established it is the basis for learning and memory. Experiments have shown that electrodes implanted in the brain, or even equipment that generates strong electromagnetic fields placed against the skull, can also set up electrical activity which generates memories. It seems likely, to our own futurologists, that a time may come when electromagnetic signals generated at a distance can impose thought patterns on the brain. If this could be accomplished, then each of us could be linked with a central communications center which could impose thoughts at will. If it contained a sufficiently vast memory bank we might even acquire direct and immediate access to all the world's knowledge, or receive learning, without having to go through ordinary education processes.

To a civilization that can keep continuous track of each individual on a planet, the monitoring and recording of every person's thoughts and the imposition of knowledge and instructions by "thought transference" would be a rather obvious development. The Scriptures seem to suggest that the Celestials' monitoring activity extends not only to individual acts but to thoughts as well. Speaking of this, Jesus reminds his disciples, "But when ye pray, use not vain repetitions, as the heathen do: for they think that they shall be heard for their much speaking. Be not ye therefore like unto them: for your Father knoweth what things ye have need of, before ye ask him" (Matthew 6:7-8).

One of the most interesting applications of such a technological development would be imparting large bodies of knowledge by instant imprinting of the brain. This would take place in much the same way that a machine can imprint an extended piece of music, which might take thirty or forty minutes of performance, in a few seconds on the surface of a compact disc. In this way a person might instantaneously learn a branch of mathematics or a foreign language.

Such a procedure could even be imposed on a large number of people simultaneously by irradiating their brains with suitable electromagnetic or other information-carrying signals. This would make the sky broadcast of our opening scenario a possibility. People all over the world would sense they were hearing a "foreign" language, yet surprisingly would understand it, no matter what their native tongue, if their brains had been programmed by a worldwide instant language course imposed as the Celestials land. We will have more to say about this in our discussion of xenoglossy in Chapter XIV.

"ONE LIKE UNTO THE SON OF MAN"

The last technological marvel which we discussed in our reconstruction of the Celestials' takeover was the use of human-like robots to carry out their plans and to enforce their will. Again our description of such a robot was not fanciful. The Scriptures give a number of detailed accounts of these devices which closely support our description.

In Revelation John tells of an encounter with one in them. "I was in the Spirit on the Lord's day, and heard behind me a great voice, as of a trumpet. ... And I turned to see the voice that speaks with me.... I saw ... one like unto the Son of man, clothed with a garment down to the foot, and girt about the paps with a golden girdle. His head and his hairs were white like wool, as white as snow, and his eyes were as a flame of fire: And his feet like unto fine brass, as if they burned in a furnace; and his voice as the sound of many waters.... and out of his mouth went a sharp two-edged sword: and his countenance was as the sun shineth in his strength" (Revelation 1:10-16).

If John's description is to be believed what he saw, like our robot in the last chapter, had a human form; had a chest and feet which appeared metallic; had burning, laser-like eyes, and was capable of emitting a sword-like beam from its mouth that could destroy whatever got in its way. Other descriptions given in the Bible also suggest these devices emit some sort of radiation which can produce drowsiness in humans and neutralize their resistance to the robot's control. In an encounter reported in Daniel, in the Old Testament, the writer tells how he saw "a certain man clothed in linen, whose loins were girded with fine gold of Uphaz: His body also was like the beryl, and his face as the appearance of lightning, and his eyes as lamps of fire, and his arms and feet like in colour to polished brass, and the voice of his words like the voice of a multitude. . .Yet heard I the voice of his words: aud when I heard the voice of his words, then was I in a deep sleep on my face, and my face toward the ground" (Daniel 10:5-6, 9).

Apparently the Celestials have a great variety of robots (or "servomechanisms" as futurologists sometimes call them), and they are not always human in form. They are generally referred to, in the Old Testament, by the Hebrew word "keruwb", which as we have already seen is translated "cherub." And although scholarly tradition has regarded cherubim as a species of angel, it is clear, as we have shown, that they were mechanical devices and not supernatural beings.

The portrait of the robot in chapter III is not fanciful; it is biblical and, according to the Scriptures, such devices will play a crucial role in the Celestials' takeover of our planet. They will carry out the drudgery of the occupation government's work; they will suppress resistance to its rule, and they will perform courier and low-level administrative duties.

Equipped with elaborate, long-range sensors, possessing advanced automotive and manipulation systems, armed with death-ray laser beams and programmed with artificial intelligence, such devices will make the Celestials' takeover of our world as swift and irresistible as the Bible claims it will be. And through them the warlike and rebellious of all nations will be brought into submission and ruled "with a rod of iron; as the vessels of a potter shall they be broken to shivers ..." (Revelation 2:27).

"TO EVER BE WITH THE LORD"

For those, however, who are caught up "to ever be with the Lord," the 1,000 year provisional government, and the permanent acceptance into the Celestial Confederation which will follow, will usher in an era of unparalleled peace, affluence and splendor. The wonders of a millennium in which the arid lands of the Earth are reclaimed to fertile abundance, pollution is eliminated, and war, famine, crime, disease and death are abolished are difficult to imagine. Looking down the long centuries to the glories of this period, the Old Testament Prophet Isaiah rhapsodizes: "The wilderness and the solitary place shall be glad for them; and the desert shall rejoice, and blossom as the rose. It shall blossom abundantly, and rejoice even with joy and singing.... Then the eyes of the blind shall be opened, and the ears of the deaf shall be unstopped. Then shall the lame man leap as a hart, and the tongue of the dumb sing: for in the wilderness shall waters break out, and streams in the desert. ... And an highway shall be there, and a way, and it shall be called The way of holiness; the unclean shall not pass over it ... And the ransomed of the Lord shall return, and come to Zion with songs and everlasting joy upon their heads: they shall obtain joy and gladness, and sorrow and sighing shall flee away" (Isaiah 35:1-2, 5-6, 8, 10).

Who are the Celestials who promise such a heritage? Why have they selected us as their heirs? What must we do to claim our inheritance? In the next chapter we will take a closer look at our benefactors.

All flesh is not the same flesh: but there is one kind of flesh of men, another flesh of beasts, another of fishes, and another of birds. There are also Celestial bodies and bodies terrestrial: but the glory of the Celestial is one, and the glory of the terrestrial is another.

– Paul, I Corinthians 15:39-40

CHAPTER V

Who Are the Celestials?

IS ANYONE OUT THERE?

In the Renaissance, when Columbus set out on his famous voyage, most educated Europeans regarded him as a dreamer and a fool. The Earth round? You could get to the Indies by sailing west? Didn't the Bible speak of the "four corners of the Earth" (Isaiah 11:12; Revelation 7:1}? How could it be round, then? And, even if it were, how could there be people on the other side? They would be hanging heads downward. Wouldn't they fall off? And wouldn't Columbus and his sailors, too, as they sailed around to the underside? These arguments seemed obvious to most good churchmen and even to the court astronomers.

The idea that there might be vast continents beyond the shores of Europe, Asia and Africa seemed as fantastic to them as the idea of other inhabited worlds seems to some of us to day. More fantastic, probably, since they believed the world to be small, flat and square. Not far beyond the familiar trade routes lay troubled seas teeming with monsters and dragons. Daring travelers had seen them rearing out of storm-tossed waves near the awful edge of the Earth where thundering waters spilled into the void below like some hellish Niagara. A few had turned back in time and lived to tell their tall tales to marveling listeners back home. How, then, could there be vast lands with millions of inhabitants beyond such horrors? Would a good God have created them there knowing they could never be reached by his true faith and church which had been revealed, once and for all, at the center of the Earth in Palestine?

Half a millennium after Columbus, we are in much the same position today. Good churchmen and self-appointed "authorities" are assuring us that the idea of millions of worlds beyond our own, containing thousands, or millions, of advanced civilizations is totally without foundation and even absurd. God created this planet as a one-time special setting for a one-time special creation. Why would he want other creations? Doesn't the Bible say that God put "lights in the firmament of the heaven to divide the day from the night; and let them be for signs, and for seasons, and for days, and years" and "for lights in the firmament of the heaven to give light upon the Earth" (Genesis 1:14-15)? Isn't this Scripture just as plain as the ones that say the Earth has "four corners"? Obviously the stars and planets are just up there for farmers' almanacs and so country people can get along without street lights.

And the idea that those stars are surrounded by worlds containing magnificent civilizations that surpass our own? How could any civilization excel our own? Haven't we already topped the wildest flights of imagination in creating computers and moon rockets and splendid atomic and hydrogen bombs?

What would a really advanced civilization do that could go beyond these things? Even our best science-fiction writers, for the most part, imagine only bigger and better gadgetry; totally automated economies; intergalactic rockets instead of moon rockets; stellar explosions instead of hydrogen bombs. But the people themselves - their social systems and laws; their art and recreation; their moral values and religions? Undoubtedly it is much harder for us to imagine a Celestial civilization millions of years ahead of our own than it was for Native Americans, without the wheel, wagons or guns, to imagine European civilization before Columbus came.

Yet a truly advanced civilization has already been here. It was witnessed thousands of years ago by a number of perceptive human scribes. Detailed accounts of their visit can be read in the collection of books called the Bible. In its pages we find a wealth of information about those ancient astronauts whom it calls the Lord God and the angels. It gives us descriptions of their physical appearance, their language, their habits, rituals and values. It tells of their architecture, their art, their agriculture, their government and their moral precepts. It describes their spacecraft, their communications systems, their weapons and their use of unknown energy forms which can perform miracles of healing, restoration and even resurrection! Let's take a look at what it has to say about our Celestial forebears.

"MANY MANSIONS"

We have already seen that the New Testament suggests there are other inhabited worlds. Jesus' famous remark that "in my father's house are many mansions" (John 14:2) was made to his disciples just before "he was parted from them, and carried up into heaven" (Luke 24:51). He prefaced it by saying, "I go to prepare a place for you" (John 14:2). The implication is clearly that the "place" he went to and prepared was off this world. It was his father's (the Lord God's) "house." The Greek word used for "house" here is "oikia", which is usually translated as a "family" or "household." Jesus' statement that the Lord God's "family" or "household" contains many "mansions" uses another Greek word, "mone", which implies specific "abodes" or "staying places." If the "household" of the Celestials is in the heavens and contains many inhabited "abodes" or "staying places," then it seems clear that Jesus' reference was to some sort of family, or confederation, of inhabited worlds to which, according to the gospel writers, he returned after his resurrection. This "family" would presumably consist of the Celestials' home planet and all of the others which they have colonized. What do modern astronomers and astrobiologists have to say about the possibility of other inhabited worlds and advanced civilizations?

Since the ancient astronaut hypothesis became popular, in the last Century, there has been a rash of critics who have tried to refute the idea of life on other worlds. Most of them either try to argue that it is impossible or take the gentler position that there is no good reason for thinking it is so. Like Columbus' critics who argued the impossibility of other inhabited continents on this world these critics have used everything, from Bible quotations and pseudoscience to sarcasm and appeals to their own "authority," to bolster their contention that the universe is a junk yard of dead matter. The single exception is our own planet, Earth.

A few examples will serve to point up the parallel between Columbus and his medieval-scholastic critics and our present day astrobiologists and their critics. The recent launching of space telescopes, including the newest "Kepler," has already revealed over 4,000 planets orbiting stars in our region of the Milky Way Galaxy. Of these, several hundred are sufficiently Earth-like to make the existence of life and civilizations a possibility if not probability. This sample makes up only about 2% of our galaxy's hundred billion stars. Further, meteorites from outer space sometimes contain amino acids that are the building blocks of life as we know it.

From these discoveries, then, we can see that the idea of life on other worlds is far more believable, in our own day, than the idea of transoceanic life was in Columbus' time and has far more evidence to support it.

Yet, as any elementary-school child knows, Columbus was right. And the elementary school children of tomorrow will know that myriads of inhabited worlds lie beyond the reach of our present-day rockets. Because of this many scientists are now recognizing the near certainty of life on other worlds.

"IN OUR IMAGE"

When it comes to the question of what these other worldly beings might be like we are not confined to guesswork. One race of them has visited us the Bible claims, and we were remade in their image. We, humankind, are the mirror in which their likeness is revealed. The best in our minds and culture faintly suggests the sublime range of their civilization and the loftiness of their moral purposes. But the resemblance is not just mental or cultural.

In the first chapter of Genesis we read that God said, "Let us make man in our image, after our likeness," and "So God created man in his own image; in the image of God created he him; male and female created he them" (Genesis 1:26-27). There are some who would argue that this passage simply means that man is like God in some immaterial way-his mind, his moral nature or his soul. They would insist that God is an immaterial, spiritual being, and therefore man could not resemble him in a physical way. Those who believe this are the victims of a misunderstanding which arose after the Bible was written.

As we will show in the next chapter, the term "God" is used in the Bible to refer to two different creators. One is the unseen ultimate Creative Power of the universe which created and sustains everything. It is often referred to as a "spirit," as when John says, "God is a Spirit" (John 4:24). But the Greek and Hebrew words used in the Bible for "spirit" simply mean a "breath" or "wind." What they imply is that a spirit, like the wind, is an unseen power. And when John says, "God is a Spirit," he means that the creator of the universe is an unseen power.

The idea that a spirit is a kind of immaterial, ghostly person was foreign to the Bible writers and crept into Christianity in the early centuries after the Bible was written. Plato, the Greek philosopher, had taught that the material world is just a shadow of a higher, immaterial world. His follower, Plotinus, taught that God, as the highest reality, must be wholly immaterial. Early church fathers, such as Augustine, wanted to harmonize Christian doctrine with this Greek thinking which dominated their world. As a result, and over the centuries, the idea developed that God and the angels, as the highest realities, are immaterial and "spiritual"; the everyday world, as the lowest reality, is mere matter, and man is somewhere in between-a godlike soul in a material body.

So when John said, "God is a Spirit," he did not mean that the Creative Power that brought the universe into being is a ghostly person. And he was not speaking of the same creator who made man in his image. That creator is also referred to as "God" in the Bible (or the "Lord God" more often), but he is clearly not an "unseen power." He is quite personal, material and humanlike (or rather, humans are like him), as we will presently see.

The confusion of these two creators-one an unseen power, the other a flesh-and-blood astronaut from another world has arisen because the first two chapters of the Bible, which tell about the creation of the world and humans, are the result of a succession of editorial efforts. Using several sources of oral tradition early editors, tried to weld them into a consistent account. Because of this it seems that these two chapters tell the creation story twice over, once in very general terms, in the first chapter, and again, in much greater detail, with the emphasis on the creation of humans, in the second chapter.

A careful study of these two narratives shows, however, that they are not two descriptions of the same creation. Even a casual inspection of their order in telling the events of creation suggests that this is so. The first account, in the first chapter, says that "God" created vegetation, marine life, fowls of the air, land animals and "man", male and female, (Genesis 1:11-26) in that order. The second, in the second chapter, says the "Lord God" formed man, put him in the Garden, made vegetation to grow, formed land animals and birds and brought them to Adam for naming, and, last of all, caused a deep sleep to fall on Adam and took out one of his ribs, from which woman was formed (Genesis 2:7-22).

In the first account life is created in the same order evolutionary biology claims-vegetation, sea animals, land animals and last of all, man-male and female. In the second, man comes first, then the plants and lower animals and, last of all, woman.

It is significant that as early as the Third Century one of Christianity's first great textual scholars, Origin of Alexandria, recognized that these two accounts in Genesis 1 and 2 could not be dealing with the same creation. He also taught that the literal sense of scripture is not always the one meant as its truth, because many texts use figurative language to convey deeper hidden truths which often becomes clearer when different passages and translations are compared with one another. He even compiled a multiple translation, parallel passage version of scripture known as the Hexipla for finding such hidden meanings.

And just as these two accounts describe two separate creations, one a general evolutionary creation and the other a special, experimental creation in the Garden of Eden, so there are two creators. And it is the second of these that interests us here, for it is in that creator's image that we were remade. Though editorial lifting and rearranging have made it seem that the statement "Let us make man in our image, after our likeness ..." refers to the evolutionary creator (since it occurs in the first narrative), we will show it could only refer to the Lord God of the second narrative, a flesh-and-blood Celestial from another world.

This "Lord God" with accompanying "angels" are the Celestials who visited us so long ago and are soon returning to complete their colonization of the Earth. They are the "gods" (elohim) whose image we mirror, for they are our ancestors and we their heirs. And it is from an examination of ourselves and clues given in the Scriptures that we can find the answer to that all-important question, "Who are the Celestials?"

In the early centuries of Christianity, after the doctrine that God and the angels are immaterial had become established, church fathers discouraged interpretations which made them too human. They reasoned that a "spiritual" being could not have a physical form. Later anthropologists called the tendency of primitive peoples to worship human-like gods "anthropomorphism" (from two Greek words meaning "human/form"). Many theologians have followed the early church fathers in viewing anthropomorphism as naive and ignorant. If, however, the Celestials are flesh and blood, then they must have a physical form, and if they made us in their image there is nothing naive in assuming that form would be human-like.

In the end, then, we come back to the simple scriptural statement that "God created man in his own image" (Genesis 1:27). And that the resemblance is physical, as well as mental and spiritual there can be no doubt, for the Lord God is quoted as saying he is a physical flesh-and-blood being a little later in Genesis. Deploring the depravity into which man has fallen, after his original sin and expulsion from the Garden, the Lord says: "My Spirit shall not always strive with man for that he also is flesh" (Genesis 6:3). Now the question this raises is "also" in addition to whom? It is clear, from the preceding passage, that the "also" refers to the Lord himself. The implication is that if the Lord and his angels are flesh and can live up to the difficult standards the Lord sets, then it is not unreasonable to ask humans to do so, too. The Lord, being flesh, knows what flesh is capable of and will not settle for less than our best. Therefore, his spirit will not always strive with human wrongdoing.

If further proof is needed on this point, there is much of it throughout the Bible. The Lord walks in the Garden in the cool of the day and calls out to Adam and Eve (Genesis 3:8)-he is sensitive to heat and cold and produces sound waves in the air. He confronts Cain and Abel and receives offerings of food (which he presumably eats) and converses with them (Genesis 4:3-15). Moses talks "face to face" with the Lord "as a man speaketh unto his friend" (Exodus 33:11) and, on one occasion, actually catches a view of his "back parts" (Exodus 33:23).

When it comes to "angels", both the Old and New Testaments tell repeatedly of how men encounter angels and mistake them for ordinary human beings. In Genesis, Abraham and Lot both entertain angels with food and drink, mistaking them, at first, for mere human travelers. Jacob is surprised by an angel, while asleep and waiting for his brother, and, mistaking him for a human intruder wrestles with him all night before discovering his mistake (Genesis 32:24-30). This is especially interesting since it implies the angel was solid enough to wrestle with and was closely matched in strength by an ordinary human. And it is evident the angel did not just take on a human form for this special occasion. The circumstances show he was taken by surprise and anxious to get on about his business, which was clearly not with Jacob. Evidently he was going about in his ordinary, everyday manner and appearance.

Speaking of such episodes the writer of Hebrews, in the New Testament, admonishes early Christians, "Be not forgetful to entertain strangers: for thereby some have entertained angels unawares" (Hebrews 13:2). Evidently then, in spite of medieval theology and contrary to medieval paintings, God and the angels are not transparent bits of ectoplasm decked out with wings. Such ideas are figments of the theologians' and artists' imaginations. The Lord God and angels of the Bible are living, flesh-and-blood beings who so closely resemble humans as to be indistinguishable from them except for their behavior and skills.

The differences between us and them lie in their achievements and civilization rather than in their nature or form. They, coming from worlds perhaps millions or billions of years older than ours, have had untold ages to perfect their natures and endowments in a civilization advanced beyond our wildest flights of imagination. As the Apostle Paul says of it: "Eye hath not seen, nor ear heard, neither have entered into the heart of man, the things which God hath prepared for them that love him" (I Corinthians 2:9).

HOW ADVANCED IS ADVANCED?

As we said earlier, our futurologists and writers of science fiction and fantasy have shown limited capacity for imagining our own future advancement or that of life on other worlds. More often than not their attempts have been confined to describing various technological wonders which they imagine these civilizations might produce. And undoubtedly truly advanced civilizations must greatly surpass us in technological capabilities. As Carl Sagan observed, they could probably "rework the cosmos." He even goes so far as to suggest we cannot absolutely rule out the possibility that quasars and high-intensity gravitational waves coming from the center of the universe might be evidences of "extra-terrestrial intelligences."

The fact that very advanced civilizations could doubtless do these things does not mean that they would spend most of their time and energy accomplishing them, however. There are other kinds of advancement that might seem more important to highly civilized Celestials. Even in our own history there are moderately advanced civilizations, such as those of China and India, that did not until recently choose the path of technological advancement taken by the West.

OTHER KINDS OF ADVANCEMENT

When we ask what other sorts of advancement civilizations millions or billions of years in our future might prefer, the problem offers a wide field for speculation. The best guide lines we have come from our own advanced non-technological civilizations and the hints given about the Celestials in the Scriptures.

Obviously one high-priority option would be the understanding and control of their own natures. The reason for this is apparent if we reflect on our own situation for a moment. We have, for example, much of the scientific know-how needed to solve our most pressing human problems, such as pollution, disease, war, crime and mental illness. Our problem is not so much lack of technology as it is lack of willingness to use our technology in a humane way when it conflicts with the short-range interests of power groups.

We could, for instance, easily eliminate pollution if we could get the auto industry, other manufacturers, the government and consumers to do the things environmental scientists tell us are necessary. But these groups will not, because it would slow business, hurt profits, take extra effort and require a more austere life style.

Similarly, we could prevent wars if we would give up our narrow national loyalties and support a worldwide system of law and disarmament. And if we stopped wars we could save a substantial part of most national budgets and apply these funds to solving other problems such as famine, disease, family decline and crime.

In all these ways we are a civilization that is technologically too advanced for its moral capabilities. We have more technology than we can wisely use for human good. As a result much of our technology is used to serve our basest and most animalistic desires and to exploit and destroy one another. When we reflect on these problems that plague us at a moderately advanced level of development, it is obvious that our greatest need is not more technology but to catch up with what we already have in the moral and social spheres.

It seems logical, then, that a truly advanced civilization would reach a point where technology would not be pursued as an end in itself, but would be limited to what could be used for truly humane purposes. And at this point it would then concentrate its major energies on developing a social order in which private morality and social justice are universal.

After developing enough gadgetry to make life reasonably secure and comfortable it would turn its attention to more important goals-eradicating the selfishness, perversion and evil in its members which nullifies the value of so much of our technology. And in their place it would try to create, probably by a combination of genetic engineering and education, a general condition of communal cooperation and benevolent concern.

The Bible makes it clear that this is one of the highest priorities of the Celestials. And this is doubtless why their concern, in leaving us a plan to share it with them, is that we develop along similar lines.

REQUIREMENTS FOR CELESTIAL CITIZENSHIP

This is also why the Bible does not suggest that the humans chosen as their heirs will not necessarily be the rich of the Earth, or those with advanced degrees or powerful positions in society. Jesus said, "Verily I say unto you, Whosoever shall not receive the kingdom of God as a little child shall in no wise enter therein" (Luke 18:17). His point was not that one must be naive, or ignorant, or simpleminded, but rather that candidates must be guileless and possess the loving, trustful nature of children.

Again, he said, "Blessed are the poor in spirit" (Matthew 5:3), "the meek" (5:5), "they which do hunger and thirst after righteousness" (5:6), "the merciful" (5:7), "the pure in heart" (5:8), "the peacemakers" (5:9). Once more his point was not that there is a premium on being a loser-it was rather that people who are genuinely humble, gentle, good and peaceful fit into an advanced society which prizes virtue and justice more than people who are opportunistic, greedy, ruthless and evil. In short, what Jesus was saying was that the Celestials want fellow citizens who are (to use a quaint and rather old fashioned term) "righteous."

MIND OVER MATTER

We can further assume that truly advanced civilizations might develop other powers we are just beginning to understand. Some of these would undoubtedly lie in the area we call "psychic" or "paranormal." If it were possible to achieve many of the technological feats we now perform with machines, by purely mental means, by what parapsychologists call "telekinesis" and "telepathy" and "clairvoyance", then this would be preferable to the clumsy and expensive hardware we presently use for these purposes. Our own researchers are beginning to suspect there are forms of power, or energy, which link mind and matter. If this is so, then it may be possible, through purely mental efforts and without gadgetry of any kind, to perform "miracles" of communication, diagnosis, healing and perhaps even the neutralizing of physical laws such as those manifested in gravitation or death. Recent studies of paranormal phenomena indicate that exceptional humans are sometimes able to insert their hands through living tissues without making incisions or leaving wounds. Others can influence sealed scientific instruments by what appear to be purely mental efforts.

The Bible indicates, in many places, that this is a line of advancement taken by the Celestials and they often use it in preference to ordinary mechanical technology. Thus Jesus speaks of such a power which he calls "faith." In describing it's awesome potentialities he tells his disciples, "... verily I say unto you, If ye have faith as a grain of mustard seed, ye shall say unto this mountain, Remove hence to yonder place; and it shall remove: and nothing shall be impossible unto you" (Matthew 17:20). In another passage, the gospel writer, John, tells how Jesus performed a feat similar to that of psychic surgeons in passing into a closed room without opening the door and apparently without leaving a hole. Of this he says: "Then the same day at evening, being the first day of the week, when the doors were shut where the disciples were assembled for fear of the Jews, came Jesus and stood in the midst, and saith unto them, Peace be unto you" (John 20:19). Other accounts by the gospel writers allege other feats in which Jesus apparently neutralized laws of nature as when he walked on water (Matthew 14:25-26).

AND HIGHER THINGS

Apart from moral, social and technical advancement we can also surmise that a greatly advanced civilization would devote much of its energies to what we call the "higher" things in life; the arts, pure scientific and philosophical inquiry, religion and social enjoyment. In the Bible there are occasional glimpses into the heavenly life of the Celestials which suggest that this is so. Evidently poetry and music play a rather large part in their activities, for there are many accounts of choral groups singing hymns or songs of praise-angels sang when Jesus was born, (Luke 2:13) and the redeemed sing around the throne of God (Revelation 5:9). Perhaps this is where the idea got started that people in Heaven spend their time singing and playing on harps. Evidently, too, they prize great vocal art. Lucifer, the alleged choirmaster of heaven, is evidently the subject of "God's" admonition reported by Ezekiel when he says "The workmanship of thy tabrets and of thy pipes was prepared in thee in the day thou wast created" (Ezekiel 25:13. The elaborate ornamentation of Eden, with its jewel-like materials and streets of "transparent gold"; and its garden with "every tree that is pleasant to the sight" (Genesis 2:9), suggest a highly developed concern for the visual arts such as architecture and landscape gardening.

In a similar way there are many suggestions throughout the Bible of the Celestials' concern for pure scientific research and philosophical inquiry. Nowhere else is the extent of their accomplishments in science or the profundity of their wisdom so dazzlingly presented as in the Book of Job. Here the Lord in reproving Job for his audacity in questioning God's purposes, says, "Hast thou entered into the springs of the sea? or hast thou walked in search of the depth? Have the gates of death been opened unto thee? or hast thou seen the doors of the shadow of death? Hast thou perceived the breadth of the Earth? declare if thou knowest it all. Where is the way where light dwelleth? and as for darkness, where is the place thereof.... Canst thou bind the sweet influences of Pleiades, or loose the bands of Orion? Canst thou bring forth Mazzaroth in his season? or canst thou guide Arcturus with his sons? Knowest thou the ordinances of heaven? canst thou set the dominion thereof in the Earth? ... Who hath put wisdom in the inward parts? or who hath given understanding to the heart?" (Job 38:16-19, 31-33, 36). In what is perhaps the most famous reproof in all of literature the Lord belittles Job's presumption in questioning him with a catalogue of the Celestials' accomplishments which is overwhelming. Over the course of almost four chapters the list continues with references to physics, astronomy, geology, meteorology, physiology, psychology, medicine, agriculture, botany and zoology. And these references do not just indicate a nodding acquaintance with these subjects but a mastery which makes human achievements seem inconsequential by comparison. Without boasting or false modesty the Lord simply asserts that the Celestials can control weather, manipulate the phenomena of life and death, move "worlds" as Carl Sagan suggests, and even "rework the cosmos" by "binding the sweet influences of Pleiades" or "loosing the bands of Orion."

Again, there are numerous references which suggest that religious ceremony and social intercourse are major preoccupations for the Celestials. At the very beginning of the Bible we are told that the Lord God instituted and observes the Sabbath himself, for when he had finished the creation "he rested on the seventh day from all his work which he had made. And God blessed the seventh day, and sanctified it: because that in it he had rested from all his work which God created and made" (Genesis 2:2-3). And again, in the last book of the Bible, we have what appears to be the description of a special empire-wide Sabbath celebration.

TO "BRING FORTH MAZZAROTH IN HIS SEASON"

One of the most remarkable discoveries to come out of our Space-Age interpretation of the Bible is that heaven, populated by the Lord God, his angels and the redeemed, is not some never-never land in a remote corner of the sky. Nor does it exist on a supernatural, rather than a natural, plane as we were taught in our childhoods. The "heaven" of the Bible is literally the heavens of our natural universe. Its inhabitants are the populations of the advanced civilizations that exist on millions of worlds throughout our own Milky Way and perhaps on other unimaginable millions beyond. In short, heaven is not a place nor a city; it is an inconceivably vast empire of worlds which embraces all of the more advanced civilizations in the Celestial empire and will one day, in the near future, embrace us. Heaven is wherever the Celestials have extended their colonization efforts and will soon, therefore, include our own planet as well. Its capitol is the home base of the Celestials, a planet which they call "Mazzaroth" whose inhabitants are called "Nazarites." From this headquarters issue the decisions and policies which direct the fortunes of a far-flung intergalactic confederation of advanced civilizations-a confederation which makes our own United Nations seem like a child's toy by comparison.

The Bible gives only slender clues as to the exact location of this headquarters. This is not surprising since its writers had only the most rudimentary knowledge of astronomy and could only use the few stars and constellations with which they were acquainted as guidelines. Such evidence as it does give, however, indicates that their capitol may be in our own galaxy. The key passage occurs in the Book of Job in a verse already quoted from the thirty-eighth chapter. "Canst thou bring forth Mazzaroth in his season? Or canst thou guide Arcturus with his sons?" (Job 38:32). Bible scholars have generally regarded this reference to Mazzaroth as one of the more obscure and puzzling references in the Bible. The Hebrew word Mazzaroth used here is commonly regarded as being derived from "Nazir", a root meaning "set apart for sacred purposes." As we shall presently see it is also linked with "Nazarite," a term used throughout the Bible to refer to particular humans set apart for the Lord's purposes as his special servants. These Nazarites are specifically instructed by the Lord, throughout the Bible, to act and groom themselves in ways which are at variance with the customs of the Hebrews from whom they came. No razor may touch their heads or faces, and they may not drink wine or strong drink. Those who voluntarily take the vows of a Nazarite, and are not set aside from birth, are also forbidden to have any contact with dead bodies, including even their closest relatives (Numbers 6:2-21). Among the outstanding Nazarites of the Bible were Samuel, Samson and John the Baptist.

Now this raises an interesting question. What connection is there between a term used to designate the Lord's special servants and another designating, apparently, some sort of astronomical or heavenly sign, or body?

Some scholars have assumed the connection is astrological. The Hebrews had learned astrology from the Babylonians during their long captivity, and the writer of Job was probably familiar with astrological lore. Since "Mazzaroth" is mentioned in connection with heavenly bodies and constellations, they argue it was probably a constellation "set apart" (therefore the connection with "Nazir") by the Hebrews, because they believed it had some special influence on the Earth. While no one has been able to identify this constellation the theory has persisted for lack of a better one.

On the surface the theory seems plausible. As so often happens with puzzling and obscure passages, however, our space age interpretation suggests quite another meaning for "bring forth Mazzaroth in his season"-a meaning which seems much more specific and is amply supported by the Hebrew etymology and by what we already know about the Celestials.

The clue to the correct interpretation of this passage lies in the custom of designating certain humans as "Nazarites." The root nazir, from which the term comes, means much more than just "set apart." It implies setting apart for special sacred, or holy, purposes-a consecration. This word was used of the unpruned vines set apart during the sacred Sabbath and Jubilee years of the Hebrews (Leviticus 25:5). It was used in the variant form of nezer for the gold plate on the front of the high priest's turban which was engraved with the words "holiness belongs to Jehovah." In the same way the official headpiece, or diadem, worn by Israel's anointed kings was called a nezer. All of these uses of nazir and nezer suggest, then, that "Mazzaroth" was not just "set apart" by humans for astrological purposes, but was rather "set apart" by the Celestials for sacred purposes.

Some inkling of what these special purposes might be can be gathered from considering the derivation of the Hebrew word used here. Ancient Jewish sources, such as the Aramaic Targum, equate "Mazzaroth" with the "Mazzaloth" of II Kings 23:5 which speaks of the "hosts of heaven," an expression later translators of the Bible have rendered as the "constellations of the Zodiac" or the "twelve signs, or constellations."

"Mazzaloth," however, is plural, and "Mazzaroth" is singular, as is shown by the use of the Hebrew personal pronoun immediately following it-"in his season." Used in this singular form it is much closer to "Mezzalah" than "Mezzaloth." And one of the meanings of mezzalah is "a planet." Accepting this derivation, we arrive, then, at the idea that "Mazzaroth" is a planet "set apart," or "consecrated," to the special use of the Celestials.

If this view is taken, the link with "Nazarites" becomes clear. If "Mazzaroth" is a planet set apart for the Celestials' special, sacred use and "Nazarite" (derived from the same root, nazir) is used to describe people "set apart" for special sacred purposes, then the implication emerges that the Celestials are headquartered, or have a way station on "Mazzaroth" and refer to their race as "Nazarites."

The use of this term for certain humans who become their special servants underscores our likeness to them. Like human missionaries, who ask their native converts to call themselves "Christians" and assume Western garb and customs when working for them, the Celestials ask their special human servants to adopt their customs of grooming and diet and to call themselves "Nazarites"-the term by which they designate the race that inhabits their home planet.

The strange grooming and life style required, by the Celestials, of human Nazarites suddenly makes sense if it is an imitation of their own ethnic culture and lifestyle. They make no sense regarded as an outgrowth of Hebrew culture and custom, for the taboos against cutting of the hair, use of strong drink and wine, and handling of the dead were not part of ancient Hebrew culture.

And if Mazzaroth was selected by the Celestials as a headquarters or way station, of their intergalactic confederation, then it would indeed be "set apart" for sacred, or holy, purposes in the way that its root, nazir, implies. If it were merely "set aside" by human observers for astrological purposes it would not.

Both linguistic analysis and what we have found out about the Celestials, then, support the idea that the Celestials call their race "Nazarites" (just as we call ours "human") and that "Mazzaroth" is a planetary headquarters or base. And if this is so, then Job 38:32 gives an obvious indication of where Mazzaroth is located. The complete question "Canst thou bring forth Mazzaroth in his season? or canst thou guide Arcturus with his sons?" links Mazzaroth with the brightest star in the constellation of Bootes-Arcturus, a star only 38 light-years from our own planet.

WHERE IS THE CELESTIALS' HEADQUARTERS?

The phrase "Arcturus with his sons" has been variously rendered by different translators of the Bible. The Hebrew word "ben", used here, can mean a literal son, or descendant, or can be used figuratively to mean a relationship in which one thing is subject to another. The Revised Version of the Bible renders the passage the "Bear with her train" because the name "Arcturus" comes from a Greek word meaning "bear." The New Oxford Annotated Bible gives the passage as "Can you guide the Bear with its children," and the Jerusalem Bible reads "show the Bear and its cubs which way to go." All translators seem to agree that ben refers to astronomical bodies dependent on Arcturus or a part of some system which it controls. Logically this could mean only one of two things. Either Arcturus has other stars which with it revolves about a common center (i.e., it is what astronomers call a "binary" star) or else it has a system of planets. Modern observation is sufficiently accurate to have ruled out the first possibility. Present day astronomers agree that Arcturus is a single-not a binary-star. The only other possible meaning of ben here, then, is that Arcturus, like our own sun, has a system of "sons," or planets, that orbit it and constitute its "train" or "cubs."

An added support for this view is found in the fact that the writer of Job knew that Arcturus has a real motion through the sky-it is "guided." This fact, not visible to the naked eye, is a cornerstone of modern astronomy. Just as our own family of planets moves around our sun in different orbits and at varying speeds, so the stars in our own galaxy, the Milky Way, move around its center in different orbits and at varying speeds. And because of this, like our own planets, they, at various times, approach toward or recede from each other.

To the naked eye these motions are not apparent. Even the nearest stars are much too far away for these motions, incredibly rapid though they are, to be noticed. Only sequences of observations, or photographs, taken over long periods of time can reveal even the slightest displacement of the stars relative to one another. Arcturus, nevertheless, has for many hundreds of thousands of years been approaching our own sun at a rate of speed which amounts to about 3 miles per second. When we consider this fact, God's challenge to Job, "canst thou guide Arcturus with his sons," becomes logical and clear. And the fact that the real motion of Arcturus was known to the writer of Job is one more startling evidence, like Bible writer's knowledge of the time-dilatation effect, that these writers had access to information which could only have come from extraterrestrials. And if our reasoning about this evidence from linguistic analysis and modern astronomy is correct then that information includes the fact that the Celestials' have a base in our galaxy on a planet orbiting the star Arcturus.

COSMIC ARCHITECTS

If this is so, the phrase "Canst thou bring forth Mazzaroth in his season?" requires some further explanation. How can a planet be "brought forth" and why would it have a "season"? Of all the facts we have so far considered about the Celestials' civilization, none, perhaps, testifies so eloquently to their scientific advancement as this quotation from the Book of Job. The Hebrew word translated "bring forth" here is "yatsa". One of its primary meanings is "bring forth," in the sense of making or creating. It is the same Hebrew word used to describe the creation in Genesis where God commands, "Let the Earth bring forth the living creature after his kind, cattle, and creeping thing, and beast of the Earth after his kind" (Genesis 1:24). Its use in Job 38:32, suggests that the planet, Mazzaroth, is not a natural phenomenon but something the Lord God and his Celestials created. Such an idea is reminiscent of Carl Sagan's remark that civilizations millions, or billions, of years in our technological future might be able "to rework the cosmos"-in short, that their citizens might be cosmic architects! What do our own futurologists have to say about the possibility of creating a planet?

The growing recognition that our own planet is a plundered one, overpopulated and with nearly exhausted resources, has stimulated space scientists and futurologists to consider the possibility of migration to bases off the Earth. In the last century Gerald K. O'Neill, a Princeton physicist, suggested that if population and pollution problems continue, by 2074 a large part of the human population could be living in "space colonies" in cities shaped like "giant cylinders twenty miles long and five miles wide." K. A. Ericke, another physicist, suggested that with their giant factories and food producing facilities [these] cities would maintain their own raw material mining centers on other Celestial bodies and be politically independent city states.

If we are already considering such possibilities, what may truly advanced Celestials have already done? Would manufacturing, or creating, a planet outright be a likely venture? If they are truly capable of "reworking the cosmos," why not? Humans, when they have the wealth and means, prefer to build homes to their own specifications and needs rather than accepting ready-built ones already on the market. Might not Celestials, capable of cosmic architecture, choose to create a planet meeting their exact specifications as to size, atmosphere, climate, distance from its sun, etc.? Would this not be even more likely if it were "set apart" as a base serving the needs of our entire galaxy?

How would they go about such a task? The science writer and futurologist Isaac Asimov already maintained the possibility of city sized "spomes," which could travel among the stars. In the same book he advances the provocative idea that natural spomes might be created by shearing moons or asteroids of out of orbit using advanced energy propulsion.

Taken together, these two proposals suggest alternative methods by which a very advanced civilization might construct an artificial planet. The first would be to assemble it from raw materials mined and transported from other planets. A mathematician, Freeman Dyson, at the Institute for Advanced Study, suggested such a scheme by which parts of our own neighbor planet, Jupiter, might, in future millennia, be broken down, piece by piece, and reassembled as a spherical shell near the Earth to capture and radiate solar energy to the Earth as a means of greatly increasing our energy supply. If we can envision such a project and discuss its engineering feasibilities it would surely not have been difficult for the Celestials to have constructed an artificial planet by methods analogous to those proposed for the Dyson sphere. A second possible method for "bringing forth Mazzaroth" would be to shear a moon or asteroid out of its natural orbit and guide it to a preselected orbit around Arcturus. The suggestion that the bringing forth was done at an appropriate season, or time, might be taken to favor this theory. Wherever it would have been, before being "brought forth," it would have been in some sort of orbit which would bring it, at times, closer and, at other times, farther from Arcturus. Shearing it out of orbit at the right time, or "season," when it was at its closest approach would accomplish this job of cosmic engineering with the least cost in energy and resources. The word used for "season" in Job 38:32 is the Hebrew "eth", meaning "time." It is derived from a root "ad", meaning a terminus in some sort of advance or enduring progression. Linguistic analysis here clearly suggests that the planet, Mazzaroth, was shot forth (to take another meaning of "yatsa") from its natural orbit at the terminus, or point in time, when it made its closest approach to Arcturus, or when, as our own space scientists put it, a "launch window" opened. So it was "brought forth" and captured as one of Arcturus's "sons."

An inevitable question raised by any assertion that such feats of "cosmic engineering" might be possible is, where would the energy needed for their accomplishment come from? This issue is so fundamental to the idea of civilizational advancement that some astrobiologists and futurologist have suggested it provides a criterion for measuring levels of advancement. So the Russian astrophysicist, Nikolai Kardaskev, has proposed a three level classification of civilizations based on the extent of energy resources that can be utilized for achieving the goals they wish to accomplish.

Level I is confined to energy resources available on the planet where it exists. Our Earth would thus be classed at level I. Level II could utilize the entire energy resources of its own solar system generated by its sun. Level III could bring the energy resources of an entire galaxy to accomplish a given task. In the case of the Celestials, since the Bible suggests they are accomplished in cosmic engineering, it would seem that over millions, or billions, of years they have learned to harness energies of stars far larger than our own sun; perhaps even the synchrotron energy generated by the rotation of galaxies and perhaps even other energy reserves such as black holes. With such inconceivable amounts of energy available they could not only redirect the orbits of heavenly bodies such as asteroids, moons and planets, but perhaps manipulate what cosmologists call space-time worm holes, allowing them to time travel backwards or forwards in time, take trips across the universe in much shorter times than light requires and possibly use still other worm holes to exit the universe itself and travel to other universes if they exist.

If Celetials possessing such technologies did indeed come to our world as the Genesis record claims then it is little wonder that our earliest ancestors perceive them as gods and the earliest authors of the Bible confused them with the ultimate creative power that brought the universe itself into existence.

And, given that the Celestials of Genesis do possess such cosmic engineering and architectural capabilities, then their federation headquarters in the Bible do justify its description of them as "Heaven."

As the Apostle Paul reminds us, in another connection, "Eye hath not seen, nor ear heard, neither have entered into the heart of man, the things which God hath prepared ..." (I Corinthians 2:9). But as the ancient Romans imitated the glories of their capitol city in the principal cities of their far flung colonies, so we may surmise that the Celestials employed architectural styles, the landscaping techniques and the jewel-like synthetic materials of construction which grace their home planet, Mazzaroth. And in the millions upon millions of other planets which make up their far-flung confederation we could doubtless find a unity of style and grace which is the mark of their civilizational influence. We have already had a faint glimpse of the glories this implies in our description of the "New Jerusalem," the space city in which they visit their vast empire and explore new worlds to be civilized like our own. This "home away from home" is evidently made to resemble their Celestial headquarters, and, though it is only a portable copy of the original, its foundation and walls of gem-like materials resembling jasper, sapphire, emerald, topaz and amethyst; its streets of transparent "gold"; its gates like pearl; its pure river of water of life, clear as crystal; its glory of inner light which requires no sun and forever banishes night-all of this suggests that the world it copies is heaven, indeed, and when their space city has once again come "down from God out of heaven" to signal their official annexation of the planet, Earth, the glories of Mazzaroth will be extended to this planet, too. Like. Mazzaroth we, too, will become a part of Heaven-the heaven of truly civilized worlds making up an inconceivably vast empire.

In the beginning God created the heaven and the Earth. And the
earth was without form, and void; and darkness was upon the
face of the deep.

– Genesis 1:1-2

CHAPTER VI

In the Beginning

With this simple statement the opening book in the Bible begins the creation story. And though this story is much like the creation stories of other Near Eastern peoples, it is very different from ones found in other parts of the world. The Sumerians, Babylonians, Assyrians and Egyptians all had similar accounts of the creation. And they all lived in, or around, the area where the Bible says the Celestials first landed and where it claims they recreated and taught humanity.

These Near Eastern creation stories all agree that the heavens and Earth started as a chaos, while creation stories from other parts of the world usually begin with mythic animals or persons who gave birth to the Earth or hatched it. Why are the Near Eastern stories so close to the actual scientific facts while the others are so fanciful and fantastic?

Why, for instance, does the Genesis account say that "the Earth was without form and void"? Many present-day astronomers also believe the universe started from a singularity "of matter without dimension, or 'form' that arose from nothingness, or a 'void'. This singularity, for reasons not understood by scientists instantaneously inflated, in a "big bang", beginning the cosmic evolution of galaxies, stars, planets and their satellites which is still going on today in a seemingly endless process of births and deaths of celestial bodies and their systems of organization.

Why again does the Bible say God brought forth vegetation, followed by sea life, followed by birds, followed by land animals and finally humans (Genesis 1:11-26)? This is the same order that is given for the evolution of life by modern biology. How did the Hebrews of five or six millennia ago know these things? Why do other creation stories throughout the world fail to reflect the scientific facts in the way Bible does? Is it because the Celestials, who knew the facts, told them to Adam and Eve, and to the patriarchs and to Moses?

And did they know them because they made them happen? Godlike as their powers are, it is difficult to believe they triggered the original big bang, or had a hand in the processes that spawned the galaxies, or personally directed the millions of variations and selections that have caused the evolution of life through the ages.

Even though their civilization may be millions, or billions, of years in our future it is not credible that they called the universe into being, for they too, like us, are flesh and blood. Like us they are within nature, they are not its creators.

Yet the first verse in Genesis says, "In the beginning God created the heaven and the earth," and in the second chapter we read that "the Lord God made the earth and the heavens, and every plant of the field before it was in the earth, and every herb of the field before it grew ... And the Lord God formed man of the dust of the ground ..." (Genesis 2:4-5, 7).

If "God" and the angels were actually astronauts from another world, is it possible to square these statements in Genesis with common sense? Either God and his angels are creators or they are creatures. How can they be both?

The answer to this question is found in a critical study of the Genesis accounts themselves. As we pointed out earlier most scholars are convinced that the two accounts of creation in Genesis 1 and 2 are taken from different sources. Yet these have become so interwoven in the Bible that has come down to us that we can no longer tell where one story leaves off and the other begins, or whether parts of each have been transferred over into the other. Only by comparing these accounts with what we know from science and textual critism can we discover the true meanting of this ancient account.

TWO SEPARATE CREATIONS

To begin with, it is obvious that the first two chapters contain accounts of two different creations, not of one told twice over. Of course some of what is said about the first creation is repeated in the second chapter, but this tells us nothing, since chapter divisions are a modern invention and did not exist in the earliest written accounts.

The first account states that "God" created vegetation, sea life, birds of the air, land animals and "man"-male and female (Genesis 1:11-26)-in that order. The second says the "Lord God" (the name is changed in the original Hebrew) formed man, put him in the Garden, made vegetation to grow, formed land animals and birds and brought them to Adam for naming, and last of all, caused a deep sleep to fall on Adam and took out one of his ribs from which he formed woman (Genesis 2:7-22).

It has been claimed, by some Bible commentators, that the first account tells of the general creation and that the second retells a special part of the same creation in greater detail. This might make sense if we assume the writers of Genesis were just careless in keeping the order straight in the two accounts except for one important problem. If we read on for the next two chapters we find statements which flatly contradict the idea that there was only one creation. For example, in Genesis 4:16-17 we read that Cain, Adam's and Eve's first son, went into the "land of Nod, on the east of Eden. And Cain knew his wife; and she conceived, and bare Enoch."

WHERE DID CAIN GET HIS WIFE?

Now if we accept that both creation stories are accounts of the same creation there had been only four humans on Earth at this time Adam, Eve and their two sons, Cain and Abel Then where did Cain's wife come from? The Bible tells of Cain's and Abel's births at the beginning of Chapter 4 but makes no mention of any daughters being born until after Cain "knew his wife." Only in Chapter 5, after Cain had already married and fathered Enoch, and Eve had given birth to a third son, Seth, is any mention made of the birth of daughters. There we find that "... Adam lived a hundred and thirty years, and begat a son in his own likeness, after his image; and called his name Seth: And the days of Adam after he had begotten Seth were eight hundred years, and he begat sons and daughters" (Genesis 5:3-4).

The argument of some scholars that Cain must have married his sister is clearly contrary to the plain scriptural record. If a sister had been born before the birth of Seth it would have been mentioned as those following his birth were. There could be no logical reason for mentioning the births of later daughters, but failing to mention the birth of a first one.

Some Bible students may object that the statement of Genesis 3:20 that Eve was "the mother of all living" and Paul's statement, in I Corinthians 15:45, that Adam was the "first man" refute the theory advanced here. This is not so. The Hebrew text for "all living" makes it clear that the reference in this scripture is confined to the experimental creation of Adam and Eve. So, too, though it is true that Adam was the first "modern" man, homo sapiens sapiens this does not rule out anthropologists' finds of earlier human types.

If this is so the conclusion is inescapable that when Genesis 4 speaks of Cain having a wife in the land of Nod it implies there were other humans on the Earth at that time besides Adam and Eve and their children. And if there were other humans, then it is obvious they were the result of a different creation from the one that produced Adam and Eve. And if this is so then the creation stories in Genesis 1 and 2 are not discussing the same creation.

It is significant that as early as the Third Century, one of Christianity's first great textual scholars of scripture, Origen of Alexandria recognized that the accounts in Genesis 1 and 2 could not be dealing with the same creation He also taught that the literal sense of scripture is not always the one meant but that many texts use figurative language to convey a deeper, hidden meaning which often becomes clearer when different passages and translations are compared. He even compiled a multiple translation/parallel passage version of scripture known as the "Hexipla" for finding such meanings.

A careful study of the early chapters in Genesis makes it clear, then, that the creation of humans occurred in two separate stages – one resulting in the natural emergence of humans, male and female; the other an artificial and experimental creation resulting in the production of a special pair, Adam and Eve.

Upon critical analysis we discover the first five chapters of Genesis clearly imply that humans originally appeared on Earth as the result of a process of creation, by "God," which involved the same stages described in the theory of evolution. But they also go on to imply that after humans, male and female, had appeared, another pair, Adam and Eve, were specially recreated by the "Lord God" in the Garden of Eden. And this happened after descendants of the first creation had already spread to other areas of the Earth, such as Cain's wife in the land of Nod.

If this is not the meaning of the early chapters in Genesis, then why are there two creation stories that disagree in telling the order of creation and why is the creator in one account called by a different name from the creator in the other? In the first account "God" is simply designated by the Hebrew word Elohim which is ordinarily used to indicate the supreme God, or power. But in Chapter 2 the same word is prefaced by another, Yehovah, which is often translated "Lord God" or "Jehovah" and means, specifically, the Hebrew national God. Could the "God" of the first account be the supreme power that produced the world and everything in it, including the Celestials? And could the "Lord God" of the second account be a flesh-and-blood astronaut, "Jehovah," who re-"created" Adam and Eve by modifying a pair of naturally evolved humans through genetic engineering?

SCIENCE VS. RELIGION

Taken literally, the Bible account seems to contradict much of what science has found out. For instance it says that God completed the creation from the heaven and Earth to man in six days. Modern astrophysics sets the timetable for the same events at almost 14 billion or more years. Genesis says man was created outright, male and female; modern biology says he evolved from lower forms of life over millions of years.

In the Nineteenth Century higher critics of the Bible suggested the creation story should be taken as "symbolic," rather than literal, fact. In this way it could be regarded as having some kind of truth and value even if it is not scientifically true. Protestant denominations, called "modernist," accepted this as a way of reconciling religious faith and an educated scientific outlook. Other sects, known as "fundamental or conservative," insisted that "all Scripture is given by inspiration of God" (II Timothy 3:16) and that the Genesis account must be literally and scientifically true. Therefore biologists must be mistaken in thinking man has evolved, and both they and geologists must be wrong when they say humans and the world are millions, or billions, of years old.

In fact, in 1650, an Irish archbishop, James Ussher, added up the genealogies in the Bible and, tracing them back from the birth of Christ to Adam, concluded the world was created in 4004 B.C. He even generously added the time and day-precisely at 9:00 in the morning, October 23 (apparently because he took it for granted that God is British and operates on Greenwich time).

The conflicts between fundamentalists and modernists became so intense, in America, that many people described it as a war between science and religion. In the southern United States, where fundamentalism was stronger, legislatures passed laws forbidding the teaching of evolution in public schools. The famous Scopes (or "monkey") trial occurred in 1925, in Tennessee, when a young high school teacher, John T. Scopes, violated Tennessee's law in his biology class. The courtroom became a showcase for the issue of the Bible against the theory of evolution and science. While Scopes was convicted, the consensus of public opinion was that science and modernism had won a moral victory because of the brilliant arguments of Clarence Darrow, the defense attorney.

Since that time the prevailing situation, in both America and Europe, has been that a majority of people (even those who are religious) accept the evolution of humans over millions of years and the fact that our world is billions of years old.

HAVING OUR CAKE AND EATING IT TOO

Our interpretation of the two Genesis accounts revives the issue of modernism vs. fundamentalism and curiously supports both sides. On the one hand, like the modernists early in the last century, we feel the first account should be taken for what it is-a poetic myth written by prescientific men of genius. In spite of its mythic form, however, it contains a metaphoric account of the creation of the universe which implies the general facts modern science has established. On the other hand, like earlier fundamentalists, we believe there are good reasons for thinking the second account is essentially literal truth. Of course, it exhibits the confusion of prescientific writers trying to describe technical achievements far beyond their understanding. It also has been intermingled with mythic material and pious rephrasings later editors and copyists have added. But, in spite of this, it contains a nearly pure descriptive account of how modern humans were created and how we acquired the rudiments of our present civilization. Further, like our fundamentalist forebears, we believe the Celestial beings who carried out this second creation set up an experimental training program for Adam and Eve intended to qualify them for sharing, as citizens, in the civilization they intend to establish here on Earth, but because of temptation by Satan (a fallen Celestial) they failed and lost their opportunity, and that an alternative plan of salvation (or citizenship) has been opened up to their descendants generally.

This attempt to take what is generally regarded as folklore and to treat it as serious scientific history and theological doctrine may appear naive and unenlightened to many who have been trained in traditional views. It may seem like the proverbial impossibility of "having one's cake and eating it, too," but we believe the scientific record (which we will review in the rest of this chapter) supports our position. We are further convinced that this position incorporates and explains the fundamental beliefs of, orthodox Judeo-Christianity.

"IN THE BEGINNING"

As we have already pointed out the first account in Genesis 1 is not a scientific one. It is poetic and mythic. For a more factual description of the origins of the universe and life, we must turn to evidence outside the Bible. This is found in the science called cosmology, a field of knowledge that cuts across astronomy, physics, chemistry and biology.

Cosmologists attempt to discover where the universe is heading at present. From this they backtrack and try to discover where it has been in the past and how it got to where it is today.

The evidence as to what the universe is doing, at present, is rather uncertain. According to the most recent evidence (including information received from radio telescopes and instruments on satellites above our atmosphere), the observable universe is more than 27 billion light-years across (27,000,000,000 X 588,000,000,000 miles). This is the observable universe.

And since we are at the center of the observable universe (observation is equally good in all directions), this means our most distant neighbors are almost 14 billion light-years away. Since light (or other radiation) from them has taken over 13 billion years to reach us, this number gives us a measure not only of the size of the universe but of its age, as well. The observable universe's outer limits are nearly 14 billion light years away.

Numbers like these are, of course, so far beyond our powers of imagination that they are virtually meaningless by themselves. Some idea of the enormous spans of space and time they measure can be grasped better if we compare them with shorter spans we can understand. Carl Sagan made one such comparison between the age of the Earth (less than a third that of the universe) and the time life has been on the Earth. He wrote that if the eons making up the lifetime of the Earth were reduced to a single year the origin of life would come at the end of January; the colonization of land in November; the rise of dinosaurs on December 15; mammals on Christmas Day; and the origin of humans at 8 P.M. on New Year's Eve. Recorded history would occupy the last 30 seconds of this last day of such a year.

And yet, vast as the age of the Earth is, and vaster still that of the universe, there is no good reason for thinking the entire cosmos may not be of greater age and expanse than those parts we can measure. In fact as the evidence continues to pour in, the debate it has generated seems to be heading toward an agreement that the cosmos may be infinite and eternal.

"WORLDS WITHOUT END"

When it comes to the question of the extent of the cosmos scientific opinion is again divided. Some astronomers believe space has limits and, therefore, the matter within it must be limited, too. Others believe it extends infinitely and that our own universe, or, perhaps, a cosmos of island universes, may extend in all directions without end. That part of the theory of relativity which implies that space is curved would seem to suggest that ultimately, if it extends far enough, it would meet itself and thus be limited. Yet a newer cosmological model known as "string theory", based on evidence coming from the field of quantum mechanics, is interpreted by some scientists as supporting a cosmos or multiverse that is perhaps infinite and eternal.

BUT WHERE DOES CREATION COME IN?

At this point some readers may be wondering where creation comes in. If the universe is eternal and infinite, where does this leave room for creation? The answer to this question is not really scientific at all, it is philosophical. It depends on what we can conceive and how we use language to explain it.

If we ask how everything started, there are only two possible answers: (1) everything comes from something that has always existed and didn't require creation; (2) everything comes from something that came out of nothing in a process of self creation.

The first possibility has been put forward by philosophers and theologians from the beginning of civilization. The eternal "something" has gone by many names: "first cause", "unmoved mover", "absolute", "ground of all being", "God", "Tat", "Tao", "Allah", and in the Bible's Genesis account of creation it is called the "Spirit of God" that calls the heavens and Earth into existence. It is a foundational belief for all the major religions except Buddhism.

The second possibility also has been advanced since the beginning of civilization and is foundational for Buddhism. It calls the nothingness it believes to be the source of everything "Nirvana".

It has been advanced by atheistic philosophers from antiquity to the present. In the last century some astronomers and evolutionary biologists known as "new atheists" have come to regard it as scientific dogma.

What is new is their false claim that scientific evidence has proved the something that came out of nothing and produced the universe in a big bang of self creation was dark energy.

Let us again see why this is so. When Maria, in the well known musical, *The Sound of Music,* sings her famous line, "nothing comes from nothing, nothing ever could," she expresses a common sense intuition that is almost universally shared.

Even those scientists who claim to believe the universe came from nothing always find it necessary to slip something into their definition of nothing that is not nothing in order to "prove" their claim something as vast as the universe could come from nothing.

They are like the magician who shows an empty hat to the audience and then proceeds to pull a rabbit out of it. No one is fooled into thinking he really pulled a live rabbit out of nothing. They know he had the rabbit concealed somewhere and only produced an illusion of taking it out of an empty hat.

A recent example of this kind of "rabbit out of a hat" cosmology is a book entitled "A Universe From Nothing" published in 2014 by Professor Lawrence M. Krauss, Director of the Origin Project at Arizona State University.

True to form he announces the universe has come from "nothing" in his title and then proceeds, in the first pages of his preface, to argue that all of "empty" space is pervaded by some mysterious, unexplainable form of energy that created the universe. It then turns out that this unexplainable energy is what most scientists call "dark energy". He however, prefers "vacuum energy" employing a kind of magician's trick with words, rather than his hands, to create the illusion that nothing is the source of the universe. To call such an energy "nothing" is the height of absurdity, this is because he goes on to claim, along with other big bang cosmologists, that it makes up a major portion of our universe, and, as its cause was powerful enough to inflate a singularity, smaller than an atom, into a beginning universe in just trillionths of a second, such an energy would have to be a tremendous "something".

In making such a claim,then, he, uninvitingly agrees with the other alternative that something has always existed that is the ultimate cause of everything else. His universe from "nothing" is not another possibility but simply a rewording of our "something has always existed." By calling it "nothing" he ends up with nonsense. Realizing this, he then tries to remedy the absurdity by suggesting it is dark, or "vacuum" energy.

Unfortunately for him, he also states the necessary conditions for scientific truth and they fail to support his claim that our universe might have come from "nothing".

His claim is unsubstantiated because neither he nor anyone else has been able to go back more than thirteen billion years, exit our present universe, and observe what might have been there before the big bang occurred. Further, any claim about what might or might not have been there cannot be tested by the two conditions he specifies for scientific truth. Nevertheless, he goes on to argue that since what we call empty space inside the universe is filled with dark (or "vacuum") energy the empty space before the universe existed must have been filled with it, too. And since it was presumably the only thing out there, it must be what brought the universe into existence.

The major problem with this conclusion, apart from its not being scientifically provable, is that other cosmologists, some of them the most eminent in their fields, have reached quite different conclusions about what may have caused the big bang and creation of our universe.

One, Stephen Hawking, whom many regard as the foremost physicist since Einstein, believed space and time, and even the laws of nature, were somehow compressed within the singularity that became the universe and they had no existence outside of it. Dark energy would therefore, be a product, not the cause, of the big bang.

This raises the question of what else might have given rise to the universe and all that is in it. Speculation among Krauss's colleagues varies. In general, however, like Professor Krauss, they avoid self contradiction or infinite regresses by advancing some form of the same conclusion slipped in by Professor Krauss; namely that "something" has always existed from which everything else has come. Nonetheless "new atheists" hold to the view that this eternal something was a mindless mix of matter and energy that, by sheer chance, gave rise to all that is.

The Bible, on the other hand, presents an opposed world view which holds that "spirit" (or consciousness) is the ultimate substrate of reality. Our archeolinguistic analysis of its texts opens a new interpretive perspective on these texts which places this claim in complete harmony with the worldview emerging from the fields of relativity theory and quantum mechanics.

In this world view neither matter or energy, nor any mix of them, as physicists understand them, can give a complete account of what science calls physical reality. There is a more fundamental underlying ingredient which must exist before we can know anything about either of them. Further quantum experiments have shown this ingredient is capable of "collapsing" mere possibilities into actualities.

This ingredient is consciousness. Without consciousness knowledge of physical reality is not possible, and, in quantum experimental setups, the very act of observing and measuring seems to create matter where none existed before.

If this is so then consciousness is also a form of energy that can create matter. And if this energy is the "something" that has existed eternally and infinitely throughout the cosmos then it could call whole universes into existence as Genesis I in the Bible claims when it states the "spirit" of God commanded "Let there be light" and it created "heaven and earth". (Gen: 1-3)

For those interested in a detailed description of the experiments that support this conclusion that conciseness can create matter a good survey is found in a recent publication by Amit Goswami, Professor of Physics at the Institute of Theoretical Sciences, University of Oregon. Its title is the "The Self-Aware Universe, How Consciousness Creates the Material World".

Of course the fact that consciousness can create matter inside the universe does not prove that it must also have done so outside the universe.

The assertion is no more a scientific one that Professor Krauss's claim that the universe came from nothing. Both belong to the domain of philosophy or theology, rather than science, and are incapable of scientific testing.

As a speculative answer to the question "what caused the universe" however, consciousness has far more plausibility than Professor Krauss's "nothing" or the claims of other "new atheists", such as Stephen Hawkings and E.O. Wilson that , the universe's cause was pure chance, a mindless happenstance that occurred in a primal soup of matter and energy. Further, such a claim fails utterly in explaining why the processes of the universe are ordered and mathematically predictable These appear to involve intelligent design.

Early in the last century Sir James Jeans, one of its most eminent astronomers, foresaw the implications of the new worldview emerging from the field of relativity theory and quantum mechanics. In his philosophical, scientific classic "The Mysterious Universe", he wrote: The universe begins to look more like a great thought than a great machine. Mind no longer appears as an accidental intruder into the realm of matter; we are beginning to suspect that we ought rather to hail it as the creator and governor of the realm of matter-not of course our individual minds but the mind in which the atoms out of which our individual minds have grown exist as thoughts…We discover the universe shows evidence of a designing or controlling power that has something in common with our own individual minds---not, so far as we have discovered, emotion, morality or aesthetic appreciation, but the tendency to think in a way which, for want of a better word, we describe as mathematical."

In the chapters which follow, particularly chapter VIII, The Experimental Creation and chapter XIV, Pentecost and Biocosmic Energy, we will examine this emerging worldview more closely and see how it is supported by a Space Age interpretation of the Bible.

Thus saith the Lord, The heaven is my throne, and the Earth is my footstool

– Isaiah 66:1

CHAPTER VII

Colony Earth

THE COMING OF THE CELESTIALS

We do not know when the Celestials first came to Earth. We can only surmise why they came. The facts are lost in the mists of prehistory.

Having overcome death, they left no bone-filled graves. Since their bases here on Earth were portable spacecraft, they took their architecture and equipment with them when they left. The only records that remain were written by humans who knew them, and we find some of the earliest of these in the Bible.

Yet, though the Bible gives no clue as to when the Celestials came and only vague hints as to why, it does tell us exactly how they came and where they first landed.

HOW THEY CAME

The Bible says the Celestials first came in the same way and to the same place they will use when they return. We have seen, in our discussion of that final return, that they will come in a spacecraft and will land at the foot of Mount Moriah where present-day Jerusalem stands. In the final book of the Bible their space city is called the "New Jerusalem." In the first book it is called "Eden."

At this point we can imagine readers who are students of the Bible saying, "But Eden was a garden. How could it be a space craft?" The confusion of their space city with the Garden arose through careless reading of the Genesis account. Genesis 2:10 says a "river went out of Eden to water the garden," and Genesis 2:8 states the Garden was "eastward in Eden." From the two passages it is clear that "Eden" is used in two different senses. In the narrower sense of Genesis 2:10 it means a center of some sort that was separate from the Garden. In the wider sense of Genesis 2:8 it included the Garden.

From this we can draw an obvious conclusion. Originally "Eden" referred to the headquarters of the Celestials when they first came to Earth. As we will show it was, in fact, their space city-a self-sufficient spome in which they were secure from the dangers of an alien world. As our own future astronauts will do, in visits to other worlds, they remained within this secure and sterile environment until they had sealed off and prepared a larger natural area outside. This area, to its east, became the "Garden of Eden." It, too, was probably isolated from its surrounding environment by a force field which kept out the hazards of alien pathogens and predators. From its safe confines the Celestials could direct the first phase of their colonization program while ensuring a totally controlled environment for the Garden experiment.

We know the Garden area was sealed off because Genesis 2:5 says that no rain fell. In its place the Celestials sent up a "mist from the Earth and watered the whole face of the ground" (Genesis 2:6). Those who live in arid parts of the world have seen long perforated pipes lying beside the furrows of farms and vineyards sending up their spray of "mist." For them there is no mystery in this passage. The Celestials irrigated their sealed Garden, ensuring, as good scientists, that no outside pollutants would contaminate their experiment.

That Eden was a sealed spome and not an ordinary land base, or city, is proved by its features. These tally identically with the holy city, the "New Jerusalem" that John the Revelator says he saw "coming down from God out of heaven" (Revelation 21:2) and that they will use upon their final return. Although Genesis 2 describes only a few of its features it is pictured more elaborately elsewhere.

Genesis simply mentions that a "river went out of Eden to water the garden," the Garden being "eastward in Eden," and that the Garden it watered had a "tree of knowledge of good and evil" and a "tree of life" (Genesis 2:9-10). In the book of Ezekiel, however, this description is greatly expanded. And this expanded one matches that given by John in the New Testament. Like John's "New Jerusalem," and the "Eden" in Genesis, it has a river flowing out of it eastward and a "tree of life." And like John's holy city it is constructed of materials resembling precious stones. Further, Ezekiel's and John's lists match closely-jasper, sapphire, emerald, topaz, amethyst, etc. (Ezekiel 28:13, Revelation 21:19-20). A careful study of all these descriptions given in Genesis, Ezekiel and Revelation makes it clear they all refer to the same thing, whether it is called "Eden" or the "New Jerusalem." And John's statement that it is a "city" which comes down "out of heaven" leaves no doubt that it is a spome-a city-sized spacecraft. As such it is self-sufficient and is capable of recycling its own air, water and food supplies and of transporting a community of Celestials across the reaches of galactic space from their world to ours.

WHERE THEY CAME

It is also the Book of Ezekiel which gives our only firm clue as to where the Celestials first established their headquarters. This Old Testament book states that its site. was "the holy mountain of God" (Ezekiel 28:14). Now though there are various "holy mountains" mentioned in the Bible, the entire phrase "the holy mountain of God" or "God's holy mountain" is used for only one, Mount Moriah, which is also called Mount Zion (Isaiah 66:20; Daniel 9:16; Joel 3:17; Zechariah 8:3). It is immediately east of Jerusalem and was later the site of Solomon's Temple, as well.

The selection of this site was a logical one. Lying within the Fertile Crescent it was one of the most favorable areas on Earth for the Garden experiment. Traditional Bible scholars have generally agreed, from the Genesis description, that the Fertile Crescent was the site of the Garden, though they have usually placed it at the extreme eastern end near the Persian Gulf.

At first this might seem in disagreement with our location of the Celestials' headquarters at Jerusalem. Once more, careful study of the text reveals that this discrepancy again arises from a failure to distinguish between Eden, as a headquarters, and the Garden of Eden as the site of the experiment. From the coast of Palestine to the Persian Gulf is a stretch of about 1,000 miles and to scholars living before the Space Age, an organized project covering such an area was not easily imaginable. Even by our own 21st Century engineering standards it would hardly be feasible. But to advanced Celestials, millions of years in our future, it would have presented few problems. To throw up a force field blanketing and sealing such an area would be child's play for a civilization that could "rework the cosmos." Its mode of production and operation might not be greatly different from natural force fields, such as the Van Allen Belt, which surrounds the Earth and shields it from dangerous radiation and particles reaching us from outerspace. And to commute, as they must have done, from their headquarters at Jerusalem to a garden near the Persian Gulf would have required little more than a two or three hour journey by present-day aircraft. With their own shuttles it probably took only a matter of minutes.

A part of the confusion about the location of Eden and the Garden is also due to the fact that the few clues given in Genesis pinpoint the Fertile Crescent, yet fit no exact geographical location within it. For example, Genesis 2:10 says that "a river went out of Eden to water the garden; and from thence it was parted, and became into four heads." It goes on to name these four branch rivers – Pison, Gihon, Hiddekel and Euphrates. Only the last is still identified by its biblical name. Scholars have identified Hiddekel as the Tigris. The others remain unidentified, as do the lands they watered. Scripture says the second one watered the whole of "Ethiopia," but no present river from this area does so for modern Ethiopia. Besides, there are no major rivers having their source near Jerusalem.

Again, though the eastern end of the Fertile Crescent is watered by the Tigris and Euphrates rivers, their source is in present-day Armenia. It has no river watering Ethiopia and is nowhere near Jerusalem.

How then can these vague and geographically unsupported statements be reconciled with the Bible's claim that the Celestials' first headquarters was at Jerusalem? Obviously the Genesis description could be factual only if there have been great changes in the elevation around Jerusalem, and if the term "Ethiopia" once described other lands. Is there any evidence this is so?

The answer is yes. Jerusalem lies near the termination of the largest rift valley on Earth, the East African--a major cause of Earth upheavals. Studies of the Dead Sea, near Jerusalem, show that it was once at least 1,500 feet higher than at present. And a river flowing south, from an elevated watershed on this location, could have watered the land of Yemen on the southern Arabian Peninsula. Interestingly, Ethiopian tradition says a large part of Ethiopia's population came from this area. That rivers did indeed once flow through the Arabian Peninsula is well established. H. St. J. B. Philby, an authority on the natural history of the area, asserts it is beyond challenge that when the ice cap of the last glacial period covered a large part of the northern hemisphere three great rivers flowed from west to east across the whole width of the Arabian Peninsula. And that the land they watered was indeed called "Ethiopia" in the time when the earliest Bible books were composed is supported by Scripture itself. For this area, now called Yemen, is identical with the land called "Midian" in the Old Testament. It is from this land that Moses' wife, Zipporah, came. The Bible states that she was the daughter of the priest of Midian (Exodus 2:16 and 21) and refers to her as "Ethiopian." Thus we read in Numbers, "And Miriam and Aaron spoke against Moses because of the Ethiopian woman whom he had married: for he had married an Ethiopian woman" (Numbers 12:1). Clearly, then, the authors of the earliest books in the Bible regarded the area south of Jerusalem, on the Arabian Peninsula, as "Ethiopia," and it could have been watered by rivers flowing southward from Jerusalem.

In view of this there seems to be good reason for accepting the biblical location of the Celestials' first Earth base. Their headquarters could have been at Jerusalem and still fit the clues Genesis gives about its river systems. Similarly the Garden could have extended from Jerusalem to the Persian Gulf and still have been under daily supervision.

WHY THEY CAME

As we said earlier the Bible gives no definitive answer as to why Celestials came to our world. The best we can do is to make educated guesses based on our own experience. Possibly the Celestials' world, like our own, once suffered a population explosion and dwindling resources, though, with their advanced technology, it would seem they could have solved such a problem without migrating. Perhaps their world was facing the sort of disaster predicted for our own in time, a runaway greenhouse effect from an accumulation of chemicals in the upper atmosphere – a barrier which traps in heat. This sort of barrier has already heated our neighbor planet, Venus, to temperatures ranging toward 800 °-900 ° Fahrenheit. Perhaps, as we have noted, being immortal they had outlived their own dying sun and were forced to seek a younger and more hospitable solar system.

Orthodox theology suggests still another answer, In the catechism many of us learned as children it says that "God created man to serve and enjoy him forever."

Actually this last motive is the one which fits best with the biblical claim that we were made in their image, for it implies that, like us, they are colonizers. In this case it was simply the thirst for knowledge and the challenge of new worlds to explore that urged them on as it is now urging our own astronauts and space scientists.

We have already seen that their choosing our world was in no way remarkable, since they are probably following a plan of expanding colonization in all directions- much as we will do in our future space explorations. If this is true we were just the next stepping stone in their line of advance, and the visit recounted in Genesis 2 is simply the first phase of a program which is applied to any planet they select. When their coming is viewed in this light it avoids one of the common objections to the idea that we have been visited by advanced civilizations.

This objection was put, in statistical terms, by Carl Sagan in his book, The Cosmic Connection. He argues that since we are only one of billions of alternative worlds in relation to the few advanced civilizations that could visit them, we may well wonder whether it is statistically likely we are among the chosen. He goes on to say that probability theory indicates it would require launching 10,000 expeditions each year from every one of his estimated advanced civilizations for us to have been visited at least once. These would be rather discouraging statistics if they really applied.

What this line of reasoning overlooks, however, is that truly advanced civilizations would not go about space exploration in the way we would be compelled to do. As often happens when writers and futurologists try to imagine what greatly advanced civilizations would be like Carl Sagan has made assumptions based on our own limited achievements. These assumptions are almost certainly unrealistic when applied to a civilization like the Celestials'.

He is assuming that extraterrestrials would launch expeditions as blindly as we would at this point, if we were reaching out toward other solar systems. Yet it is likely such civilizations would have methods of information gathering that would permit them to select the most suitable worlds before they attempted any launches. Rather than sending expeditions toward any world that might exist, as we would have to do, they could pick only the very few that met their specific requirements. From neighboring solar systems they had already reached or, perhaps even from their home base, they would survey the world they were considering. They would determine its position and orbit in relation to its sun, its physical and chemical properties, its life-supporting capabilities and its technological development.

In the case of our own world they probably did this thousands of years before we were actually visited. And, because they were colonizing innumerable other worlds at the same time, it would probably be further thousands of years, after their initial visit, before they would return to carry out the final stages of their plan.

Carl Sagan's argument from probability theory fails, then, because he applies it to a situation that almost certainly involved choice and planning rather than chance. We were not visited because our number finally came up on the wheel of fortune but because their line of advance made us next on their list.

As we have already seen clues in the Bible suggest they have a base that is only about 38 light-years away-a distance not quite ten times that of our nearest stellar neighbor. And since their technological advancements suggest they have been colonizing space for millions, or even billions, of years it is likely their explorations have been extensive. When we combine this with the fact that ours is a world capable of supporting life and technology we can see that our eventually being selected was not only probable, it was virtually inevitable!

A more recent book by one of today's leading biologists exhibits a similar kind of limitation in reasoning regarding the likelihood of colonization by extraterrestrials. In his The Meaning of Human Existence Edward O. Wilson gives a "portrait" of what extraterrestrials might be like by carrying over what we know of life here and applying it to life on other worlds. He concludes the portrait with the dogmatic assertion that our "poor little planet" has not been colonized and "never can be", because the systems of microorganisms that our bodies depend on for survival would not match the ones extraterrestrials might have developed and the species of plants and animals we depend on for food might be toxic and even fatal for their very different metabolisms.

Such an argument calls to mind other "leading" scientists of the past who have made unbelievable mistakes in disregarding or dismissing scientific developments that were just around the corner or even happening in front of their unseeing eyes. Just before the end of the 19th Century William Thompson, Lord Kelvin, one of the most eminent physicists of his time, is reported to have announced to a conference of his scientific colleagues that all of the important scientific discoveries in physics had already been made, and that all that remained was to now apply these discoveries to ever widening ranges of phenomena. The first three decades of the last century proved him to be dead wrong. Einstein's publication of his theory of relativity, and the opening up of the field of quantum mechanics by Max Planck and Erwin Schrodinger accomplished the proof. Rather than all scientific discoveries having already been made the new perspectives on physical reality afforded by their discoveries constitute one of the greatest revolutions in the history of scientific thought – a revolution that was "just around the corner" when Lord Kelvin made his infamous announcement.

An even more egregious blunder was made by Simon Newcomb, a Canadian American astronomer who, just a year before the Wright brothers made their historic first airplane flight, solemnly announced that "flight by machines heavier than air is unpractical and insignificant, if not utterly impossible." Of course he only had to look around him to see "heavier than air" living objects with wings and feathers flying and even quietly floating on currents of air. Within half a century of his dismissal of human air travel intercontinental aviation had become a major industry and saturation bombing from aircraft had paved the way for defeat of Nazi Germany in WWII. The dropping of two atom bombs from aircraft then led to the surrender of Japan. And within less than a normal lifetime "heavier than air" spacecraft carried a team of astronauts to the moon and brought them safely back to Earth.

Professor Wilson's dogmatic pronouncement that colonization of our planet by extraterrestrials is an impossibility involves the same sort of miscalculation in evaluating scientific trends and their possibilities. Again he looks with unseeing eyes at the progress our own very rudimentary level of advancement has already made in immunizations against pathogens in various regions of the Earth. These allow us to safely travel in peace and war without risk of infection or death. He looks with unseeing eyes at our botanical gardens and zoos where we create controlled climates and biome ecologies that allow plants and animals to flourish where they originally would have perished. He sees genetically modified foods growing in our farms and on market shelves that have acquired properties making them more nutritious, rid them of harmful qualities and fails to project where such technologies might take us, or inhabitants of other worlds, in the next ten thousand, or hundred thousand, or millions of years and, having done all this he assures us interplanetary colonization is a pipe dream.

For the same reasons he assumes it has never happened and can never happen here or anywhere else. Because it is impossible for us today it will remain, in Simon Newcumbs phrase, "utterly impossible" for all time. It is not clear how "utterly impossible" differs from "impossible" but it probably has to do with how badly the utterer wants it to be true.

That being the case for E.O. Wilson he badly needs us to be "alone" for all time and insists we must remain so "forever". It serves to maintain the religion he has helped make out of the "new atheism" supported by Neo-Darwinists such as Stephen Gould and Richard Dawkins. It requires believing we have pulled ourselves up by our own bootstraps in our struggle for survival, as individuals and as a species, without the assistance of God or extraterrestrials. He wants us to be alone and to remain so "forever".

It would be difficult to climb further out on a limb than Professor Wilson has done with this line of reasoning. The technologies that would be needed to adapt us to environments or to alter them to where they would be adapted to us are well known to the scientific community. Funding and political opposition are the prior problems that must be solved first, but enough is known to make it reasonably certain that our colonization of other planets will be done.

What Professor Wilson has in mind however, is not the problem of our migrating to other planets, but their colonization of us. This he declares to be "forever" impossible, because they might not be able to cope with our alien microorganisms. The other problem of their not being able to subsist on the plant and animal foods our world has to offer would be his second reason for believing such colonization has never succeeded and never will.

The Bible, however, as we have already shown, claims such a colonization has already occurred and that it is succeeding. It describes the technologies that have made the success possible and they completely nullify Professor Wilson's objections.

The Bible claims the Celestial's colonization of Earth brought humanoid robots with them capable of carrying out all the first steps of preparation for their occupation. The Celestials remained within the sealed sphere that brought them, or the protected area sealed off by their robots, until the natural environment of Earth was altered enough to make it hospitable for them to enter it. Further they modified existing species of plants and animals to take advantage of the natural resistance to Earth's pathogens they already had and to make them safe and nutritious for Celestial consumption. It is also probable they made alterations in the Earth's atmosphere and climate that would make it safer once they moved out of the area they had sealed off and sanitized when first arriving. They also probably began setting up ecological areas outside the sanitized zones to be used for biome farming which would grow needed microorganisms suitable for supporting their own life forms and the new ones they were recreating.

By using robots they avoided the principal problems Professor Wilson claims unsolvable. Robots are not harmed by pathogens. Robots do not require food and cannot be harmed by it. Further by modifying Earth's plant and animal life they could use their natural immunity to Earth's hazards and with immunizations of themselves they could secure their own immunity.

Once again, as with Carl Sagan's assumptions, Professor Wilson's claims are irrelevant. Like Carl Sagan he assumes advanced Celestials would be handicapped by the same limitations we would face if we were in their place. Earth's colonization by Celestials, hundreds of thousand or millions of years in our technological future, is completely feasible and, in fact, could easily be accomplished with technologies just a little more advanced than those we are already have. His arguments are totally without scientific support. His claim that we must remain alone on this planet is as illogical as Simon Newcomb's claim, a century ago, was that we must remain earthbound, "crawling like wingless insects on its surface".

Since Professor Wilson's claim that colonization of Earth is a scientific impossibility is itself clearly groundless we will turn now to a more detailed examination of the Celestial's plan for colonizing "Earth: as revealed in the Bible.

THE CELESTIAL'S SPACE PROGRAM

On Earth our own first steps into space have required vast bureaucracies and gigantic industrial projects. In these the organization and funding of government are linked with industrial facilities and human resources to create programs of awesome dimensions such as the administrative colossus, NASA, and the space exploration programs it has directed.

Yet impressive as its achievements are, overshadowing even the construction of the Great Pyramid in antiquity, they doubtless would seem crude and primitive to a civilization like the Celestials'. For in spite of the fantastic expenditures of money and energy these projects required they have just begun the exploration of our own solar system.

When compared with the problem of bringing a space city a mile square and containing a community of Celestials over vast distances of many light-years, the Apollo Moon Project pales into insignificance. And when we find the

Celestials' journey from Mazzaroth to Earth was probably only a neighborhood jaunt compared with many they have made to far more distant worlds we begin to appreciate the real meaning of the term "space exploration." Indeed, if we believe the Scriptures, the space mission recounted in Genesis was only the first phase of a single colonization effort to a small planet which is one among millions that make up their larger space program. What sort of administration, specialists and resources would be necessary to organize and sustain space efforts of this magnitude?

Though we have only hints, here and there, it is possible to piece together some overall conception of the Celestial's equivalent to NASA. "Equivalent," however, hardly applies to an organization that embraces "worlds without end" and organizes the highest levels of natural and artificial intelligence in projects that extend over millions of light years' distance.

As might be expected, like its earthly counterpart, the Celestials' space administration is organized into many levels. Its highest decision making is carried out, on their home planet, by a general staff of senior administrators who serve as aides to their empire's chief, Jehovah.

Several passages in the Bible picture this general staff in action. Typically they are shown grouped around Jehovah in the command center and surrounded by the communications equipment and computers needed to monitor and direct their far-flung space empire. The most detailed of these descriptions comes from the pen of John the Revelator who claimed he was granted a possibly televised view of their headquarters. Speaking of it he says: "... and behold, a throne was set in heaven, and one sat on the throne.... And round about the throne were four and twenty seats: and upon the seats I saw four and twenty elders sitting, clothed in white raiment; and they had on their heads crowns of gold. And out of the throne proceeded lightnings and thunderings and voices ... And before the throne there was a sea of glass like unto crystal: and in the midst of the throne, and round about the throne, were four beasts full of eyes before and behind" (Revelation 4:2-6).

Bible scholars have been puzzled by this and similar passages. The reference to a throne suggests command, but the surrounding "sea of glass" and "beasts" with "eyes before and behind" combine seeming metaphors in a strange mixture which has proved impenetrable to traditional textual analysis.

Now, in our own Space Age, the passage can be seen for what it is. Without Bible dictionaries or commentaries its descriptions immediately call to mind video images, like John's, which are familiar to anyone who watches daily television. How many times, in newscasts and documentaries or science fiction movies, have we all viewed space centers like the one John is describing? Filled with white-suited "elders" and technicians, their walls a "sea" of glassed television panels, they bustle with the pandemonium of flashing lights and "thundering" loud speakers.

Like John's four "beasts," with "eyes before and behind," they are studded with the consoles of data-processing equipment and computers. Their lighted dials and instrument panels do indeed resemble "eyes" in grotesque mechanical monsters.

To a First Century Christian the term "beast" would be a proper one to apply to something which is inhuman yet "alive" with intelligent function. Its whirring activity as questions were addressed to it, and its thunderous voice as it responded, would suggest animal vitality. It could hardly be called a person, since it lacked human form and dignity. Yet to a person who had never seen a computer or heard of artificial intelligence, it would be undeniably "living." The Greek word John used for "beast" is *zoon*, which simply means "something alive." It was not the more common "therion", which he would have chosen had he really meant an ordinary wild, or dangerous, animal.

Even in our own age, script writers, like the John of Revelation, are prone to invest intelligent robots in their sci-fi movies with living characteristics giving them names like "Hal" or "R2D2" and attributing benevolent or rebellious motives to them as they aid or attempt to overthrow humans.

HOW ABOUT LONG-DISTANCE CALLS?

It might at first seem doubtful that a central headquarters could coordinate the interests of an intergalactic empire. How could information be conveyed over vast distances, measured in light-years, quickly enough to be of use? How could responses be sent to far-off worlds in time to serve the purposes which had prompted them?

Yet, even in human history, there are parallels that suggest the problem is not insurmountable. The Roman Empire was one of the largest and most enduring the world has known. In its time communications traveled slowly. Often many months were required to send messages from its remote borders to Rome. Directives and commands returned even more slowly. Yet it functioned with an efficiency which has hardly been surpassed in modern times. In a similar manner it would seem that an empire of galaxies might function efficiently, in spite of the distance problem, provided its colonies had sufficient autonomy and flexibility.

There is reason to believe, however, that the Celestials may not find delays in communication a problem at all. Modern physics teaches us that the speed of light is an absolute limit for all forms of energy that could carry messages. Information transmitted by radio or television cannot exceed a velocity of 186,202 miles per second. At this rate dialogue between galaxies might require millions or even billions of years for completion. How could an efficient exchange of information take place among societies separated by such distances? The answer may lie in the science of parapsychology. In recent years experiments in this field have produced impressive evidence for the existence of nonphysical energies which can transmit information. Unlike electromagnetic signals they do not diminish with distance and can apparently span great reaches of space instantaneously.

Numerous experiments, both here and abroad, have shown telepathy and clairvoyance can be as effective over hundreds, or even thousands, of miles as when operating within the confines of a single room. Such studies point clearly to some as yet unexplained energy form which transcends the conventional laws of spacetime. J. B. Rhine, a pioneer researcher in extra-sensory phenomena at Duke

University has pointed out that a large body of evidence now exists that supports the hypothesis that our minds can communicate or gain knowledge of the world around us, not confined by space/time/mass limitations and independently of our ordinary sense organs.

More recently our own Apollo space missions, as well as those of the Soviets, have been used to study the effectiveness of telepathy for communicating in outer space. Initial results have been reported as encouraging.

Experimental studies on extrasensory perception indicate that psi energies, as yet unharnessed by humans, provide a means by which an advanced civilization might carry on running dialogues or maintain instantaneous surveillance across the vast distances of interstellar space.

Similarly experiments in present day quantum physics have shown sub atomic particles which were once closely associated can, when separated over vast distances, continue to influence one another so that changes in one are mirrored in the other. This suggests such quantum effects might be used to communicate information across cosmic distances instantaneously.

Apart from the scientific evidence there are numerous passages in the Bible that imply Celestials do maintain interplanetary dialogues and surveillance. Others even give detailed descriptions of the equipment they use for this purpose. We shall examine some of these in chapters which follow.

All of this lends plausibility to John's description of a command headquarters from which Celestials could control a vast space empire.

COLONIAL ADMINISTRATION

Fragmentary clues in the Scriptures give further details concerning the Celestials' interstellar space program. In addition to Jehovah, as chief, and the "four and twenty" regional directors, the headquarters staff also includes archangels who perform command and liaison functions. While the Bible names only Gabriel, who acts as emissary and deputy for Jehovah, Lucifer, who directed the Garden experiment, and Michael, who led the victorious forces against Lucifer's rebellion, the roster is filled out in the apocryphal literature. In the first Book of Enoch five others are added: Raphael, Uriel, Raguel, Saraquel, and Remiel. Though Lucifer is not specifically mentioned as an archangel before his fall, his description as "perfect" in the day he was "created" (Ezekiel 28:15), his position as director of the Garden experiment (Ezekiel 28:14), and the reference to him as the "prince of this world" (John 12:31) would all indicate he belonged to the highest rank of Celestials.

At a lower level there are other orders of Celestials who perform intelligence and caretaking functions (Daniel 4:13 and 23, Psalms 91:11 and Matthew 4:6, for example). In addition they also carry out space exploration and assist in the work of colonization. Aiding them are the seraphim and cherubim. Traditional biblical commentators have assumed these to be orders, or ranks, of angels. As we have already shown there is good reason to suppose this is not correct. A critical study of the texts describing these aides indicates they are not even living creatures but rather robots-servomechanisms. Some have been constructed with human form; others resemble animals or are simply automated pieces of machinery. The more complex are programmed with artificial intelligence and can substitute for Celestials in performing the routine work of an advanced civilization. They are variously depicted, throughout the Bible, as flying through the air, transporting Celestials, collecting and carrying, guarding and protecting or attacking and destroying.

Last, and of greatest importance at the planetary level, are the melchisedecs – local administrators in charge of individual colonies, or planets. These again have proved a source of puzzlement to traditional scholars and commentators. The only one mentioned in the Scriptures appears first in Genesis where he is described as "the priest of the most high God" (Genesis 14:18). Interestingly this is before there was a Hebrew priesthood and even before Abraham had fathered the Hebrew nation. Abraham, however, visited this melchisedec (called simply "Melchizedek" in Genesis) and paid tithes to him, receiving his blessing and acknowledging him as the high priest of the true God.

Now this raises some interesting questions. Abraham was a stranger to the land. How did he know "Melchizedek" was the priest of the most high God? And what God? Certainly not one of those worshipped in the country from which Abraham came. And what was "God's" priest doing here in Canaan long before he had chosen a people, revealed his law or set up a priesthood of human ministers under Moses? Who made him a priest that Abraham would acknowledge?

Some additional light is thrown on these questions by the Book of Hebrews in the New Testament, where "Melchisedec" is mentioned. Here we are told Jesus, too, was made "a priest for ever after the order of Melchisedec" (Hebrews 7:17)- as though the name referred to a class or rank, rather than an individual. Then, speaking of "Melchizedek" in Genesis, the writer of Hebrews informs us that he was "without father, without mother, without descent, having neither beginning of days, nor end of life; but made like unto the Son of God"-one who "abideth a priest continually" (Hebrews 7:3).

Puzzled commentators have suggested that this description was applied to the Genesis melchisedec because, being a Gentile Canaanite, he was not included in the Hebrew genealogies-hence his lack of recorded parentage and his being without a birth or death date. Unfortunately for this theory it fails to explain why the writer of Hebrews would have gone on to say he was "made like unto the Son of God" and how, being mortal, he could remain a priest "forever." Obviously this condition could be fulfilled only if he were "like unto the Son of God" in the sense of being a Celestial and hence immortal.

In their eagerness to give "Melchizedek" a human lineage, Jewish commentators, in the Targums of Jerusalem and Jonathan, suggested that he was Noah's son, Shem. This view has been adopted by a number of Christian scholars, as well. There is, however, not a shred of scriptural evidence to support it.

The fact of "Melchizedek's" high priestly office, before there was a Hebrew priesthood, and his perpetual tenure in that office ("continually" or "forever"), make it clear that the writer of Hebrews regarded him as Celestial rather than human. Further, the suggestion that there is an "order of Melchisedecs" coincides with linguistic analysis of the term itself. The word "melchisedec" comes from two Hebrew roots: "mehlek", meaning a "queen or king," and tsedeq, meaning "right" or "just." In other words the etymology of the name shows that it is a descriptive title, not a proper name-a "king of righteousness." One final piece of evidence serves to clinch the argument. "Melchisedec" ruled at "Salem," according to Genesis, and Bible scholars agree that "Salem" was the site which later became Jerusalem.

If this was the Celestials' first headquarters on Earth, as the Book of Ezekiel claims, then it would be logical that upon their withdrawal they would leave one of their numbers in charge of the new colony. And it would be convenient that he would govern from their former headquarters-Eden, or Jerusalem. He would be the priest, on Earth, of the "highest God" before there was an Earthly priesthood. And he, being created immortal, would be "without father, without mother" and "without end of life."

All this makes it clear that the Melchisedec of Genesis and Hebrews was one of an order of "kings of righteousness." Among its members is also included Jesus of Nazareth. Like the first "Melchisedec" he, too, is ultimately destined to rule this world when the Celestials return.

And, by an extension of the same line of reasoning, it is logical that other members of the "Order of Melchisedec" rule other worlds. As we shall see later there is evidence that "Melchisedec" was not even the first ruler here. Lucifer, the director of the Garden experiment, was the first and would have remained so except for his rebellion. In all probability his successor was the Celestial who led the loyal forces responsible for his defeat. This was the archangel, Michael, who is described as "one of the chief princes" (Daniel 10:13). The Hebrew words used here for "chief" and "prince" mean "ruler" and "high priest."

The Bible identifies no further melchisedecs specifically. The Genesis "Melchisedec" and Jesus are the only ones it clearly identifies. But we do have two references, in the Book of Job, to gatherings of what appear to be other melchisedecs. In these we find "sons of God" attending scheduled staff meetings to receive work assignments. And among them Lucifer appears! Oddly this is after his fall and expulsion from the Garden-apparently his membership among them is still in effect by virtue of his office, a right which has not yet been revoked by the appointment of a successor. And so we read: "Now there was a day when the sons of God came to present themselves before the Lord, and Satan came also among them" (Job 1:6). And again in Chapter 2 we find another meeting which recurs as a regularly scheduled event: "Again there was a day when the sons of God came to present themselves before the Lord, and Satan came also among them to present himself before the Lord" (Job 2:1). The Hebrew word for "present" here is "yatsab", which means to "offer" oneself, presumably for service.

Apparently, then, the administration of particular planets or colonies is the work of melchisedecs. These, with the assistance of watchers and guardian "angels" (a work force of cherubim and seraphim), carry out the decisions of the empire's leader and regional directors. In addition they also rule on local matters falling under their jurisdiction.

COLONIZATION – THE PROGRAM BEGINS

The colonization of our own planet began in an uneventful way. It followed a pattern which had been well established over millennia of space exploration. At first, and until Lucifer's rebellion, the administrative machinery functioned smoothly as it had with thousands of worlds before.

Once they had selected our world, the course they followed can be reconstructed with a fair degree of certainty. We can chart its progress by comparing it with the history of human colonization, our present space program and clues given in the Scriptures.

Their initial visit was the first phase of a long-range plan for permanent settlement. Because of this they had to bring enough supplies to establish a long-term base. It was also necessary to bring a sizable population of Celestials, themselves, who could carry out the preparations. It seems likely they brought plants and animals, or at least genetic blueprints for species and biome ecologies. These were later used to introduce new plants and animals in the same way as our own New England colonists did when they settled the New World. Evidently they also brought equipment to remodel and domesticate native life forms. Probably they included instruments for studying the Earth, its resources and its native life with thoroughness impossible from their home base or other space colonies. They may also have brought equipment to set up forces which could alter the Earth's surface, its atmosphere, climate, and even its orientation to other heavenly bodies. Such planetary engineering would explain the puzzling balance of life supporting conditions known as the "anthropic principle". William Hartman, as astronomer, has written a book, "Mars, the Mysterious Red Planet" explaining our own plans to reengineer the Red Planet for temporary settlement of scientists in this century.

How long these preparations took we can only guess. In the next chapter we will try to pinpoint the time when their most critical experiment took place-the remodeling, or recreation, of humans. From the fossil record and clues given in the Scriptures this can be determined with some accuracy. But how many years, or even centuries, may have preceded this crucial experiment is impossible to determine. Similarly, biblical evidence indicates they remained on Earth, or at least visited at frequent intervals, for centuries after the Garden experiment. But the Bible gives no hint as to when their space city, Eden, first arrived and no certain occasion for its withdrawal.

The scriptural evidence that does exist suggests their program of colonization has gone through three stages. Stage I, a period of indeterminable length, was the time when their headquarters was actually located on the Earth. Its site was within the area they had sealed off-the Garden. Within this Garden they created, or remodeled, various forms of life to "seed" the Earth in preparation for their final return. It seems likely they also used this stage to make extensive studies of our world and, perhaps, to reconstruct some of its basic features.

STAGE II – THE PLAN IS REVISED

Stage II began with the withdrawal of Eden and was a period when they monitored their experimental work closely – the more so since their original experimental design had been upset by a rebellion and power struggle within their own ranks. The director of the Garden experiment and chief assistant to Jehovah, Satan, had betrayed his trust and attempted to use created man as a tool in a scheme to overthrow Jehovah and seize command of the colony.

In a society which had renounced evil and injustice for untold millennia, such an act, though possible, could not have been foreseen, and its effect on the colonization project was disastrous. Nevertheless, Satan and the Celestials who sided with him, were overthrown and marooned in our region of the galaxy along with the created humans they had betrayed. To prevent a total aborting of the colonization plan it became necessary to revise it. The revision was a supplemental program for retraining and salvaging the experimental humans.

As a result this second stage was marked by frequent visits to Earth and the selection of human leaders, or "prophets," through whom the Celestials directed and taught humanity. During this period they also found it necessary, occasionally, to interfere in the course of human events. They did this to preserve the groundwork they had laid and guide their corrupted heirs back to the course they had originally planned. The third stage was launched to bring about the fulfillment of their revised program. The descendants of their corrupted creation proved to be a "stiff-necked" and intractable lot. The results of genetic tampering by Satan, and their interbreeding with inferior evolved humans, had produced an unstable psychological makeup. The wickedness of humans created a problem unique to this planet and required a unique solution.

STAGE III – "FOR GOD SO LOVED THE WORLD"

Drastic measures were called for, and Jehovah made a startling decision. Like human anthropologists who find out about an unknown culture by going to live among its members, Jehovah decided to send one of their own. He would be a Celestial born into the human situation where its enigmas and perversities could be studied from within. By sharing the weaknesses and temptations of human, and triumphing over them, he could demonstrate the possibility and value of the Celestials' way of life. And he would do it in a manner indirect guidance by human leaders and prophets could not. He would demonstrate the redeeming power of total love and its ability to lift men above the woes of the human condition. Through his knowledge and mastery of the Creative Power, or "Holy Spirit," he would show men the way to an inner wholeness of spirit which can regenerate fallen human nature and enable humans to conquer wrongdoing, disease and even death. And, yes, he could even go through the ultimate experience of death and be resurrected-a final proof of the reality of eternal life and the Celestials' power over humanity's greatest enemy.

The Bible tells of Jehovah's decision in a single dramatic sentence: "For God so loved the world, that he gave his only begotten Son, that whosoever believeth in him should not perish, but has everlasting life" (John 3:16). At first it might seem that such concern on the part of extraterrestrial strangers is improbable. But we must remember we are their heirs. They had created, nurtured and trained us and ultimately failed to protect us against ruination by one of their own. Their lack, as immortals, of natural offspring, and their sense of unfulfilled responsibility to us, dependent creatures made in their own image, make the extent of their concern and love understandable. And even though it may surpass its human counterparts the circumstances make it believable.

The die was cast. A DNA information print of Jehovah was used. One of his most trusted aides, Gabriel, was dispatched and supervised the imposition of it on the ovular chromatin of a human virgin, Mary. She and her husband had been selected because of their direct descent from the original created stock and their observance of the Celestially taught religion.

Nine months later an identical twin to Jehovah was born to the human mother, Mary. Jehovah's final step in the salvation of his wayward creation was underway. The clone, Jesus of Nazareth, lived an exemplary life according to high standards set by the Celestials. He taught and manifested the redemptive power of love as a remedy for the ills of the human condition. Finally, in his death and resurrection, he demonstrated the genuineness of the Celestials' offer of eternal life and citizenship to humans who prove themselves worthy.

As a parting gift, before returning to the home base, he initiated a select group of followers into the use of the ultimate Creative Power. He called this his "baptism" and showed them how to use the power (which present-day parapsychologists call "bioplasmic," or "biocosmic") to heal illness, reform character disorders, transcend so-called laws of nature and even resurrect the dead. Most important, he taught that the voluntary opening up of one's life to this power can regenerate fallen human nature and give men a "new birth." By being "born again" humans can not only achieve righteousness in their external conduct but, more important, wholeness (or "holiness") within. .Only through such a "rebirth" can fallen humans become worthy of Celestial citizenship.

With the launching of this third phase a workable solution was at last reached for salvaging a remnant of humanity. The promise of a redeemer made to patriarchal humans after the fall and carried, by their descendants, into religious legends and myths throughout the world had at last been fulfilled. After Jesus' death, resurrection and return to the Celestials' home base his disciples began the work of bringing this solution to the world at large.

"UNTO THE ENTIRE WORLD"

At Pentecost they experienced the formation of a new religion, Christianity, which has played a major role in the spread of this final plan throughout the Earth. At Pentecost over 3,000 people, drawn from the farthest reaches of the Empire and beyond, experienced the "baptism of the spirit" - the crucial parapsychological and spiritual transformation which suddenly swept humans into a vast evolutionary leap into the future. By setting up the conditions for a mass experience of biocosmic power, and its effects on human nature ordinary men became, in a significant new sense, "sons of God." Paraphysical manifestations accompanied this outpouring. Some emitted visible auras as they were charged with the "Holy Spirit," or cosmic power. "Tongues of flame" came and rested on their heads, reminiscent of the halos painted around saints in early church art. Parapsychological manifestations and charismatic "gifts of the spirit," such as xenoglossy broke forth. Men from many nations spoke in "tongues" and understood one another's speech without knowing the languages they heard. Extraordinary psychic healings took place, and a new faith that was to prove the most widespread in the history of humanity sprang into being. The spread of the good news of salvation was underway.

All signs predicted in the Bible proclaim that the third stage of the Celestials' colonization plan is now rapidly drawing to a close. With the rebirth of the nation of Israel their return is, as Jesus dramatically put it, "Even at the doors."

Shortly they will return in the manner, described in the opening chapter of this book, to set up a thousand-year reign of peace and justice. During this time the nations of the world will be molded into a peaceful unity which can be included in the Celestials' intergalactic empire. At the end of that probationary period full citizenship will be conferred on the human remnant that has survived the training and qualified for eternal life. They will begin a new existence, in immortal bodies, as citizens, not just of this world, but of Heaven, the confederation of advanced civilizations the Celestials have created.

This, in brief, is the reason why the Celestials came to Earth. It explains why they created us, and the course their plan for us has taken. It leaves many questions unanswered, however, questions which preoccupy our scientists today as we stand on the threshold of our own space age. What specific techniques were used in our creation? What is the proof that we are not the result of biological evolution alone? Does the fossil record support our claim? How does our Space Age interpretation modify current scientific views on the origin of humanity, of races and the beginnings of civilization? We will consider these questions next in the chapter which follows.

And the Lord God formed man of the dust of the ground, and breathed into his nostrils the breath of life; and man became a living soul.

– Genesis 2:7

CHAPTER VIII

The Experimental Creation

In the Nineteenth Century higher critics of the Bible ridiculed such passages as the one quoted above. "Man" created outright from dust-preposterous! Hadn't Darwin proved man evolved over millions of years, and was descended from ape-like ancestors? What did God have to do with it? Obviously the Genesis account is just a curious bit of Hebrew folklore.

Today, at the beginning of the Twenty-First century, we are not so sure. Space Age anthropology has tried hard to document Darwin's theories, yet curious gaps and puzzles remain. The immediate ancestor of modern humans has never been found though fossils of our more remote ancestors exist in profusion. We are not even exactly sure when or where contemporary humans arose or how we spread so rapidly throughout the Earth. The origin of races remains an enigma. Most puzzling of all is our miraculous ascent, over five or six millennia, from an animal level of existence to full-blown, urban civilization in ancient Sumer. What caused our sudden elevation from the state of a savage, living in caves and using crude stone tools, to that of a sophisticate who lived in grid-pattern cities, constructed monumental architecture we cannot duplicate today, charted the heavens, projected the periods and times of comets and eclipses with great accuracy, philosophized about the mysteries of the universe and created remarkable sculptures and literature?

Did the blind, natural selection of chance variations elevate us, or were we assisted in our upward climb? Today, as we stand on the threshold of space exploration, the idea that we have been visited and assisted is not preposterous. The Genesis account of "man's" creation begins to look more like futurology than folklore.

And yet the fossil record and the proofs of humanity's evolutionary history remain. How can we disentangle the conflicting lines of evidence that support such opposed views of our beginnings?

NOT FROM THE APES

In the late Nineteenth Century battle lines were drawn sharply between religious fundamentalists and evolutionary scientists and philosophers. Fundamentalists attacked the theory of evolution and evolutionists attacked the Bible. Today the battles are largely forgotten. Many conservative Christians who are scientifically literate recognize that the fossil record cannot be denied. Fossils of earlier humans and prehuman hominids exist in abundance, and their hundreds of thousands and millions of years of age have been irrefutably established by dating techniques. Such specimens can be seen in almost any local museum of natural history.

On the other hand archaeologists and textual scholars are increasingly confirming the accuracy of the Bible. Persons, places and events mentioned in it are almost daily being verified by new archaeological finds. Discoveries such as the Dead Sea scrolls prove considerable accuracy of translations which have come down to us.

Where then does the truth lie? Were we created outright, as the Bible claims, or did we evolve by the stages shown in the fossil record?

MODERN HUMANS – A RECREATION

One of the most important discoveries to come out of our Space Age interpretation of the Bible is its claim that humans evolved and were then recreated by extraterrestrials. The Genesis account of our beginnings far from denying our evolutionary origin actually affirms it in mythic form in Genesis 1 and recounts our recreation in Genesis 2. In fact if one accepts the stories in Genesis as being literally true, as Bible based opponents of evolution generally do, the Genesis story of a universal flood, if examined carefully, compels belief in evolution because it claims all the millions of species alive today are descended from the few Noah could have brought onto the Ark.

The fossil record proving human evolution stands then. It cannot be denied. Yet modern humans also stand. And as they stand they cannot be accounted for by the evidence in the fossil record. In the final stages of our emergence we became too much too fast to be explained by existing understanding of evolution. Some added agency is needed to explain the strangeness and, in particular, the extraordinary over-endowments that set us apart from every other animal on this planet.

The Bible tells us this added agency was the activity of Celestials who refashioned us in their own otherworldly image. Unfortunately it tells us little more. How they refashioned us, their motives in doing so, the techniques they used-all these we must reconstruct from other sources. In this chapter we will attempt this reconstruction from the fragmentary hints given in the Bible and two other sources – the emerging science of genetic engineering and paleoanthropology. The story that emerges is a truly astounding one, for it proves we are indeed not from the apes but the heir of a very different sort of ancestor. Let us see, then, how this ancestor went about our reconstruction.

THE GARDEN EXPERIMENT

When the Celestials first reached Earth they began the preparations necessary for a genetic experiment of great complexity and importance. An area of our alien world was prepared by isolating it and modifying it to resemble their own. Just as our space missions take elaborate precautions to avoid contamination of samples and quarantine astronauts upon their return, so they guarded against alien microorganisms and pollution. This would be necessary, both for themselves and the plants and animals they created, if they were to achieve predictable results. They did this by marking off a large area and throwing up a force field around it to seal off pollution by air or water and to repel invading predators. The dimensions of this area are not given in Genesis, but they are given for the "New Jerusalem" in the book of Revelation and we have already seen that it is almost certainly identical with "Eden" in Genesis.

If the two accounts are of the same area, then the overall length of the Garden was about 500 miles to a side-"twelve thousand furlongs" around the "foursquare" perimeter, as John the Revelator tells us (Revelation 21:16). With its base at Jerusalem, the square would just about cover what geographers call the Fertile Crescent assuming its diagonal ran from the area of present day Jerusalem to the tip of the Persian Gulf. This area, in which historians locate the earliest of human civilizations, extends from the eastern seaboard of the Mediterranean, past the foothills of Kurdistan and down to the shores of the Persian Gulf. Within this area there was ample room to create the plants and animals they needed for food and domestic help.

HOW DID THEY "CREATE" PLANTS AND ANIMALS?

In terms of our coming biological revolution we can make likely guesses at the methods they employed. They could, of course, have brought plants and animals with them as our own colonists did in the Renaissance. A more efficient method, however, would be to bring genetic blueprints of their own desirable species or to modify those already here by genetic engineering.

By bringing DNA records of life forms of their own world they could simply replicate them from raw materials, as they were needed, without having to keep and feed them in the meantime. Modifying our own native species would be even better, where possible, since they would already be adapted to the Earth's environment. In the case of their most crucial experiment, humans, they almost certainly used the latter method. As we have seen the Cain story in Genesis tells us there were already other humans on Earth at the time of their coming. In looking for a native animal to domesticate and leave in charge of their program the selection of one of these hominids, primitive but not unlike themselves, would be a logical choice. With improvements and training humans could be given the responsibility of the Garden, "to dress it and to keep it" (Genesis 2: 14), after they had left. Once the new plants and animals, including humans, were established they could spread throughout the Earth to make it more hospitable for the Celestials' return.

DO WE HAVE LOOK-ALIKES ON OTHER WORLDS?

This assumes, of course, that beings from another world would resemble our early ancestors closely enough so that they could easily be remade into a reasonable facsimile of the alien beings. Is this likely and how much remodeling would be required?

What do scientists who investigate the question of otherworldly life think? Is it really likely that life here would so nearly duplicate life on an alien world? Science-fiction writers have reveled in imagining bizarre forms which intelligent life might take on distant planets. Scriptwriters have fascinated movie audiences with shots of ant-like creatures flying spaceships and balancing relativity equations, and of little green men with antennae, or gelatinous blobs that pursue humans like superhuman sleuths. Isn't it extremely unlikely that intelligent life on an alien world would resemble us – especially if it had had millions, or billions, of years to evolve beyond our own stage of development?

Carl Sagan expressed this skepticism when he pointed out that evolution of life on Earth was a product of random events, chance mutations, and many unrelated adaptations. Consequently, he argued, it is highly unlikely life elsewhere would so duplicate human processes as to resemble life here.

At first glance this argument has a certain common-sense plausibility. Since life takes such myriad forms here, is it not reasonable that it would assume even more varied forms elsewhere? Especially if conditions on the alien world were very different from our own? Why, of all the millions or billions of forms it could take, would intelligent life elsewhere assume the one specific form we associate with advanced intelligence and civilization here?

Unfortunately the argument will not stand up under scientific scrutiny. In the first place there is no good evidence that evolution is as blind and random as Sagan supposes. We have already seen that some astrophysicists, such as James Jeans, believe cosmic and biological evolution take place in ways that are meaningful or even mathematical. The adaptive mechanisms of many forms of higher life so nearly duplicate machines and electronic devices we have invented it is difficult to suppose they, too, are not the result of intelligent design working through nature.

Further, biologists know that many similarities between life forms here on Earth are due to structural properties which characterize the basic chemicals of life. As has been pointed out living organisms are the greatly magnified expression of molecules that compose them. For example the fact that many animals are made in matching right and left halves is thought to be due to the right-left symmetry of certain molecules that compose them. Similarly, primates (monkeys, apes and humans) have five-fingered and five-toed extremities because of the pentodal (five-featured) structure of other organic molecules. Even the location of sense and movement control in the head rather than the middle or tail end of some animals is thought to be due to the way cells balance and organize themselves at a chemical level in the developing embryo.

Now since meteorites from outer space contain the same chemicals that form building blocks for life here is it not reasonable to suppose there may be life forms elsewhere which resemble our own? Further, if these chemicals function there as they do here then it could well be that some of these alien creatures would have bilateral symmetry, five-fingered and five toed extremities and heads containing sense organs and controls for their bodies.

And if they visited our Earth because they had chosen it for its similarity to their own it might well be that they would find life forms here that closely resembled themselves. In fact they might very well discover that the Creative Power that had produced them had duplicated its efforts on this planet. For if our world is similar to theirs then it would be reasonable to suppose evolution here would parallel the course it had taken there.

Even on Earth this parallelism between life forms having completely dissimilar origins is sometimes found. Biologists call this "convergence" of dissimilar types because of a common environment. For example, the cetacea (a group of mammals including porpoises, dolphins, and whales) have the same evolutionary origin as cats, dogs and apes, not to omit ourselves. Yet because of the millions of years they have spent adapting to a watery environment they have come to resemble fish. The parallels are so striking that many people assume they are fish. They have even developed fishlike tails, finlike forelimbs and a hairless surface.

So the idea that Celestials came to Earth and found evolved hominids here who resembled them is not improbable. Nor would their added millions or billions of years of development necessarily have carried them beyond the characteristics we regard as human. For anthropologists point out that even with our own race the little technology we have developed has so shielded us from natural selection that evolution has virtually stopped for us. In a biological sense we are not demonstrably different from the cavemen who lived throughout Europe 30,000 to 40,000 years ago. Our evolution has become primarily cultural and technological rather than biological.

In the same way the Celestials would have reached a limit of biological evolution when they achieved our present level of civilization. The added millions or billions of years they have had to develop would have made few changes in their physical natures, except as they artificially improved them by genetic engineering. Their development from that point on, like ours, would lie principally in the mind and spirit. So they arrived on Earth, closely resembling our human ancestors, and decided to make the resemblance even closer.

HOW CLOSE IS CLOSE?

Just how closely these hominids resembled the Celestials is open to speculation. If the Bible is correct in saying the remodeled version reflects their image, then we can get an approximate idea by comparing ourselves with our own fossil ancestors.

Such a comparison suggests the differences were minimal. Probably the hominid selected by them would have been more hairy than ourselves. It may have had a smaller brain, and almost certainly it was less efficient. Perhaps there were minor cosmetic differences-a lower or more receding brow, a more protruding jaw or a less upright posture. Many of the changes the Celestials made might not be evident even if we could examine a fossil of their re-creation and compare it with the prototype from which it was taken.

Yet the changes they made, subtle as they may have been, revolutionized human nature and made us a biological improbability-a sapient animal endowed with skills and aspirations no earthly development could have given us. How did they accomplish this incredible transformation?

IN OUR IMAGE

The operation, itself, would have been a simple one. Tissue samples were taken from a hominid of the selected species. A scanning device ,could record the DNA pattern of its cells. The record would then be modified. A slight sequence change here, in the code symbols of the information record, would ensure its hairlessness and cause it to resemble them more closely. Others would provide extra brain cells in critical areas related to memory, abstract thought and creative productivity. One would enlarge the convolution of Broca and make more elaborate and grammatical speech possible. With a few simple substitutions of this sort the genetic "surgery" would be complete.

Now the modified record could be fed into a replicator, along with a quantity of raw chemicals. The result would be a man recreated from the "dust of the ground" (Genesis 2:7) by the Lord God just as the Bible says. This man, "Adam," would be an improved variety of the hominid from which he was taken – a man recreated in the "image" of the Celestials. Not quite as dramatic as Michelangelo's version, perhaps, but fully as effective, The Lord God would then breathe "the breath of life" into him, and he would become "a living soul" (Genesis 2:7). The Hebrew word used here for "breath" is *"nshamah"*, which means a vital breath or wind-a power. The technique of vivification was probably not different from our own use of electric shocks to restart the heartbeat in cardiac arrest.

A female companion could then have been provided by repeating the procedure. The matching of their genes, however, if they reproduced by the method used on the outside, would introduce an element of unpredictability undesirable in a controlled experiment. Parents who have tried to anticipate characteristics of their own children are aware of this uncertainty. A more satisfactory method would be to clone the companion. This could have been done by taking a doctored record and making one more change-the one determining sex. The Lord, however, chose a more dramatic method. He anesthetized Adam and removed a "rib," so Genesis 2:21 tells us. The cellular material of the rib was then evidently scanned, modified for sex-chromosome pattern, and replicated. The reason for this clumsier method was apparently psychological rather than genetic. The Lord wished Adam to value Eve, the clone, so he made him give up something for her. Thus Adam is moved to remark, "This is now bone of my bones, and flesh of my flesh: she shall be called Woman, because she was taken out of Man" (Genesis 2:23). Adam got the point, and the Lord's object lesson was effective.

As a clone of Adam Eve was his identical twin (except for sex). The characteristics of their offspring could be predicted with absolute certainty – a necessity in this sort of experiment where so much was to be entrusted to their care.

THE CELESTIALS' FIRST ARTIFACT

Whenever human colonists have migrated to new lands they have generally domesticated plants and animals they found there. In refashioning humans to make them more useful the Celestials followed a similar course. Unlike our own colonists who used slow and inefficient methods such as taming and selective breeding, the Celestials simply remade their domestic life forms to order on the spot. And in the way they refashioned us they demonstrated their vast civilizational and moral superiority to human colonizers. For while we have usually destroyed, enslaved or at least exploited natives in our colonies the Celestials elevated humans to their own level. In making us near equals they ruled out the possibility that we could become mere "beasts of burden." They created us not just to serve them but to enjoy them and be enjoyed by them, and to be co-equal in their civilization. And in being so designed we were set apart from all other animals on this planet in ways which give irrefutable proof they were here and we are their heirs. Humans are the most dramatic artifact they left behind, an artifact of unquestionable extraterrestrial origin.

HOW TO RECOGNIZE AN ARTIFACT
FROM ANOTHER WORLD

The old hymn which says, "This world is not my home; I'm just passing through" expresses a feeling most reflective people recognize and contains at least half a truth. We are indeed, as Christian theology maintains, dual-natured beings-infused with the other worldly gifts of a Celestial race, yet linked by ties of evolutionary descent to the beasts of the Earth. Thus the Apostle Paul was moved to lament: "O wretched man that I am! who shall deliver me from the body of this death?" (Romans 7:24). This is the very essence of tragedy in the classical sense – humans doomed to yearn and strive for more than we can be, yet knowing our ultimate fate is death with the doom of all our dreams. The very gift of reflective thought which enables us to imagine and long for perfection and immortality is the fatal power which also reveals our bestiality and our doom. Small wonder modern philosophers have called this insight "existential despair." Like Prometheus we hold the gift of Celestial fire yet are chained to the rock of our animal ancestry.

Perhaps this is why the Celestials have shown such long suffering patience with their wayward creation-their strange offspring who is half natural child and half bestial stepchild. And perhaps this is why they have gone to such lengths in revising their original plan.

Their motives in creating us were not just those of trainers domesticating beasts, or colonists exploiting "savages", or superior beings amusing themselves with pets. They were not even those of missionaries who have sought to elevate "heathen" people by bringing them the gift of a "superior" civilization and religion.

Their real motives include a higher interest so obvious it seems almost human, for we also share it as we reflect their image. Since they do not reproduce sexually they have no children. Being busy with the pursuits of a highly advanced civilization, yet possessing the humanlike need for relaxation and play, they crave the enjoyment children can bring. Like us they have a highly developed need to care for the immature and helpless. Like us they have the need to invest themselves in the growth and development of dependent beings under their care. And like us they enjoy reliving their own development vicariously and taking pride in the achievements of offspring as they fulfill the hopes and expectations of their parents. So they have transferred these needs to those they create and domesticate in their course of space colonization.

Wherever they go they create, or re-create, heirs in their image-heirs whom they can love, instruct, guide and ultimately welcome into their civilization as equals. It is this fact which provides the startling proof that we are not just products of earthly evolution. Unlike any other animal we were remade according to an unearthly pattern. In the process they over endowed us with traits of no earthly use. They could only be of use as their companions or co-citizens.

Because of this we not only have traits necessary for survival (the only kind earthly evolution can give us), but we possess numerous others which are irrelevant to survival. These could not be the product of natural selection, for they often distract us from the sordid business of surviving and divert our attention to higher matters. As Jesus points out in the New Testament, "man shall not live by bread alone" (Luke 4:4).

Interestingly, though they do not contribute to survival, these traits are prized as the "highest" qualities of our species, and they single us out from every other earthly kind. They could only have arisen on another kind of world or as a means of sharing with beings from one, and this is precisely where and how we acquired them.

We will presently examine these unearthly traits which set us apart. They include the capacity for philosophical reflection, for religious experience with its yearning for immortality, for disinterested or "pure" scientific investigation and for artistic creation.

Before looking at these, however, it will be helpful to consider the structure in which they are housed-the human body. For even here, at a purely physical level, our nature already shows oddities that give us an unparalleled strangeness among earth's inhabitants.

THE "FEATHERLESS BIPED"

The peculiarities which set us apart from other animals are typified by the whimsical definition which is sometimes given of the human being as a "featherless biped."

Though our walking on two legs and lacking feathers is indeed a peculiarity it is by no means the strangest or most significant of our oddities.

Among those which have attracted the attention of zoologists none is harder to explain than our nearly equal lack of hair. Among some 4,000 species of land mammals, including our closest relatives, the monkeys and great apes, man alone is nearly hairless. He is, as Desmond Morris so aptly put it, a "naked ape."[3]

Our loss of a furry pelt defies an evolutionary explanation, for it would be a distinct advantage in most climates and as a protection against a scratching and abrading environment. In fact, we have had to compensate for its loss by the wearing of clothes. Our lack of it is antievolutionary. How then did it come about? Was it engineered by Celestials to make us more like them? Did they remove our pelt, much as we clip, groom and shave our own domestic animals, because they found it more aesthetic?

Again, in curious contrast to our overall hairlessness is our luxuriant mop of head hair. All the great apes, our nearest biological "cousins", are bald or nearly so. Interestingly, the Lord's special servants, Nazarites, were required to leave hair uncut (Numbers 6:5), and Paul describes it as a woman's "glory" (I Corinthians 11:15). Were these ideas handed down by Celestials who have luxuriant hair and fashioned us in their image?

Another remarkable difference that sets humans apart from the rest of the higher animals is our capacity to engage in sex for expressive and pleasurable purposes, rather than as an exclusively reproductive act. The human female is alone in lacking the estrus (or "heat") cycle which confines female lower animals to mating only when they are ovulating and can reproduce. A woman can enjoy love and sex even when reproduction is not the goal. Similarly the human male alone, among higher mammals, lacks a penis bone. Because of this, sex for him must be preceded by arousal and cannot be quickly completed as a starkly reproductive act-as it so often is for animals in the wild. And both men and women are peculiar, among higher mammals, in forming pair bonding, the tendency to make lifelong, monogamous unions. Are these differences gifts of the Celestials who gave them to us, because they wished to train us in the responsibilities of nurturance, fidelity, sympathy and love so important in their civilization?

THE BRAINY BIPED

Of all the characteristics that set humans apart from other animals none is more baffling or utterly inexplicable than the brain and its remarkable capacities. By itself it is an overwhelming evidence of Celestial interference in our development.

As a functional instrument it is unrivaled by anything we know not only in the animal kingdom, but in the entire universe. It contains over 100 billion cells. Almost as many as there are stars in our galaxy.

It contains natural forms of almost every electronic device known to man. It has conductors, resistors, capacitors, transformers, relays, filters, memory-storage units and retrieval systems.

Unlike the best computers designed by humans it can create superb poetry, compose immortal symphonies, envision over-powering paintings. Yet it is so miniaturized it is usually housed in a cavity of only about 1, 300 cubic centimeters and weighs barely three pounds. How did the naked ape come by such a tool?

To suppose that such a device could have "evolved" by a simple mechanical selection among millions of chance variations is, as Darwin himself observed, "absurd in the highest degree." It is about as plausible as that the plays of Shakespeare would accidentally assemble themselves out of discarded newsprint tossed into a trash bin.

More than any other structure we know the human brain seems to show that nature does not work by blind and mechanical processes of chance, as some scientists have argued, but involves a purpose and intelligence that works toward meaning and wholeness. The human brain, regarded as an artifact, is perhaps the most compelling evidence we know of to support the idea that the designing and controlling power of the universe is creative intelligence. It is, in fact, an eternal, infinite consciousness which the Bible calls "God". Philosophers have seen it as an all-pervading reality underlying both mind and matter out of which all that has been and is has emerged.

Yet, even if we grant that such a power might create intelligent hominids and even Celestials million of years in our future, an enigma remains, for such developments take time.

The paleontological record shows that major species changes require hundreds of thousands, or even millions, of years to accomplish. The rise and fall of dinosaurs, for example, occurred over a period of 150 million years. And one of our earliest hominid ancestor, homo habilis, lived several million years ago. Yet the changes that separate us from it are insignificant when compared with those that distinguish us from our nearest living cousins, the great apes.

Normally, then, even hundreds of thousands of years are insufficient to produce major changes in a species. Yet in the case of modern humans we find a most astonishing exception to this rule. For our ancestors of only a little over 30,000 years ago lived scarcely above the level of beasts around them. They used only the crudest of tools, made by flaking stones, and lived at an animal level of existence. And the fossil record shows they had lived at this same level since they first appeared around 250,000 years ago.

THE MODERN HUMAN'S CELESTIAL BRAIN

Recently, however, somewhere between thirty to fifty thousand years ago, a subtly different *Homo sapiens* appeared. Though their fossils look much the same as those of earlier humans the quality of their intellectual functioning shows an incredible leap into the future. For within a bare 30,000 years they spread throughout the world and lifted their species from a common lot with animals to the level of urban civilization. Within a tenth of the time the species had taken to produce crude tools and a rudimentary use of fire. In that brief time they invented writing, mathematics, religion, literature, philosophy, medicine, agriculture, trade and commerce and the use of money. They left records and monuments showing they understood the orbital periods of the planets and cycles of eclipses and comets. They catalogued hundreds of herbs, mastered techniques of surgery, learned the art of embalming, built pyramids and other wonders that could hardly be duplicated today. The statuary and poetry they created compare with the best in the world today.

Why did the human species suddenly begin to do all these things? Was it because their brains, produced over eons by the ultimate Creative Power, had suddenly been altered by visiting extraterrestrials? And was their sudden knowledge of science, art and religion taught them by these same god-like extraterrestrials?

The common assumption by anthropologists and historians that we discovered and developed all these refinements in a mere 30,000 years, as a result of biological and cultural evolution, seems, to quote Darwin again, "absurd in the highest degree." Nothing in the fossil record, or our knowledge of developmental biology, suggests that evolution has ever produced so many profound transformations in such a moment of time.

One conclusion seems inescapable. We were fashioned in the image of godlike Celestials. Our incredible brains are not just the result of natural selection operating on chance variations. They required a deliberate and artificial improvement. The mechanisms postulated by biologists to explain our explosion of brain function are simply inadequate to account for the results.

Our achievements cry out for a better explanation. They tell us that we are heirs of a Celestial race, and our minds and civilization are the result of their intervention. To see more clearly how this is so we will now give some final consideration to the unearthly traits we mentioned at the opening of this chapter. These traits, more than any others we have, show the nature of our minds and the extent to which their development has gone beyond the survival needs of our ancestors or even of ourselves today.

In examining them we will show why they cannot be the product of natural selection but exceed what it is capable of producing and bear witness that we are indeed heirs of a Celestial race.

OUR UNEARTHLY OVERENDOWMENTS

One of the most firmly established principles of evolutionary biology is that natural selection doesn't equip living creatures with traits they do not need or give them excessive amounts of those which are necessary. Natural selection works only with variations which occur spontaneously in the course of reproduction. It can preserve only those which are necessary for existence-and only in degrees or amounts which are useful for survival.

Over endowment cannot be produced by natural selection alone. If that were the factor that produced our three million year leap from apelike to human intelligence it would have left us at the level of apes, because for most of those three million years, we needed little more than the apes to survive. We lived in the open or in caves, ate raw foods and used only the crudest of tools.

Then, suddenly, we appear on the pages of history, 6,000 years ago, in ancient Sumer. And when we appear already knowing more than we need, even now, to survive in the Twenty-First Century. In fact, it is not demonstrable, in many areas of knowledge, that we know more now than our ancestors knew then. By any reasonable critical standards their reflective thought, their literary expression, their political skill, their moral sensitivity and their spiritual aspirations were equal to our own. Only in areas of technical and scientific accomplishment is there any real evidence of a superiority on our part.

How did such an unbelievable overendowment occur, and why? Some anthropologists, attempting to explain this anomaly, have suggested that natural selection somehow created a "reserve" of intelligence in Stone-Age humans, beyond what was actually used. So Bjorn Kurten, of Helsinki University, asks why we should be able to grasp advanced mathematics and philosophy and enjoy intricate poetry and music-things that had no place in the life of paleolithic humanity?" The answer, he says, is quite simple. It is that "untutored brains" use only a small part of their potential. So that Paleolithic humans could survive, natural selection had to "call forth a vastly greater unrealized capacity, which remains dormant in the savage but can be activated by education."

Unfortunately for Professor Kurten this argument is simply not supported by the facts. Anthropology and archaeology show, beyond question, that early primitive humans were able to grasp advanced mathematical relationships and to philosophize about the great perennial problems of the universe without a formal education. In the Valley of the Kings in Egypt, at Machu Picchu in Peru, at Stonehenge in England and at many other places throughout the world we have overwhelming proof of this. Similarly Paul Radin, early in the last century, showed that the myths of contemporary primitives come to grips with the great philosophical questions which preoccupy "educated" people. Clearly it does not require a formal education to call forth these abilities in homo sapiens sapiens, nor are they dormant without it.

Our incredible over-endowment of intellect, then, is not a reserve created by natural selection. Nor was our creation of civilization, a few thousand years ago, the product of evolution alone. The quality of the human mind, and the civilization it created, are without parallel in any other species on Earth.

They are unparalleled even in the one other sapient species of hominid known to have existed on Earth. In his book The Social Conquest of Earth, sociobiologist, E.O. Wilson proposes a more recent theory concerning how we, homo sapiens, sapiens became so much more intelligent than any other animal on Earth. The answer he writes, is because as social animals we are caught in a "clash" between our need for individual survival and our need to work for the survival of the social group to which we belong. These sometimes conflicting needs, he argues, imposed dilemmas on our evolving brains. They required even greater adaptive capabilities that could only be achieved by a more complex and diversified neural infrastructure. And it is plausible that this conflict did play an important part in lifting us to a rudimentary level of civilized living including the use of fire, tools, weapons fashioned by flaking stones and the development of language as a means of social cooperation.

It fails utterly, however, to explain an additional set of extraordinary endowments which natural selection could not give us. Nor does it explain why Neanderthals who had the same need for individual and group survival went into decline and extinction while we went on to become urban sophisticates.

These opposed stages of decline and progress are still a source of puzzlement today. The more so because the Neanderthals also shared much more with us than just the need for individual and group survival. Fossil finds show they had brains as large or larger than ours. They occupied many of the same territories as we did and even mated with our ancestor homo sapiens sapiens. Why then did they fail to go on to create a civilization of their own?

Professor Wilson suggested it was because of something they lacked that handicapped them in their competition with us for territory and resources. He admits, however, that what that deficiency was remains a mystery.

Archeolingustic analysis of the Genesis account in the Bible suggests it was rather the improvements the Celestials gave our recreated ancestors that set them apart from all other animals including the Neanderthals. These allowed our ancestors to become the only animals on Earth to create civilization. The Bible offers an alternative and more plausible explanation of our uniquely over-endowed brains. We will now turn to a closer examination of the traits that have made this accomplishment possible.

OUR UNEARTHLY OVER-ENDOWMENTS

It has often been pointed out that the more general forms of philosophical speculation have little bearing on the conduct of life. Whether the world is ideal or material, machinelike or organismic, is not a matter about which we can do anything or which requires any sort of response. Yet we have always been compelled to puzzle about such questions. Why?

If we are the product of evolution one of its strangest ironies is that it has endowed us with the capacity to criticize its handiwork. So Bertrand Russell commented on the strange mystery that nature has gifted us with sight, with knowledge of good and evil, with the capacity of judging its works and that in spite of death, the mark and seal of parental control, we are yet free, during our brief years, to examine, to criticize, to know and in imagination to create. We alone have this freedom.

And ironic and mysterious it is if this strange endowment is the work of natural selection. But if it is a gift of the Celestials it is as inevitable as night and day. How could heirs of a god-like race show less than "divine discontent" and existential despair having their human lot? Could they show less than discontent with the souls of gods imprisoned in the bodies of beasts? Could they feel less than despair knowing the ties of evolutionary kinship doom them to share, with the beasts of this Earth, their dark instinctual urges and their mortal doom?

With such a prospect it is small wonder that "*homo philosophicus*" broods about the meaning of human existence and destiny. Our unearthly capacity for philosophical reflection makes it inevitable that we "cherish, ere yet the blow falls the lofty thoughts that enoble our little day" to quote Bertrand Russell's cynical appraisal.

Yet in spite of our existential tragedy we are also a child of hope. And among our "lofty thoughts" one persists that is peculiarly indicative of its givers. It is the curious mixture of belief and feeling we call religious aspiration, and it is our only hope of escape from our mortal prison.

It is strange that an endowment which seems to have no earthly survival value should be our only hope of immortal survival-yet it is so. For religion, in one form or another, has always had, as its central theme, our possibility of sharing with the gods. We will defer until later any discussion of whether all religions discern a common vital truth. But it is clear from the most casual inspection of the Bible, that its central theme is our hope of sharing in the Celestials' secret of eternal life. In scripture after scripture, throughout both the Old and New Testaments, the hope and the promise of eternal life is repeated again and again. An unbiased study of the Bible leaves no doubt that immortality is the Celestials' most prized possession. The first glimpse we catch of them, in Genesis, reveals a tree of life in their midst. And the final, glorious view we have of them, in Revelation, shows a holy city come "down from God out of heaven" (Revelation 21:2), with a "pure river of water of life ... proceeding out of the throne of God" and the tree of life growing on its banks (Revelation 22:1-2). Wherever Jehovah is mentioned we are reminded that he is the "Alpha and Omega, the beginning and the end, the first and the last" (Revelation 22:13) – who "liveth for ever and ever" (Revelation 15:7). And the final promise given in the Bible is the promise of life everlasting: "And the Spirit and the bride say, Corne.... And let him that is athirst come. And whosoever will, let him take the water of life freely" (Revelation 22:17).

Is this hope, man's oldest and fondest dream, the product of natural selection? Or was it implanted by a Celestial race that has every intention of fulfilling it in the future? No other animal, not even our closest primate relatives, has any conception of life everlasting or yearns for it. Zoologists and students of comparative psychology have never produced a shred of evidence to support such an idea.

Humans alone, of all living creatures, aspire to the godlike condition of immortality. We alone regulate our lives according to its otherworldly promise of survival even when it flies in the face of natural survival as it has for countless martyrs to faith. Is religious aspiration and yearning for immortality the product of nature, or is it a Celestial gift? Will they return to fulfill this aspiration? In a later chapter we will examine the scientific facts and theories which support such a hope.

The most distinguishing characteristic of homo sapiens sapiens, according to biologists and anthropologists, is the capacity for manipulating symbols with their extraordinary brain. This is why they have named us homo sapiens sapiens. No other animal on Earth has our peculiar ability to use mental representations as indicators of abstractions. As a result, no other animal has the capacity for abstract thought in any but the most rudimentary form.

When thought is tied to the concrete environment around us it is limited to what is immediate and present. Foresight, planning, multistep problem-solving and creative thought such as theorizing, fantasy and aesthetic composition are all impossible. Humans alone, so far as we can tell, can react to inner images, rather than external stimuli, as symbols of complex relationships and long-range consequences. They alone can conceive of labels for classes of objects and experiences so that generalized thinking about relationships, rather than things, becomes possible.

It is these abilities which have earned us the description of "sapient." Even at their lowest levels they so far exceed what other animals can do that the difference becomes one of kind rather than degree. A rat, or a chimpanzee, can solve simple problems such as psychologists' mazes. But their problem-solving, when compared with that of a chess grandmaster or a theoretical physicist, differs as a horse and buggy does from a moon rocket. When this ability is directed toward what Francis Bacon called "interrogating nature" it becomes science-the ability to construct abstract inner models, in terms of mathematics or logic, which mirror the structure and relationships of the universe.

Our ability to do this separates us from all other animals. Even more, however, we are separated from them by our desire to do it. Only we have this "disinterested curiosity." A cat, or dog, or ape will examine something if it shows promise of satisfying an immediate need. But only the sapient human will toil through years of patient research, follow endless blind leads and suffer ridicule, rejection and even privation in the search for objective truth.

This capacity for the disinterested pursuit of truth is one of our most Celestial traits, for it elevates us above the merely animal business of surviving and making a "living." It enables us to discover our place in the universe and gives us a sense of identity. It helps us realize our oneness with all things and promotes that largeness of view which makes the immediate problems of life endurable.

And in their unending search for truth the great scientists of the past and present have helped us grasp the immensity of the universe and the intricate harmony of life. They have deepened our sense of kinship with all natural things and given us purpose and hope for the future.

In the infinite patience of the experimenter and the cosmic breadth of the theorizer, pure science represents us at our unearthly best. Only Celestial motivations could have driven Marie Curie to sort through tons upon tons of pitchblende, over thousands of experiments, during long years of privation, because prejudice and her sex barred her from a university position. When she at last glimpsed the faint smudge of radium, too slight even to weigh, glowing in the darkness of her homemade laboratory, she regarded the years and sacrifices as completely rewarded. There was no way of knowing her discovery would have practical usefulness, but her Celestial aspiration for truth had been satisfied.

When visitors at the Princeton Institute for Advanced Study would ask Albert Einstein where his laboratory was he would tap his head, and when they inquired about his tools he would extend his pencil. His Celestial brain and pencil wielding hand were all he needed to probe the depths of the universe as no man before him had done. The beauty and almost divine simplicity of the equation in which he expressed his insight brings it close to the mysterious symbols of the ancients which were believed to indicate the supreme reason underlying all things. To grasp that a simple combination of abstract symbols, $E = MC^2$, could express the ultimate interrelationships of space, time, energy and matter must surely be one of the most profoundly creative intellectual feats ever performed by the human mind.

Did Marie Curie and Albert Einstein inherit the inspirations that drove them to unique heights from millions of chance variations in subhuman ancestors? Could the gradual accumulation of skills permitting the survival of tree shrews and lemurs and apelike primates eventually add up to an ability to unlock the secrets of nuclear energy or to capture the universe in an equation? Could such incredible over endowments be generated by such simple mechanisms? Or were they outright gifts matured on other worlds over the hundreds of millions, or billions, of years evolution has not had to produce them here?

Perhaps the sense in which we most mirror the Celestials, the sense in which we best share with them their godlike nature, is our ability to create. Like God the Creator, who called the worlds into existence, like the Lord God who called us into existence, we can call the creatures of our own celestial minds into being and give them objective expression.

No primate, no ape, not even the chimpanzee, has this ability, even in the most rudimentary degree. In humans it is over endowed beyond the widest conceivable limits of usefulness-far beyond. The mind of a Beethoven could conceive symphonies that rival the heavens in their complexity. Shakespeare created hundreds of humans, in his plays, as real as those we meet in daily life--more real, in a deeper sense, for they are quintessential. They embody, in their single selves, what is most typical of the whole range and diversity of humanity throughout human history. Michelangelo could recreate the creation in such staggering splendor that throughout the ages it remains the event, itself, the infinite captured in finite paint and mortar on the vault of the Sistine Chapel

Is this strange gift a product of natural selection acquired because of its survival value? Can any accumulation of chance variations over any number of generations for any conceivable practical reason explain the bursting of genius in the mind of a Beethoven, or a Shakespeare, or a Michelangelo? Or is it a blaze of Celestial fire? Do humans create and express their artistic dreams because, like their Celestial ancestors, they possess other worldly creative natures? Do humans compose, paint, sculpt, declaim and poeticize because "The Spirit itself beareth witness with our Spirit, that we are the children of God. And if children, then heirs; heirs." (Romans 8:16-17)?

We believe the answer is evident. Yes, humans are a celestial artifact housed in a natural body-the product of a Celestial experiment. As Shakespeare has Hamlet say: "What a piece of work is a man! How noble in reason! How infinite in faculty! In form and moving how express and admirable! In action how like an angel! In apprehension how like a God! The beauty of the world! The paragon of animals!"

If this is so, however, one important question remains. Apart from the Bible, is there any proof that our incredible over endowments of mind and unearthly gifts of spirit are the work of an experimental creation? We have already referred to the fossil record. Scientists who study this record tell us it documents the evolution of humans by gradual and progressive stages to the present state. Is there any point in this record, any discontinuity or gap, where the Celestials could have made their experimental modification in a way that is supported by the fossil evidence? We will consider this important question last.

THE FOSSIL RECORD AND HOMO SAPIENS SAPIENS

The field of paleoanthropology is concerned with the bones, their deposits in layers of earth, sand and stone and the various cultural relics of ancient creatures. It has been a field of endless controversy and debate since the time of Darwin. From the beginning imposing theories have rested on the minimum of hard evidence, a tooth, a jaw fragment, a piece of skull or a bit of chipped or flaked stone. Gradually, over the decades of recent centuries, more refined methods of investigation have been brought to bear on the products of the pick and shovel. These include delicate instruments for reassembling bone fragments, casts and models, biochemical analyses, radioactive carbon and potassium-argon dating and computer analyses based on refined measurements. Above all, the fossil finds have continued to pour in from all over the world. The record now contains many fairly complete skulls, relatively intact skeletons and tools of all sorts-cutters, choppers, scrapers and awls.

At the same time geologists, paleontologists and other specialists have been filling in our knowledge of the early environments in which humans developed, the climate changes, the ice ages, the drift of continents and the rise and fall of land masses.

And out of all this data an increasingly clearer picture of human evolution has emerged. Yet curious gaps remain. We have never identified our immediate ancestor, though it is much closer in time than many others we have found. As a result, we are not sure where modern humans first arose or how they spread throughout the world. Nor have we explained the development of races.

THE HUMAN FAMILY TREE

Yet in spite of this the main outlines of our family tree are clear. As it has been reconstructed by paleontologists and anthropologists it can be quickly summarized. A little over 2 million years ago our first clearly human ancestor, *Homo habilis* ("handy man"), appeared-so called because of its flaking and use of stone tools. It apparently hunted, stood erect and had a brain capacity of around 800 cubic centimeters. Beyond this little more is known about its way of life. Its remains have been investigated, in the last century, by the famous Leakey family in Kenya, Africa.

About a million years ago its descendant, homo erectus, took the next step forward in human evolution. Around five feet in height, this race had a truly erect posture and used a wider range of tools. In their most advanced form their braincase averaged about 1,100 cubic centimeters. They were originally found in Java but findings eventually spread to most of the tropical Old World.

Then, around 500,000 years ago, a new type of human destined to become sapient appeared on the scene-the neanderthal race. At first they differed little from homo erectus, but as millennia passed their braincase expanded to over 1,400 cubic centimeters (larger than our own average). Unlike modern humans they were long-headed, barrel-chested and powerful individuals with curved arm and leg bones in their later sapient form. They used a rich assortment of tools, lived in the open or caves and buried their dead in a way which suggests the beginnings of religious belief.

Around 250,000 years ago another sapient human also appeared on the scene. This race was also large-brained (around 1,300-1,400 cubic centimeters) but actually predated the sapient neanderthals. Their remains were first found in the riverbed of the Thames, in England, and at Fontechevade, in France. Computer analysis of the skull taken from the Thames (called "Swanscombe man") shows that its owner was undoubtedly an early homo sapiens. Bjorn Kurten suggested this race may have been ancestors of both sapient neanderthals and modern homo sapiens sapiens.

However that may be they spread throughout much of Europe, for similar remains have been found at Steinheim, Germany, and Vertesszolos, Hungary. Though these finds are fragmentary, they reveal an individual that lacked the exaggerated rear skull of sapient Neanderthal and had a high, well rounded brow like our own.

With these finds the record of a non-neanderthal homo sapiens is interrupted until about 40,000 years ago, when a very similar type reappears which anthropologists variously call Cro-Magnon man, homo sapiens sapiens or "modern man." Taller than the neanderthals this race was, and is, also more slender and graceful. Their high, well-rounded forehead surmounts a braincase that averages around 1,250-1,350 cubic centimeters. From the first they used a wide range of tools, buried their dead and left elaborate cave art.

They rapidly carried tool making far beyond the late neanderthal stage and, at the end of the stone age, suddenly developed into communal dwellers. Within the next 5,000 years they created villages, domesticated plants and animals, and developed metallurgy and pottery. Around 4000 B.C. they produced, at the eastern end of the Fertile Crescent, a full blown urban, civilization with the flowering of major arts and sciences. This is the account present-day social scientists and historians give of our origins.

ENTER THE CELESTIALS

This brings us back to our original question. Is there any point in this record, any discontinuity or gap, where the Celestials could have made their experimental modification? Even such a brief review reveals one startling discontinuity, or gap. It is the strange appearance, disappearance and reappearance of the non-Neanderthal homo sapiens. Well-known students of human evolution and the fossil record have commented on this puzzling phenomenon. So Theodosius Dobzhansky wrote that before Europe was inhabited by neanderthals there were humans more like ourselves than the neanderthals, and the neanderthals were then replaced, abruptly, by a race of homo sapiens whose bones were much like our own. So it looks as if homo sapiens appeared, disappeared and reappeared again. Could the conjurers behind this abrupt reappearance have been a race of extraterrestrials? Did they refashion this moribund race into a superior type that quickly spread throughout the world and displaced the neanderthals who had previously coexisted and interbred with them?

As we saw, in our brief review of human evolution, early homo sapiens spread as far east as Vertesszolos, Hungary. In fact, the specimen found there had the largest brain of the lot -about 1,400 cubic centimeters.

It is a short distance from Vertesszolos to the eastern end of the Fertile Crescent. A migration moving in that direction could well have carried a small population of this race to the Garden of Eden site. And though they declined, as sapient neanderthal rose to dominance, representatives would, in all probability, still have been there when the Celestials arrived. These large-brained survivors would have been logical candidates for the Celestials' genetic experiment. Is there any scientific evidence that our undiscovered immediate ancestor arose from such a type or in the area we have identified as the Garden of Eden site?

THE MT. CARMEL FINDS

The answer to this question may lie in one more set of fossil clues, one of the most ambiguous ever uncovered. They were found between 1929 and 1934 near Haifa at Mt. Carmel-the general area the Bible assigns to Eden itself. They consisted of two sets of fossils in two caves, Tabun and Skhul. The older set, at Tabun, were neanderthal and were dated at around 41,000 to 42,000 B.C. The later set, at Skhul, showed a curious mixture of cro-magnon and neanderthal features. This is puzzling, since the neanderthal type had already disappeared from that area by 35,000 B.C. – the date assigned to these fossils.

THE "ANCIENT MODERN"

While various theories were offered to account for the problems these fossils presented, one explanation is of special interest to us here. It proposed that the later Skhul fossils represented descendants of the Tabun neanderthals-descendants produced by interbreeding with an unknown ancestor of cro-magnon man. According to the theory, this ancestor had "evolved" to the east and then migrated to Mount Carmel. Speaking of this C. L. Brace and Ashley Montagu wrote of a "solution to the puzzle" which assumed the existence of an "ancient modern" who arose "farther east, perhaps".

If this "solution of the puzzle" is the correct one the "ancient modern" could well be the Lord's experimental creation who migrated from their point of origin "farther east"-the Garden of Eden site. Though the Bible makes no mention of such a migration it is interesting that one of the apocryphal books, The First Book of Adam and Eve, tells how, after their expulsion from the Garden, Adam and Eve went to dwell in a "Cave of Treasures" on the western border of the Garden. Could this "Cave of Treasures" have been one of those located on Mt. Carmel such as Tabun or Skhul?

Whatever the answer to this question is the ideas suggested by the Mt. Carmel finds are further supported by the Bible itself. To appreciate the full significance of this we must now turn, once again, to the Genesis account. This provides another clue which may link the Lord's experimental creation with Brace and Montagu's "ancient modern" and the Mt. Carmel finds.

"GOD'S" SONS AND "MEN'S DAUGHTERS"

We have earlier seen, how soon after the Lord's experimental creation of Adam and Eve, their son, Cain, went into the land of Nod and "knew his wife." Could this have been the first instance of the sort of interbreeding C. L. Brace and Ashley Montagu suggest might have occurred between "ancient moderns" and less advanced races around them?

The idea becomes more significant when we read a little past the Cain story in Genesis and find that "... it came to pass, when men began to multiply on the face of the earth, and daughters were born unto them, That the sons of God saw the daughters of men that they were fair; and they took them wives of all which they chose" (Genesis 6:1-2).

Some commentators have suggested these "sons of God" were angels who were lured into unions with the mortal "daughters of men"-in spite of Jesus' assurance that angels "neither marry, nor are given in marriage" (Matthew 22: 30). Others have proposed that the "sons of God" were descendants of righteous Seth and the "daughters of men" the offspring of murderous Cain. Yet they fail to explain how righteousness and ungodliness are inheritable or why God would make such a prejudicial distinction among Adam's innocent grandchildren.

Our space age interpretation offers a better explanation of this most curious passage. The "sons of God" were the descendants of the Lord's experimental creation, and the "daughters of men" were evolved homo sapiens around them.

If this is so, then Brace and Montagu's "ancient modern" was, in all likelihood, the Lord's experimental recreation. And the Skhul fossils are those of its descendants, who represent crossings between "God's sons" and the "daughters of men," or homo sapiens sapiens and sapient neaderthals.

WHEN DID THE CELESTIALS' EXPERIMENT OCCUR?

On this assumption we can pinpoint the time of the Celestials' recreation rather closely. It could not have occurred after 35,000 B.C., since "ancient moderns" had already ancestored the Skhul descendants.

Allowing them time to migrate from the eastern end of the Fertile Crescent, where they were recreated, to Mt. Carmel we can set a somewhat earlier date for their recreation. Yet it would not have been long, for their descendants replaced the neanderthal race only after it was in a decline. Now this occurred around 40,000 B.C. The experimental creation would, therefore, probably have occurred a little while before-long enough to allow the "ancient moderns" to "multiply," to outgrow their subsistence and to move on to Mt. Carmel. How long was this? We have no way of knowing exactly. But their success in competing against neanderthaleans suggests a very late date in the period of neanderthal decline-probably a few thousand years at most. Weighing all these considerations a date between 50,000 and 40,000 B.C. seems realistic.

If anthropologists ever find the remains of the "ancient modern," conjecture will be at an end. Unfortunately this is unlikely because of what anthropologists call the "Sewell Wright effect." The causes of fossilization are complicated and occur rarely. As a result, small populations seldom leave fossils and the "ancient moderns" were too quickly hybridized to ever have become numerous. Their hybrid descendants, however, left their mark on the fossil record throughout the Earth, for they are ourselves-homo sapiens sapiens!

THE MYSTERIES OF RACE

One of the major problems in current anthropological investigation is the mystery of race. If homo sapiens sapiens emerged only 30,000 to 40,000 years ago, how has there been time for them to differentiate into the races one finds today? Our space age view of the modern human, as a hybrid, offers a reasonable explanation for this mystery.

Since the "daughters of men" had an evolutionary descent stretching back over two, or more, millions of years, there was ample time to develop racial differences. During the time when the small population of "God's sons" interbred with these "daughters of men" they would quickly have absorbed these racial differences as they spread throughout the Earth.

Is there any evidence that racial differences did not arise in *homo sapiens*

sapiens, but already preexisted in his evolutionary ancestors? The answer is given by Carleton Coon. Speaking of Choukoutien man (an early homo erectus found in China and dating from 360,000 years ago) he pointed out that though definitely homo erectus they differ from the Javenese specimens racially. Instead of sloping gradually their foreheads stand out sharply from their eyebrow ridges. They had cheekbones and jaws which protruded forward and their teeth were "shaped like shovels." These peculiarities are still seen in mongoloid teeth from China to Cape Horn and anthropologists refer to them as "shoveled teeth."

The evidence cited by Carleton Coon, then, makes it clear that races already existed among early humans who were ancestral to homo sapiens sapiens. In them they had the hundreds of thousands of years necessary for natural selection and interbreeding to do their work. When created humans interbred with their sapient descendants they acquired these genetic differences they had not had time to produce on their own.

AN OVERVIEW

It appears, then, that our interpretation of the biblical account of human origins is consistent with anthropological facts. It further suggests hypotheses which could, if verified, clear up present gaps and mysteries surrounding our beginnings.

In concluding our examination of the experimental creation it may help to summarize the agreements between the Bible's account and what science has discovered in the fossil record. These agreements give strong support to a Space Age interpretation of the Genesis story of humanity's creation.

1. The Bible says "man" was "created" to the east of Jerusalem. The Mt. Carmel finds suggest that an "ancient modern" who ancestored us did indeed come from "east" of Jerusalem.

2. The Bible says "God" created man in his own "image." If modern human reveals that image it is so unlike most of our fossil ancestors as to defy a natural selective explanation. Yet genetic engineering could bridge the gap-if "creation" means modifying something like Vertesszolos man.

3. The discovery of this type of human, in Hungary, makes it likely that a descendant may have occupied the eastern end of the Fertile Crescent 40,000 to 50,000 years ago. The Bible says the Celestials created "man" here, and anthropologists have found *homo sapiens sapiens* fossils nearby that date just after this period.

4. The findings at Skhul Cave suggest the "unknown" ancestor of modern humans interbred with neanderthals. This has been further verified by DNA analysis which shows neandethal genes widely spread in the present human population. The Bible says the "sons of God" took wives from the "daughters of men" after they became numerous.

5. Our interpretation of the Genesis account suggests an explanation of the origin of races which is a problem for more traditional theories.

The Space Age interpretation of our recreation, then, reconciles the biblical
and scientific accounts. In addition it suggests a theory which fills the gaps and
clear up puzzles in our present scientific knowledge. Only further fossil finds can
establish or refute this theory.

We will now turn away from the scientific record and take up a question which
is primarily moral and theological: How did we lose our recreated state?

And when the woman saw that the tree was good for food, and that it was pleasant to the eyes, and a tree to be desired to make one wise, she took of the fruit thereof, and did eat, and gave also unto her husband with her; and he did eat.

– Genesis 3:6

CHAPTER IX

The Experiment Fails

THE "ORIGINAL SIN"

In the grammar schools of colonial New England the Puritans taught their children to read from Bible-story readers. Infants learning the ABCs were greeted with the announcement, "A is for Adam; in Adam's fall we sinned, all."

The English poet Milton composed what may be the greatest literary epic of the language, *Paradise Lost*. Though his imagery and conception were infinitely more elevated than the Puritans' Bible readers, the message is the same.

She gave him of that fair enticing fruit
With liberal hand. He scrupled not to eat,
Against his better knowledge, not deceived,
But fondly overcome with female charm.
Earth trembled from her entrails, as again
In pangs, and Nature gave a second groan;
Sky loured, and, muttering thunder, some sad drops
Wept at completing of the mortal Sin
Original ...

Since its composition Genesis has puzzled thoughtful readers with its telling of this immortal legend. Is it fact or fiction? It has been compared with the Prometheus myth of the Greeks a Titan stealing Celestial fire from the gods, incurring their wrath and being chained to a rock eternally with a vulture tearing his liver for punishment.

What do such stories mean? Is sapient humans' wisdom its own punishment, because it enables them, alone of all the beasts, to realize their end is death? Or does the Adam and Eve story have some more factual basis? Did our ancestors commit some actual folly which demoted them, and us, from a higher state of existence? If so, what was it? Was it literally eating an apple? The Bible makes no mention of apples-it only mentions a "fruit." Was the "forbidden fruit" symbolic of some other act? Was it, as Milton thought, sexual intercourse? Did the Lord God have some other plan for reproduction in mind for humans which Adam upset by his lustful transgression? Could this have been the original sin?

Whatever the "original sin" was theologians and scholars have been even more puzzled by its relation to us-Adam's and Eve's descendants. The Bible seems to teach the "doctrine of original sin"-the idea, so quaintly put forth by the Puritans, that "in Adam's fall we sinned, all." But how could we be responsible for what Adam and Eve did even if the story is literally true? Yet the Bible does seem to say we are. So the Apostle Paul observes, "Wherefore, as by one man sin entered into the world, and death by sin; and so death passed upon all men ... by one man's disobedience many were made sinners ..." (Romans 5:12, 19).

How could an advanced civilization of Celestials with "lofty moral purposes" reason in this way? Probably no doctrine in the history of Christianity has caused more revulsion among morally sensitive men and women. How could a just God condemn billions of blameless humans to death for the transgression of an ancestor whom they never knew?

A MORAL RIDDLE AND A POSSIBLE SOLUTION

This is the great moral riddle which the story of humanity's fall poses. It has no answer in terms of enlightened morality and justice. And according to our method this suggests it may be in need of reinterpretation. Isn't it possible the whole Adam and Eve story has been misunderstood by both theologians and mythologists? May there not be another interpretation of it which makes sense and does not outrage our notions of morality and justice?

In this chapter we will try to discover what the "original sin" was by analyzing the story in the light of modern thinking about genetics and psychology. We will start by reexamining the story itself. The first thing to notice is that though Adam and Eve were denied the tree of "knowledge of good and evil" they were denied no other.

Early in Genesis we read that "the Lord God planted a garden eastward in Eden" and out of the ground made "to grow every tree that is pleasant to the sight, and good for food; the tree of life also in the midst of the garden, and the tree of knowledge of good and evil" (Genesis 2:8-9). Next, we find the "Lord God commanded the man, saying, Of every tree of the garden thou mayest freely eat: But of the tree of the knowledge of good and evil, thou shalt not eat of it: for in the day that thou eatest thereof thou shalt surely die" (Genesis 2:16-17). Later the "serpent" tells Eve that "God doth know that in the day ye eat thereof [of the tree of knowledge of good and evil] then your eyes shall be opened, and ye shall be as gods, knowing good and evil" (Genesis 3:5). When God discovers they have succumbed to the "serpent's" temptation he counsels with the other Celestials, saying, "Behold, the man is become as one of us, to know good and evil: and now, lest he put forth his hand, and take also of the tree of life, and eat, and live forever ..." (Genesis 3:22).

In "eating" of the "tree of knowledge of good and evil" they did something which denied them this immortality and gave them another godlike attribute in its place-an attribute the Lord felt they were not ready to receive. To prevent its misuse he barred them from further eating of the "tree of life" so that they could not achieve immortality and misuse the godlike power they had stolen.

If this is so it follows that, while the "original sin" was disobedience to the Lord God's command, the specific act of disobedience involved something more. Its "sinfulness" lay not just in its opposition to the Lord's will but in something it did to Adam and Eve-something which made them and their heirs forever after "sinful" and caused all their descendants to inherit death. What this actually was we will speculate on shortly. In the meantime the important point to make here is that the act, described as "eating" forbidden fruit, resulted in Adam's and Eve's being able, for the first time, to know "good" and "evil."

The Hebrew word used here for "know" is a derivative of "da'ath", which has the meanings of "cunningly" or "wittingly." Unlike the primary root "yada", "know," from which it comes, it narrows the meaning to imply purpose. It is one thing to know, but quite a different thing to use knowledge purposefully ("cunningly" or "wittingly") to achieve moral results.

What the "forbidden fruit" gave Adam and Eve, then, was not a mere ability to distinguish between "good" and "evil" as traditional Bible scholars have thought. It was, rather, the power to regulate their conduct according to the knowledge that they already had (they knew they were not to eat of the forbidden tree). What they acquired, in short, was not moral knowledge but moral responsibility-the ability to choose between good and evil.

MORAL RESPONSIBILITY

Up until this time they had been like the evolved animals from which they came. Like our lower animals their large brained, earthly ancestors were governed by animal instincts and conditioning. There is no evidence they regulated their behavior by abstract notions of "right" and "wrong."

The ability to do so is peculiar to modern humans and is one more unearthly trait which proves our Celestial origin. For moral responsibility has no survival value. Since it allows us to choose our responses freely, according to abstract notions of right and wrong, it can lead us to go against survival as readily as with it. In fact, moral values often require self-denial and may dictate courses which jeopardize survival.

The Genesis account makes it clear that moral responsibility was evidently a trait which was not included in Adam's and Eve's original equipment. The Lord intended to add it later after they had been trained to understand the values he wished them to follow. He had created them, like animals or infants, so they would follow the strongest influence. They had no real ability to choose.

And to protect the experiment he had placed them in a controlled environment where they would receive only the right sort of influences-his and those of his trusted director. We can understand the implications of the situation better by considering how human trainers teach animals. They train them to do "right" by rewarding good behavior and punishing bad. But if they are humane they do not hold them morally responsible for their actions. When they punish them it is because they are trying to change their behavior, not because they are "guilty" of anything. They can have no guilt since they have no self-control. They merely respond to the strongest influence.

In the same way Adam and Eve were being conditioned to do what was right. Since they had inherited a "bestial" nature from their evolutionary forebears it was necessary to counterbalance it by training them to live according to higher ideals. Since character cannot be inherited it could not be included in their original DNA blueprint. It had to be taught.

But until they had learned it there was danger in allowing them moral choice. They might choose the wrong course and ruin the experiment. If they were to be helpers and eventual citizens they must develop as virtuous beings who were good from choice-not as programmed robots like the cherubim or seraphim. Keeping these distinctions in mind, we are now ready to reinterpret the "original sin" and its consequences.

THE "ORIGINAL SIN"

To do this we must start with the idea that Adam and Eve were in an animal, or childlike, state of innocence before the fall. If we accept this seriously it poses a strange paradox. Since they were "innocent", as infants and animals are, they could not use "knowledge of good and evil" in regulating their behavior. They could not "sin" in the moral sense of that term. They were not morally responsible.

Just as animals and infants are not morally responsible for their behavior, so the Lord could not hold Adam and Eve morally responsible for "eating the fruit." They simply yielded to the strongest pressure--Eve to the persuasiveness of the "serpent" and Adam to Eve's example. At the moment these were more powerful influences on their behavior than the fear of punishment by the Lord.

They could only "sin" in the literal and moral sense after they had "eaten" the fruit and acquired moral responsibility. The "eating," itself, was not a morally responsible act. To hold them guilty of a moral offense would be applying what, in law, is called an "ex post facto" judgment-a judgment which could fairly be made only after the fact to which it is applied.

Since this is true our earlier suggestion that their "sin" and "guilt" were figurative, rather than literal, has to be correct. No other interpretation could vindicate the Lord God of a double injustice-holding them responsible when they were not and holding us responsible for what they did.

They "sinned" in the sense of doing wrong, disobeying a command of their parent. But it was a "sin" for which they were not morally responsible. It was like the "sin" of a naughty infant or a mischievous animal, except that they were adults, and the consequences of their "sin" were enormous. In this respect it was more like an act of murder committed by an idiot. They murdered themselves and us, their descendants, through their lack of moral restraint. The "original sin," then, was not a literal moral lapse. It was, rather, something which gave them, and us, a "sinful" nature-one capable of sinning. And, as Milton put it, it was a "mortal" sin, for it prevented their immortality and passed death on to us, their descendants. In this way we literally inherited their figurative guilt and punishment – death.

THE "FATAL APPLE"

Now let us see if we can discover what act they could have performed to invite these dreadful consequences. What did they really do in "eating forbidden fruit", and what were the circumstances surrounding their folly? As in so many passages that refer to the Celestials it would not have been possible to understand this part of the story before the Twentieth Century. Only since the development of molecular biology have we gained some insight into the processes by which living creatures develop the structures and traits that make up their natures. The writer of Genesis 3, knowing nothing of this, could only describe Adam's and Eve's fatal misdeed as "eating a fruit."

We know now that to acquire a new trait, such as the ability to exercise choice, we must undergo two specialized developments. First there would have to be a suitable specialization of the cerebral cortex itself-the seat of abstract thought. This would be necessary so that the brain could store memories of rewards and punishments, abstract what these have in common and label their relationships by the terms "right" and "wrong." As we saw in the last chapter this development had already taken place in the evolution of Adam's and Eve's large-brained ancestors.

But the capacity to use these conceptions to regulate behavior would require a further development having to do with voluntary action. This can perhaps be understood better by considering the case of humans who presently fail to exhibit this further development. Apparently this second specialization, which Adam and Eve underwent by "eating forbidden fruit", failed to take place in them. Psychologists and psychiatrists in the early part of the last century used to refer to such people as "moral imbeciles." Later they were called "psychopaths" or "sociopaths." Today we often use the phrase "character disorder" or "disorder of impulse." But whatever name is used the nature of their defect is clear and enables us to understand, by negative example, what it was that Adam and Eve acquired in committing the "original sin."

Like Adam and Eve before the fall, and unlike normal human adults, they cannot choose to ignore impulse and self-gratification in favor of higher moral values or long-range interests. They lack the capacity for moral responsibility.

This brings us to the key question. What could Adam and Eve have "eaten" that would stimulate this development in their brains? The field of microbiology gives a possible answer. It lies in the fact that we constantly remanufacture our own bodies according to instructions which are built into the heart of every cell. As our body cells die they replace themselves by means of these instructions-a process called "protein synthesis." This is a natural, built-in sort of replication not unlike the artificial process the Celestials used to recreate our first ancestors. By means of it we restore our bodies and maintain health and life until aging and death overtake us.

During the last half-century biologists have been experimenting with improving this natural replicating process. Some studies are concerned with keeping it perfect indefinitely without rejuvenation losing effectiveness. This could eventually lead to control of aging and even immortality.

Others have focused on artificially changing the instructions so that the cell does not manufacture a duplicate but makes an "improved" version of the original. This is a start toward genetic engineering. Ultimately, it could lead to feeding an animal or plant specific nucleic acids and producing new traits at will-traits such as moral responsibility. Our own biologists have already taken tentative steps in this direction in what is called "recombinant DNA" research.

This "doctoring" of the code is similar to what the Lord must have done when he created Adam, except that to produce a whole man outright, he would have needed to use an artificial replicator.

Once humans had been recreated and the new model tested the desired trait could then be added at a later time by ingesting a prepared "fruit". It would be "organ specific" and would make the necessary change in the instructions to produce the desired trait. The "fatal apple," then, was probably a preparation of nucleic acids which stimulated Adam's and Eve's brains to develop moral responsibility.

THE UNFORESEEABLE

Yet, if the Celestials understood genetic engineering and had controlled their Garden experiment as carefully as the Bible says, how did it go wrong? The failure of the Garden of Eden experiment seems improbable. If the Celestials were hundreds of thousands, or millions, of years in our technological future, if they had mastered the secret of conditional immortality, if they created modern humans, how then could they have miscalculated their behavior so badly? Why would the Lord have put the "tree of knowledge of good and evil" where Adam and Eve could reach it if he did not wish them to eat from it? Being their Creator, could he have overestimated their ability to resist its temptation?

Many of these problems which obscure the Adam and Eve story become clear when it is reinterpreted in the way we have suggested. The Lord did not miscalculate Adam's and Eve's behavior, nor did he make a mistake in allowing them access to the "tree of knowledge of good and evil." The "mistake," which led to the failure of the experiment, occurred at a much higher level and was made long before Adam and Eve. It was in predicting the behavior of his favorite archangel,

Lucifer (or Satan), the director of the experiment. And such a prediction would not have been possible-even for the Lord. The Celestials are free moral agents. Like their image reflectors, humans, they have the capacity for moral choice. Long before the Garden of Eden experiment, on another world, they had removed the influences from their society which cause humans to misuse their power of moral choice. Theirs was a utopian society without injustice or evil.

It would be natural for the Lord to believe that any member of the Celestial society was beyond doing evil. It had probably been millions of years since a single evil or unjust act had occurred in their civilization. How could the Lord anticipate that it would suddenly appear in his chosen leader, Lucifer-the one he had trusted with the direction of this vital experiment?

The solution to this problem is provided by our space age distinction between "God" the Lord of the Celestials and "God" the ultimate creative power. If by "God" we mean the Lord of the Celestials (and in the Garden story we do), then he is not the infinitely perfect being of medieval theology. He is vastly superior to us. but he too "is flesh" and fallible. He could create a being, such as Lucifer, whose conduct he might be unable to predict. It seemed that the Garden experiment was foolproof, but it was not. His failure to foresee the defection of Lucifer does not raise the "problem of evil" because he was not the ultimate creator of power.

THE "PROBLEM OF EVIL"

If we mean the ultimate creative power there is no obvious answer. The "Problem of Evil" has never been satisfactorily explained. According to Ezekiel, Lucifer was regarded by the Lord as his created masterpiece. Speaking of him the Lord says, "Behold, thou art wiser than Daniel; there is no secret that they can hide from thee ... Thou wast perfect in thy ways from the day that thou wast created, till iniquity was found in thee.... Thine heart was lifted up because of thy beauty, thou hast corrupted thy wisdom by reason of thy brightness ..." (Ezekiel 28:3, 15, 17).

The medieval picture of Satan as the Devil, complete with horns, cloven hoofs and pitchfork tail, is obviously not a copy of the portrait given here. This medieval view is the result of later pagan influences that crept into Christianity. The Lucifer (and Satan) of the Bible is a highest-level Celestial, next to the Lord in his intelligence and wisdom, gifted with an exquisite musical voice, beautiful of form; the Lord's favorite archangel-an "angel of light" (II Corinthians 11:14). Why, then, was there evil in his nature?

The only possible answer seems to lie in the nature of moral freedom-the ability to choose between good and evil. It is a fact that we do have the choice between good and evil. The Bible tells us we mirror the Celestials in this respect.

While this accounts for the evil humans do, it does not address the larger problem of the coexistence of "cosmic evil", such as death and natural disasters, with an ultimate creative intelligence. Further three millennia of theological effort has failed to find a satisfactory answer to the problem of evil.

This is paralleled in science, since a century of experiments and theorizing has failed to find a "final theory" that explains how quantum indeterminacy and paradoxes can coexist with a universe that, in large scale, seems predictably ordered and whole.

Perhaps the answer to this larger problem is that our finite minds are incapable of grasping an ultimate creative power that is infinite and eternal, The Bible, in the book of Job, says this is true as we have seen in the chapter, In the Beginning.

This is why Job's declaration of faith, in his extremity of undeserved suffering has seemed the only answer possible to the undeserved suffering of other believers during the long Judeo-Christian experience. So the unknown author of Job has his hero proclaim "though he slay me, yet will I trust him." (Job 13:15)

"THE BEST-LAID PLANS"

Coming back to, Adam and Eve they were created, childlike, so they followed the strongest influence. The Lord had isolated them in the Garden so they were removed from every evil influence in the strange new world from which their animal ancestors came. They inherited a "carnal" (or bestial) nature from them, but they had godlike minds capable of controlling it once they had received the capacity of moral choice. This the Lord intended to give them as soon as they were "trained" by him to know the right choices.

As future members of the Celestials' society he wanted them to live morally and justly from choice, not just as programmed robots. Good conduct which is forced has no virtue, and he and the Celestials could welcome only virtuous humans as fellow citizens and equals. The situation is similar to a powerful king, who can command his beautiful subject to submit to his embraces but wants her to love him from choice. Her love means nothing unless it is freely given. So he courts her patiently, trying to win by love, rather than taking it by force.

Perhaps this is why, throughout the Bible, the righteous humans who will eventually be welcomed into the Celestials' society are compared to a bride and the Lord to the bride groom. So Isaiah says,"... as the bridegroom rejoiced over the bride, so shall thy God rejoice over thee" (Isaiah 62:5).

The final control was set by the Lord in putting Lucifer, his trusted aide, in charge. He would see that nothing went wrong with the plan for creating a race of intelligent and moral beings who could assist in taming the new world. Afterward they could be welcomed as heirs and compatriots.

The Lord could have created more angels for the job as he had created Lucifer and others. Replication or cloning would have provided Celestials in any numbers he desired. But the idea of making citizens out of the most superior natives of the new world seemed more appropriate. The motive again was not unlike that of human colonizers who employ or marry residents of the areas they colonize. Adaptation to a new environment is hastened by using the adaptations already present among its natives.

And the only way humans could be trained to prize the good was to give them some opportunity to reject the evil even though, at first, it might not be a real choice. In the same way, earthly parents train children, even before they have developed moral responsibility, by conditioning them to do what is "good" and avoid what is "naughty." The "That's a good boy (or girl)" and the "No, no!" (with a pat of the greedy hand reaching to touch) can teach the child "moral" values even before it has the actual power to choose them.

So the Lord had set a moral value, obedience to proper authority, as a training feature in the experiment even before Adam and Eve could really choose. Like earthly parents, he said, "Don't touch-don't eat," with the threat of death. He could have made the tree of knowledge of good and evil inaccessible, but in a moral vacuum his creations would have had no opportunity to learn the value of obedience before they were given the power to choose or reject it.

As the experiment was set up their obedience seemed guaranteed. All influences worked to ensure it. As an added precaution, however, the Lord inserted an additional control-he had added a "self-destruct" feature to the experiment. As our own Earthly scientists build a self-destruction feature for rockets that abort launching, so he had built the possibility of death into this experiment. If they "ate of the tree," in spite of his command (and their bestial heritage did perhaps leave some uncertainty), then their immortality would be canceled out. The Celestials could not permit a race of immortals, prone to evil, to share their world with them. If the "fruit" was "eaten" before the Lord had removed this feature, humans would forfeit immortality by acquiring "aging genes" which had been added to the mix. With these, and their exclusion from the tree of life, an experimental failure could be humanely dealt with without endangering Celestial society. Without the tree of life the remodeled humans would quickly revert to the mortal state of animal existence from which the Lord had recreated them.

"THOU SHALT NOT SURELY DIE"

But in spite of all these controls, in spite of the Lord's warning Adam and Eve about the self-destruct feature, in spite of the trusted leadership of Lucifer, in spite of the Lord's indulgence and parental guidance, the unforeseeable happened. Lucifer, the created masterwork, had been given too much. "Thine heart was lifted up because of thy beauty, thou hast corrupted thy wisdom by reason of thy brightness" was the Lord's postmortem judgment on Satan's defection. Pride, a virtue in moderation, had become a vice when inflated to excess in a being capable of freely making a wrong choice. Satan decided he was the Lord's equal-no, his superior. He was more worthy of the position of leadership.

He would first subvert the weakest link in the Lord's plan. Adam and Eve, the childlike experimental hybrids incapable of moral choice, would yield to the most immediate and powerful influence. He would use all of his brilliance, his charm, his charisma, to dazzle Eve. She, in turn, would subvert Adam. In the first domestic environment her attention had been occupied with matters other than the technical details of the DNA mix. She would be easier to convince that the Lord's caution was groundless. Adam, taught by the Lord and with more understanding of the self-destruct feature, would be harder to persuade. Later, after Eve had eaten and not immediately died, he could be moved by her charms. He would want to believe her and share her experience. Like today's drug enthusiasts she would want to "turn him on." With a little urging he would be only too glad to share her forbidden adventure.

Afterward, once Lucifer had shown he could flout the Lord's authority in this matter, it would be easy to sway the other Celestials to his side in the power struggle. He would persuade them that the Lord should have made more Celestials rather than creating these undependable humans to do his work. The Lord's fitness to command would be called into question; his pet creation, the humans, would be on the way to extinction, and the field would be clear for a takeover by himself. He would assume the position of leadership to which his gifts entitled him.

His plans laid Satan made his move. Genesis 3 says, "Now the serpent was more subtle than any beast of the field which the Lord God had made." Going to Eve he said, "Yea, hath God said, Ye shall not eat of every tree of the garden?" Eve replied that they might except for the tree in the midst of the Garden. "Ye shall not eat it, neither shall ye touch it, lest ye die". And the serpent said unto the woman, "Ye shall not surely die: For God doth know that in the day ye eat thereof, then your eyes shall be opened, and ye shall be as gods, knowing good and evil" (Genesis 3:1, 3-5).

With skill he seized on the weakest point in Eve's psychology, her vanity. She and Adam had admired and been awed by the brilliance and achievements of the Lord and the other Celestials. To be like them would be the greatest achievement she could imagine. And to be equal to the beautiful creature now flattering her with his attentions would be heaven!

"THAT OLD SERPENT CALLED THE DEVIL"

In the Genesis account the "serpent" appears as a literal snake, possessed by Satan, and used as his mouthpiece. Whether it was actually Satan himself or some automated device or robot through which instructions were ordinarily relayed to Adam and Eve we cannot tell. But it is evident, from the context, that it was not a literal serpent. Eve's succumbing to such a "Dr. Dolittle" – like device has been traditionally explained by the argument that the "serpent" was far different from its present form-walking upright, beautiful, next to man in intelligence. It is small wonder that such a fable finds little acceptance in the Twenty-First Century.

The word "serpent" used here comes from a Hebrew root, *nacash*, meaning "to hiss" (or whisper a spell, as magicians often did). It is likely then that the original version of this story blamed Eve's misconduct on an enchanter, not a snake. The association of this hissing enchanter with a "snake" came about later as editors gradually wandered away from the original meaning.

In view of this it seems likely, then, that the "serpent" was actually Satan, or a robot through whom he spoke, and not a literal "beast of the field" as the Genesis story implies. That he did not magically assume the form of a serpent on this one occasion, as literal-minded commentators often argue, is further supported by the fact he is referred to, throughout the Bible, as a "dragon" or "serpent" (as in the heading of this section, Revelation 12:9). The curse later put upon him by the Lord also shows that this is a figurative description. He says, "Because thou hast done this, thou art cursed above all cattle, and above every beast of the field; upon thy belly shalt thou go, and dust shalt thou eat all the days of thy life ... " (Genesis 3:14). This seems literal but is shown to be figurative by the following declaration that "I will put enmity between thee and the woman, and between thy seed and her seed; it shall bruise thy head ... " (Genesis 3:15). Even the most literal-minded interpreters have agreed that this is a figurative reference to the son of Mary, Jesus, overcoming death in the resurrection. The Bible says Jesus died that "through death he might destroy him that had the power of death, that is the devil" (Hebrews 2:14). Thus, he, the seed of a woman, "bruised" the "serpent's" head.

"IN ADAM'S FALL"

And so it was that Satan, "that old serpent," was the direct cause of the fall. Being the director of the experiment he had access to the DNA mix that could confer moral responsibility and death. It was a simple matter for him to beguile the child-like Eve into "eating" the mix (probably by oral administration rather than injection). That accomplished, she implicated Adam. Whether it required just one ingestion of the nucleic acids or whether it required a number is not clear. But after they "ate," the "eyes of them both were opened, and they knew that they were naked; and they sewed fig leaves together, and made themselves aprons" (Genesis 3:7). Whether their shame was for literal nakedness or for the nakedness of their guilt is not clear; and whether they literally tried to hide behind "fig leaves" or whether these are symbolic of behavior defenses they used in a futile attempt to conceal their new-found moral perception can only be surmised. Whichever it was the Lord saw through their disguise. Humanlike, his first reaction was one of shocked disbelief-"what is this that thou hast done?" (Genesis 3:13).

"UPON THY BELLY"

From that point the narrative moves rapidly to a conclusion. The serpent was cursed first. All sorts of fanciful zoological myths have been employed to explain the declaration, "upon thy belly shalt thou go." Imaginative fundamentalists have suggested that previous to this time snakes walked on legs. A more probable interpretation, in view of our claim that the "serpent" was Satan, is that the curse meant that when the other Celestials left Earth Satan and his followers would be confined to the local region of the Galaxy containing Earth. To be confined to this local part of the galaxy, after knowing the freedom of ranging intergalactic space, would be a punishment comparable to earthly sailors marooned on desolate islands by their comrades.

The righteous Celestials took their spacecraft with them and apparently set up controls which prevented Satan and his angels from manufacturing craft that could reach the Celestials' outer space empire. The rebellion of the fallen Celestials had led to warfare in which Michael was victorious over Satan. "And there was war in heaven: Michael and his angels fought against the dragon; and the dragon fought and his angels, and prevailed not; neither was their place found any more in heaven. And the great dragon was cast out, that old serpent, called the Devil, and Satan, which deceiveth the whole world: he was cast out into the Earth, and his angels were cast out with him" (Revelation 12:7-9).

Being occupied with founding and oversight of innumerable other colonization programs they chose to quarantine rather than immediately dispose of the rebellious Celestials. This would avoid contamination of the workforce that had already led to the defection of a third of their population and avoid neglect of other colonization programs. Upon their final return to colony Earth disposition of the fallen Celestials and humans who chose to join in their rebellion could be dealt with. The peace terms evidently stripped Satan and his followers of long-range spacecraft and confined them to Earth's region of the Galaxy.

"HOW ART THOU FALLEN!"

The ignominy of Satan's fate is summed up by the words the Prophet Isaiah attributes to Jehovah when he exclaims, "How art thou fallen from heaven, 0 Lucifer, son of the morning! how art thou cut down to the ground, which didst weaken the nations!" (Isaiah 14:12).

His gifts and leadership experience would enable him still to dominate the other rebellious Celestials who shared his fate. And, together, they could easily influence and dominate a majority of the human hybrids they had duped. So, marooned, stripped of rank and place among the Celestials, Satan, who had aspired to replace Jehovah himself, would thereafter have to be content with dominating a handful of felons and a degraded population of humans. As the ruler of a penal colony in the trackless backwaters of outer space he could contemplate the irony of Jesus' contemptuous description of him as, "the Prince of this World", and while he did so the human hybrids he had betrayed would work out their destiny by his side.

SORROW AND TOIL

Adam and Eve's fate was less inglorious, though equally harsh. Eve was dealt with first as the initial wrongdoer. "I will greatly multiply thy sorrow and thy conception; in sorrow thou shalt bring forth children ..." (Genesis 3:16). Turning to Adam he continues: "... cursed is the ground for thy sake; in sorrow shalt thou eat of it all the days of thy life ... In the sweat of thy face shalt thou eat bread, till thou return unto the ground; for out of it wast thou taken; for dust thou art, and unto dust shalt thou return" (Genesis 3:16--19).

Even though this curse seems harsh, in view of their child-like innocence and Satan's wiles, it should be remembered that it was built into the experiment-these penalties were automatic, and they had been warned.

That the Lord was compassionate, even in his frustration and disappointment, is evident, for immediately after this he took them both and made them "coats of skins, and clothed them" (Genesis 3:21). This was evidently to prepare them for the harsher weather outside the sealed environment. Immediately after he "drove out the man; and he placed at the east of the garden of Eden cherubim and a flaming sword as we have already seen in Chapter II.

The automatic nature of the penalties can be explained readily in our Space Age interpretation of the original sin. Fundamentalists have speculated on what exactly the Lord did to make women "bring forth children" in sorrow. And zoologists and anthropologists have puzzled over the fact that the human female alone, of higher mammals, seems to suffer greatly in the process of giving birth and is unable to resume normal functions at once.

The answer would seem to be that the Lord did not originally intend human reproduction to be sexual. That he created humans to enjoy sex and express love through it we have already seen. But the possibilities of mutation and genetic accidents; which attend sexual reproduction, would make it undesirable for eugenic reasons. It is more likely the Lord intended to reproduce humans by the same method used for the Celestial's, replication by cloning.

But now that the experiment had been spoiled, they were on their own. Outside they would revert to the method used by their evolved ancestors sexual reproduction. Unfortunately, the large brains which their ancestors had evolved had enlarged the cranial cavity as well. As a result the skull was too big for easy passage through the pelvic opening. This had to remain small, because the hips must be close together in a creature that walks upright. Clearly our large-brained ancestors found giving birth a painful process. This could have been avoided if replication or cloning had been used for Adam and Eve as the Lord evidently intended. Now, however, they were back to a state of nature, and so the necessity of natural birth, with a painful labor, became an inevitable consequence of Eve's fall. Like her ancestors she and her descendants would ever after pay the evolutionary penalty for developing upright posture and a large brain at the same time. They would "bring forth children" in sorrow.

And with both Adam and Eve the problems of diet and food gathering were built into their physiology. Unlike most animals of Earth they had developed as omnivorous creatures living on a varied diet of animal and plant products. This complexity was probably necessary for their more complex brain functions, since the complete range of amino acids are found naturally only in both animal and plant sources.

At any rate it meant their high standard of living would require an elaborate economy involving both hunting and domesticating plants and animals. Unlike simple creatures which can subsist on a single natural source of food; humans would ever after earn their bread by the "sweat of their face." Within the Celestials' controlled society these problems had doubtless been solved by the production of synthetic foods. They had developed beyond the necessity of "earning a living" and could devote themselves to higher things. On the outside humans could subsist only by unrelenting toil until they returned to the "dust of the ground" from which they were taken.

"CHERUBIM AND A FLAMING SWORD"

And with the Lord's curse upon them Adam and Eve were driven out of the Garden, and the Lord placed "cherubim" and a "flaming sword" to keep them from the tree of life and the achievement of immortality.

Again traditional interpretation has pictured winged angelic beings standing day and night with glittering swords drawn ready to strike down Adam and Eve if they attempted to return. As we have already seen, however, the word "cherub" and its plural, "cherubim," refer not to angelic beings, but to servomechanisms, or robots, which perform the drudgery of the Celestials' civilization. The cherubim posted at the entrance to the Garden of Eden were evidently a sort of erect barrier, armed with "a flaming sword", a rotating beam (probably a laser), which "turned every way" (Genesis 3:24) and was capable of wounding or killing anything that attempted passage.

But some Bible-wise readers may be objecting "Doesn't Scripture also use "cherub" to mean "angels"? Doesn't Ezekiel 28:14, for example, say that Satan was the "anointed cherub that covereth" in the Garden, and doesn't this prove some cherubs, at least, are Celestials?" The answer to this question can be found in a critical examination of the derivations of the words themselves. And it serves to point up the problems of translation.

In this case the fault lies with the King James translation. The phrase "anointed cherub" is used for the Hebrew word "mimschach". It is derived from a root meaning "rub with oil," or "anoint," but the primary sense intended is the spreading connected with rubbing oil. For this reason "mimschach" is usually translated as "expanded" or "outspread." This was taken into account when the King James translators added the phrase "that covereth"-"thou art the anointed cherub that covereth." Yet, although the words "anointed" and "covereth" do convey the essential ideas, and the phrase follows the Hebrew word order, a number of modern translators feel they miss the real point. Thus the New English Bible gives the passage as "I set you with a towering cherub as guardian." The Jerusalem Bible gives it, "I had provided you with a guardian cherub." And again the New Oxford Annotated Bible gives the same sense when it says, "With an anointed guardian cherub I placed you."

If these modern readings are correct then the King James translation completely misses the point. Satan is not called a cherub anointed or otherwise. It is rather that a "guardian cherub" spread its protection over him and his headquarters at the Garden. This guardian cherub was probably similar to the one the Lord set at the gate of the Garden, a laser device which "covered" the experimental headquarters. This was where the director stayed with his precious stores of genetic mixes-the laboratory at the Garden's center. A revolving laser generator on its roof would have "covered" its entire perimeter to keep out intruders. Only Satan could have penetrated it to put Adam and Eve and the forbidden "fruit" together.

PARADISE LOST

With these guarding cherubim, then, the access to the Garden and its secret of immortality was permanently shut off for humanity. From the moment of their expulsion Adam and Eve reverted to the state of nature from which their unreconstructed ancestors had come. Like them they now had to make their way amid hostile predators, alien evolved humans and the fallen Celestials who had access to their world.

The story of their struggles in the strange and savage world outside the Garden is told in the briefest of narratives in the later chapters in Genesis. It is elaborated, sometimes plausibly, and sometimes fantastically, by accounts given in the apocryphal literature. Secular history can tell us little of this period, for it precedes any written records.

In the next chapter we will try to reconstruct the trials and progress, the failures and triumphs, of our human ancestors as they took up a precarious existence in their demoted state.

... when the sons of God came in unto the daughters of men, and they bare children to them, the same became mighty men which were of old, men of renown.

– Genesis 6:4

CHAPTER X

The Bible and History

AFTER THE FALL

"And Adam knew Eve his wife; and she conceived, and bare Cain, and said, I have gotten a man from the Lord. And she again bare his brother Abel" (Genesis 4:1-2). With these lines Genesis picks up the thread of narrative after Adam's and Eve's expulsion from the Garden. For the next nine chapters the Bible continues the story we traced in the fossil record in Chapter VIII. No other section in the Bible compresses so much in so short a space, unless it is the account of the original creation in Genesis 1. According to our earlier estimate these chapters must encompass nearly 30,000 to 35,000 years for they end with the call of Abraham, after his migration from Ur; where the ancient Sumerian civilization arose. History sets this event at around 4,000 years ago.

In these chapters the Bible recounts epochal happenings: the first murder; the multiplication of men and wickedness throughout the world; the genealogies of the patriarchs and their descendants; fantastic life spans of almost a thousand years; mortals being carried to heaven alive; a catastrophic flood that destroys all but one family and the dispersion of humanity throughout the Earth with the development of races and languages.

GENESIS AS HISTORY

Unfortunately, there is no way to recover an exact historical record from these legends. It is generally agreed by scholars that the biblical narrative is highly selective. Further, its accounts have doubtless been reworked as countless generations passed them down in oral traditions from father to son. Yet this does not mean the events are imaginary or the people fictitious. To believe this goes against the informed opinion of most mythologists and historians. The narrative is essentially historical, but it is not the kind of history we associate with textbooks and courses in high school and college. It is folk history, legend, the record preserved in the consciousness of the race by the process of parents telling their children of their heritage and by priests and bards reciting, or singing, more solemn accounts on ceremonial occasions. If we are to believe what the Bible tells us it may also be that these narratives reflect the editorial influence of the Celestials themselves. We have its assurance they communicated, to the writers, those special insights they wished preserved in human memory as symbols of their redemptive plan.

THE PROBLEM OF THE GENEALOGIES

The real problem in trying to reconstruct a history from these genealogies is that they are selective rather than complete. Though the Genesis editors tried to make them seem complete by giving exact lines of descent, ages of parents at children's births, and life spans, these mean little.

Bishop Ussher's attempt, in the Seventeenth Century, to add them up to a total, giving the date of creation, was doomed to failure. Other scholars using the same methods have arrived at dates quite different from Ussher's. This is because of textual discrepancies. In some genealogical passages no ages are given at all, and in different versions of the Bible, such as the Hebrew Masoretic text and the Greek Septuagint, ages given do not always agree. Further, the Hebrew word for "son of", "ben", can mean a remote descendant as well as an actual son. So, too, "yolad" – "begat"– doesn't necessarily mean "father of" but can be used for a more remote ancestor.

This can be confusing, as Matthew 1:8 shows. There we read that "Joram begat Ozias." What the passage fails to mention is that three generations passed between Joram and Ozias -Ahaziah, Joash and Amaziah. The Ozias "begat" by Joram was not his son but his great-great-grandson! This is not evidence of carelessness on the part of biblical writers, it was custom. Genealogies often mentioned only the more important members of a family tree.

From this it is evident that adding up Bible genealogies cannot clarify whether Adam and Eve were created in 4004 B.C. or 40,004 B.C. Any serious effort to date Bible events must rest on outside evidence such as that of archaeology or the fossil record.

In spite of this there is increasing evidence, from history and archaeology, to indicate that the heroes and places of the Bible are usually based on real lives and actual times and places. Finds in the last century at Ebla in Syria have unearthed over 15,000 clay tablets which mention such names as Abraham, Esau, David, Saul and even Israel. The time and place of these finds would be right for these Bible patriarchs and kings.

In this chapter we will therefore assume that the biblical narrative is essentially historical. And we will take it for granted that biblical characters, such as Adam and Eve, Cain and Abel, Enoch and Noah, were real in the sense that they refer to real people, or peoples, of whom they are representative. Further, we will assume that those they represent were descendants of the Lord's special creation and were real actors in the drama of the Bible.

We believe that the record of their doings is true in the special sense that folk history is generally true. In this chapter we will try to discover the role they played in the development of humanity and in the larger biblical narrative as told to our first ancestors by the Celestials.

REDEMPTIVE HISTORY

In discussing the doings of the Celestials, up to this point, we have been mainly concerned with what could be called secular history-history of the sort created by the folk process or history that is written by specialists called historians. While much of the Bible began with the first sort of history, and many parts have been reworked into the second, the intent of its writers was to create still a third kind. It is what we may call "redemptive history" – history that reveals a plan for the redemption of humanity.

Time and again the Bible tells us it is not just ordinary history and that its purpose is not just to tell a story. In almost every book it directly states, or at least implies, that the stories it contains are intended as revelations and examples. They reveal the Celestials' plan for us and instruct us in how to follow that plan so that we may be redeemed. Once again we are reminded of the famous passage from II Timothy which tells us: "All scripture is given by inspiration of God, and is profitable for doctrine, for reproof, for correction, for instruction in righteousness: That the man of God may be perfect, thoroughly furnished unto all good works" (II Timothy 3:16-17).

The attempt to square this claim, made by Bible writers, with scientific history has been a major problem for theologians of the last hundred years. If we cannot know the events told in the Bible actually happened, and if we are not sure the people in its stories were real, how can it reveal anything and how can it make any demands on us to live in a particular way? This has been a central issue in Bible criticism for both religious leaders and skeptical critics (and many recent theologians have been both). An answer to this difficult question has been worked out by certain German theologians over the last two centuries. They call their solution "heilsgeschichte" – redemptive history.

According to this notion events can be really understood only in terms of their history, and their history is complete only if it shows their relation to God. We have already used this concept in Chapter VI, In the Beginning. If we acknowledge the creative power in nature as God, and our dependence on it as its creatures, then our view becomes a religious one – our history is a sacred one and our participation in that history becomes redemptive.

But even more we are the product of a special history not shared by the rest of the natural creation. We are the special recreation of the Celestials and their heirs. This special history has placed upon us demands unique in the natural world. We, alone out of all living things, have a special calling to prepare the world for their return and to make ourselves worthy of sharing in their rule of it.

The Bible is a record of this special history. It discloses their purpose in coming to our world and it challenges us to share their plan for its future. As such it is a call to action. And it is precisely this call to action which distinguishes it from ordinary history.

As the Danish existential philosopher, Kierkegaard, pointed out, it is as though we sit observing a great epic drama on a cosmic stage. Suddenly the principal actor, who is also the director of the drama, steps up to the front of the stage, points at us, and calls out, "You, you're wanted. Come up here. Take your part."

THE BIBLE AS REDEMPTIVE HISTORY

So it is that the Bible is more than a record of people and events. Through its characters and narratives it reveals a plan and calls out to us to fulfill a special destiny and to prepare for a unique inheritance.

Of course the question immediately comes up, "By what authority does the Bible issue this challenge and hold out these promises?" The answer is given again and again in the story we will follow. It claims that the Lord and his assistants, the other Celestials, not only came at one special time to recreate us, but have continued a watchful care throughout history. Throughout the entire Bible we will see the repeated claim that they have often directly intervened to produce events serving as types and symbols of their plan for us. At other times they have selected special people, or even whole peoples, to act as emissaries and messengers to tell of their plan and to inspire and reprove humans as they carried it out or ignored it. In many cases these special people were the writers of the Bible. And it is their special relation to the Celestials, and the revealing events in which they participated, that give their writings a claim to inspiration and sacred authority.

HIGHER CRITICISM AND THE BIBLE

Much of the higher criticism of the Bible, during the last two centuries, has tried to show these claims for inspiration and authority are worthless. Critics have argued that parts of the Bible were not written by the people claimed to be their authors; they have attempted to show that the ideas in their writings were taken from folklore and mythology of other peoples whom they knew. They have invoked the folk and myth-making processes to debunk extraordinary or miraculous events of the Bible and to show they were really just ordinary experiences that seemed miraculous to ignorant nomads and illiterate fishermen. Or they have claimed they were the inventions of later copyists and editors who inserted them into the record, after the fact, to support their own special doctrines and views.

Anyone who examines the Bible carefully and critically cannot doubt these things have sometimes happened. Books claimed to be written by certain authors show usages and name locations which would have been known only to later writers. Bible stories do parallel the myths of other cultures, but this may be because they both come from a common source and not because they influenced each other. Some of these stories are told as though they were of universal, world shaking events when it is clear, from the context and secular history, that they were only of local importance. And certain passages, in our current translations, are not even found in the earliest surviving manuscripts.

WHAT REALLY MATTERS

All of this is unimportant, however, if we accept the idea that inspiration and authority do not require the Bible to be literally and scientifically true in a word-for-word sense. What does matter is that, in spite of growth and change and the problems of translation, the essential revelation has been retained. With the aid of archaeology and textual analysis scholars have discovered such a solid core of historical fact. Now our space age interpretation adds a new tool for getting at this core. Its discovery that incredibly advanced extraterrestrials were principal actors in the drama of the Bible gives new dimension to our understanding of its pages.

The inspiration and authority of the Bible does not lie in its word-for-word dictation by Celestials, nor in its literal scientific truth. Neither of these is necessary, or even possible, considering how the record came into being and the people who wrote it. What matters is that the revelation of the plan is there and that we perceive it and respond to its challenge. For this reason it does not particularly matter whether Adam and Eve were actual individuals or symbols for the race created by the Celestials. The message of the Celestials' watchful concern over human affairs is communicated whether the flood was a local event, destroying the small world known to the Genesis writers, or a truly worldwide catastrophe as the record seems to claim. The unique nature and history of the Jews is not changed whether Abraham was called by the angel of the Lord or the inevitabilities of his own life. And the significance and validity of the Mosaic law, as a revelation of righteousness, is not altered whether Moses was the unacknowledged son of a Pharaoh's daughter or a Hebrew slave who was divinely chosen to receive a revelation on Mount Sinai.

It is this disclosure of revelation and its challenge which is the true work of interpretation. And a Space Age interpretation, by bringing new knowledge to bear on ancient mysteries, unveils their hidden treasures.

In this sense, then, our interpretation of the Bible's meaning is valid. Its explanations make the timeless truths of the Bible timely. Even more, a Space Age interpretation of the Bible's challenge gives it urgency as we stand in the second decade of the Twenty-First century. It says, "They're coming back soon! An advanced civilization will soon arrive here on Earth – a civilization without crime, war, injustice or death. Are you ready for citizenship?"

A LIVING FAITH

But, some readers may be thinking, since different interpretations are possible how can we know which one is right? The answer to this is that none is right, in the sense that matters, unless it speaks to you. If, by looking at the Bible from some particular viewpoint, its authors step up to the front of the stage, point their finger at you and say, "You, you're wanted. Come up here. Take your part!," then that is the right interpretation for you. And, if you respond by taking your part, you will do so, not because you have been convinced by arguments, but because you have been moved by the power of revelation-a power which challenges you to a personal commitment.

Such a response is based on religious faith, and your action makes it a living faith. Only by a living faith, discovered in this way, can you know revelational truth. Without such a practical test, proof is impossible and with it, proof is unnecessary. "The proof of the pudding is in the eating" as the old adage says. The Bible is largely a record of the doings and sayings of people who found the Lord pointing his finger at them and responded to the challenge with a living faith. Some of the first and most important of these are introduced in the first dozen chapters of Genesis.

MEN OF RENOWN AND MIGHTY EVENTS

The personalities in the first dozen chapters of Genesis are an impressive "Who's Who"-the founders of the present human race, the first murderer, the first human to escape death, the longest-lived human, the only surviving family from a catastrophic deluge, and the founder of the most remarkable people in history. The biblical heroes, Adam and Eve, Cain and Abel, Enoch and Methuselah, Noah and his family, and Abraham are figures of epic grandeur.

As we said earlier, however, it is impossible to reconstruct the beginnings of the race from the accounts of their deeds and the genealogies linking them with lesser figures. Their deeds are representative and the genealogies are selective. They leave many questions unanswered.

Where did Adam and Eve go after they were driven from the Garden? When did they, or their descendants, move to other areas? When did settled community living begin and where? How did the institutions of civilization begin – agriculture, building, art, social and religious ceremony? If these are mentioned at all they are already highly developed when we first encounter them in the Bible.

Adam tills and keeps the Garden (Genesis 2:15). His sons, Cain and Abel, carry on the tradition. Cain brings the fruits of the ground and Abel the firstborn of his flock to the Lord. Cain murders Abel when the Lord prefers Abel's offering (Genesis 4:2-8). Farming and animal husbandry are already developed arts as the Genesis narrative opens. In Genesis 4:17, we learn that Cain "builded a city"-architecture and city planning were recognized human skills. In Genesis 4:21, we find that Jubal "was the father of all such as handle the harp and organ." Musical art was a recognized tradition. In Genesis 4:22, Zillah gives birth to Tubal-cain, who instructs men in the crafts of brass and ironwork. Zillah's husband, Lamech, boasts that he has slain a man who wounded him and another for hurting him, and asserts that if Cain was avenged "sevenfold" he will be avenged "seventy and sevenfold" (Genesis 4:23-24). Fighting, as organized warfare, is on its way. In Genesis 6:14-16, we find Noah building an ark half the size of a modern ocean liner. In Genesis 11:4, men build a tower that reaches into the heavens-monumental architecture is already highly advanced. In Genesis 12:1, Abraham is called, by the Lord, out of a city which modern archaeology has shown was already highly civilized a millennium before Nebuchadnezzar.

Can any of these developments be set into a chronology? Archaeologists and prehistorians have estimates as to when the domestication of plants and animals began, but it would be much later than the time of Adam and Eve and their two sons-if the experimental creation was over 35,000 years ago. If Tubal-cain taught iron and brass work when historians think the use of these metals began, it would have been millennia after the Bible genealogies date him in the seventh generation from Adam. If the Tower of Babel was a ziggurat, as some archaeologists have contended, it must have been built when the early civilizations of the Fertile Crescent were flourishing. Yet this would have been much too late for the spread of humanity and development of languages which are linked with its defeat. Clearly, these stories involve tremendous telescopings in time.

GENESIS AND LONGEVITY

And this telescoping involves another fascinating problem, one of the most puzzling in the Bible. This is the problem of the incredible ages attributed to the preflood patriarchs. All but one are claimed to have lived over 700 years, and one, Methuselah, is credited with an age of 969!

Are these ages to be taken seriously or are they merely attempts, on the part of the priestly editor, to close the gaps left by selective genealogies?

It is interesting that later genealogies give ages that drop to more believable averages. For example, until Eber, no patriarch after the flood lived less than 433 years. But now, in one generation, the life span drops to 239 years and never exceeds that amount again. In fact, a steady decline continues, with Abraham dead at 175; Moses dying an old man at 120; and in Psalms 90:10 we find that, by David's time, "three score and ten" had become the expected human span.

Because these genealogies are selective there is no way to set up any kind of continuous chronology that would permit checking these age spans against one another for consistency. Yet, if the Adamic race did start with a superior longevity, due to their having fallen from a condition of immortality, the decline Genesis shows is exactly what we would expect as a result of interbreeding with the short-lived "daughters of men." Lacking evidence independent of the Bible record, then, the case for an extreme lifespan in the first created humans remains uncertain.

BIBLE HEROES AND OTHER RECORDS

Little more is told about the preflood heroes in Genesis. Beyond the bare genealogical framework, only an occasional human interest item breaks through from Adam's and Eve's expulsion from the Garden to Noah's building of the Ark. We read of Cain's slaying Abel over the Lord's choice of offering; Enoch's "walking with God" and then ceasing to be; Methuselah's unbelievable durability; Noah's justness and perfection and his "walk with God"-these fill out the account. The richness of detail we find in the folklore and epics of other peoples is notably lacking in these early Bible stories. Unlike Homer's poetic magnificence we have no elaborate descriptions of weapons and costumes, or, curiously, even of the heroes themselves. This lack of personal description is a strange feature throughout the entire Bible, for there is scarcely a hint as to the physical image of any important figure. We have no scripturally based idea of the appearance of Adam and Eve, Noah, Abraham, Moses, Elijah, John the Baptist, Jesus or Paul. Our ideas are almost wholly derived from the conceptions of relatively modern artists such as Leonardo Da Vinci, Michelangelo and Gustave Dore.

Perhaps this is the reason a large body of literature grew up, in early Judaism, to fill in historical gaps and elaborate on biographical and descriptive details. By the time the priest Ezra and his fellow scribes began reconstruction of the Hebrew scriptures which were lost or scattered during the exile (around 440 B.C.), there was a much larger body of oral traditions and writing than they actually selected. Much of this had, at one time or another, been regarded as sacred and set down in scriptural form. In attempting to reconstruct a text from these fragments they decided to make a division of the materials. A part was selected for publication and the rest was reserved for special purposes. This led to a distinction between those writings which were officially recognized for public use (the "canon") and others which were reserved for use by scholars and teachers, the apocrypha.

THE APOCRYPHA

It is probably this idea that the books outside the canon were to be kept secret, or hidden, which led to their later designation as "apocryphal" (from a Greek word meaning "concealed" or "hidden away"). However the term arose it was later adopted by Christians and used to designate not only books which the Jews had left out but a newer collection of Jewish and Christian literature that these later church fathers and councils rejected when they were selecting the Christian canon of scripture.

It is this body of apocryphal literature (older and newer) which has, for both Jews and Christians, served to fill in the details of the belief system based on the Bible. At first, among the post-exilic Jews, it was regarded as a source of religious instruction and wisdom intended to supplement the Pentateuch and other canonical books. In the centuries just before and after the beginning of the present era, however, there was a tremendous increase in apocryphal literature. This was largely due to the influence of Greek ideas on religious thought of both Jews and early Christians. These Hellenized Jews and Christians were often developing strange ideas in conflict with the traditions of their faiths. They also frequently raised questions which the Scriptures in common use did not answer.

As a result they began to search for the old "outside" books which had been lost, or deliberately destroyed, in the hope of answers. New versions of the old books appeared, and new books were sometimes forged to promote strange beliefs or present new solutions to unanswered questions. To get these forgeries accepted, the writers would often claim them as the work of some famous hero or patriarch or even a Bible writer. Since many of the original outside books had been lost, it was not easy to distinguish between restorations and outright forgeries, and often a given book might involve both processes. This is how the Christian view of apocryphal writings as spurious, or false teachings arose. As a result, both Jews and Christians developed a mixed attitude toward the apocryphal writings. They continued to cherish and enjoy them for a number of centuries, and both the Septuagint and early editions of the Christian Bible included them. Even the early editions of the King James Version, published after 1611, included some of them. On the other hand, as the Masoretic version of the Hebrew Scriptures and the formation of the Christian canon developed, in the early centuries of the present era, there was a growing tendency to regard them as a source of false doctrine. This led to neglect and avoidance of their use. Gradually they were excluded from most modern versions of the Bible. The common belief that they were rejected as "uninspired" at some specific time by official groups of Jewish or Christian leaders, after prayerful consideration, is simply not true. When such groups made decisions on what was canonical or excluded they were generally only acknowledging what had already been announced by some revered rabbi or early church father or giving official recognition to what had become an unofficial acceptance or rejection.

There was, of course, a general feeling among the Masoretes and the early Christian fathers that outright forgeries were not "inspired." As Christian doctrine began to be unified it was also felt that books teaching "false" doctrines (or views which had been declared "heresies") were not inspired. These views influenced some of the exclusions. But others seem to be without any foundation in reason. Even today it is difficult to see why Esther was received and Judith excluded. As a basis for religious instruction it is hard to show the advantages of Ecclesiastes and the Song of Solomon over the Book of Wisdom or the prophecy of Baruch. It is hard to explain why Jews and Catholics recognize the books of Maccabees while modern Protestants reject them. Yet all three accepted the authority of Chronicles. It is also difficult to explain why Hebrews is included in the New Testament, though its authorship still remains unknown, when other well authenticated letters of the apostles were rejected.

THE BIBLE A GROWING AND CHANGING WORK

From this we see that the present canon of the Bible is the result of historical growth in which chance, the changing ideas of people, as well as careful study and prayerful searching all played a part. Some of the Bible's present books have been recognized almost from the beginning. Others, such as Hebrews and Revelation, were doubtful and were rejected by some and accepted by others well into the present era. A few, like the Maccabees, still remain in dispute among Jews, Catholics and Protestants. Of those finally rejected, a number are authentic writings from the hands of Bible writers or principal characters in the drama of the Bible. Others are patchworks of traditional writings combined with forgery. Still others are outright forgeries. Among them is much that is historic, spiritual and wise, as well as what is fantastic, absurd and unsound.

There is no sure approach in separating the wheat from the chaff in the apocryphal writings. That they can be useful in rounding out our picture of the Bible's meaning is beyond doubt. But they can also be a source of confusion and misinterpretation, as can conflicting passages in the Bible itself. In the last analysis, it seems the only sure method is one which the thousands of believers, scholars, fathers and rabbis who founded our present canon employed. Each student of the writings, inside or outside the canon, must decide. We must each repeat the process which those who have gone before have gone through if we would experience the full revelation of the Bible. Whether we find it in the Masoretic text, in a Catholic version with the Maccabees or a Protestant version without them, or even in rejected books which speak to us must be a personal decision.

There is no simple rule of thumb which can make this decision easy. Are we to reject all writings not known to come from the pen of inspired writers? Several of the books in the canon are from unknown authors. Are we to reject whatever shows the influence of pagan idolatries and heathen superstition? Some have argued that the account in Genesis 22 of Abraham's near-sacrifice of Isaac is evidence that Canaanite child-sacrifice practices influenced Jewish thought. Others have found the account in II Kings 2:23-24 which implies that God sent two she bears to destroy forty-two children who mocked Elisha an evidence of heathen superstition.

An impartial reader must surely agree that it would be odd if the God of the law were to test Abraham's faith by seeing if he was willing to engage in the idolatrous practice of his neighbors. And it is very hard to imagine the God of universal justice and truth, portrayed in Jewish and Christian belief, lending himself to child slaughter on the whim of an old man's annoyance.

From all this it is evident that the Bible is not a fixed body of words unchanging for all time. It is the product of a history which will continue into the future. It was not produced, like ordinary books, by one writer during a single lifetime. It was written, a book at a time, by many writers over many centuries and in many places. Even individual books were sometimes the joint product of several writers over a period of time. The Bible grew as it passed from Jewish to Christian hands. Its content and form fluctuated during the centuries its canon was being fixed, and its outline is still unclear from one faith to another. It has continued to undergo subtle transformations as it has passed through successive translations. Today, chameleon-like, it continues to assume different appearances to different viewers in the perspective of various interpretations.

DOUBTFUL DEEDS AND CURIOUS CHARACTERIZATIONS

Returning to the books outside the canon, we find a bewildering array of material to fill in the history omitted from the record in the first dozen books of Genesis. We find, in the books of Adam and Eve, that, after expulsion from the Garden, Adam and Eve crossed the rivers surrounding Eden. These had been frozen when the archangel Michael touched them with a rod. At God's command they went to dwell in the Cave of Treasures. Later, in their despair over losing Paradise, they attempted suicide. In time Cain and Abel, as well as daughters, were born to them, and Cain stirred up enmity in the family circle. After Cain slew Abel, God placed seven curses on him. During all this time Satan continued to appear to Adam and Eve, as well as to their children, and tempted them to further sin. Once he appeared to Adam as a beautiful woman who attempted his seduction.

Later Satan induced Seth to marry away from his family, but Seth remained steadfast and, after Adam's death, became the head of his clan. In Adam's old age he prophesied the coming flood and instructed Seth concerning his death and funeral. As generations passed descendants of Adam and Eve continued to keep the Cave of Treasures as a family shrine, and leadership passed through a succession of heroes to Enoch.

In the Book of Enoch we learn that this hero was a seer noted for his great wisdom. He instructed humanity with religious teachings and prophesied concerning times to come. He told his son, Methuselah, of two visions he had in which the destruction of mankind by flood was revealed, and the whole human history from his own time to the end laid before him. The chronology of these events, and the signs and wonders which accompanied them, are an interesting hodgepodge of astronomical and astrological lore, as well as an excursion into numerology and angelology (the study of orders and functions of angelic beings). The occult knowledge and prophetic powers claimed for Enoch may be the origin of ancient views which credited him with secret wisdom later attributed to such figures as Thoth, Hermes Trismegistus, Pythagoras and Plato.

The Book of Jubilees goes on to tell how, after inventing writing and instructing the human race in learning, Enoch set down a testament to enable them to know the seasons and keep track of time. Finally he was conducted by the angels, "in majesty and honor," to the Garden of Eden, where he remained to write down "the condemnation and judgment of the world" and "all the wickedness of the children of men." The book then goes on to give the births and biographies of Methuselah, Lamech and his son, Noah. It interrupts the narrative to tell of the death of Adam, after Noah's birth, and states that he was "the first to be buried in the Earth." Soon after this it tells how Adam's son, Cain, died when his house collapsed on him, moralizing, "for with a stone he had killed Abel, and by a stone was he killed in righteous judgment."

The account then takes up the life of Noah and begins an elaboration on the story of the flood. And with the deluge we reach a great divide in the biblical story of our race. For after its waters recede life is never again the same for the Celestials' recreated heirs.

Life spans are dramatically shortened, races emerge and mankind is scattered throughout the Earth. Diverse languages bar communication, and the Celestials' role in Earthly affairs becomes more remote and dependent on human leaders and prophets.

BIBLE LEGENDS AND PREHISTORY

And, out of the mists which shroud the periods following the flood, the beginnings of secular prehistory emerge. The attempt to relate the Bible to other legends and myth systems is one of the most fascinating puzzles in the field of historical research. It has also been a recent subject for a variety of provocative books on prehistory.

As we saw in Chapter VIII, homo sapiens sapiens emerged on this planet 30,000 to 40,000 years ago. Yet the earliest truly historic records we have go back no further than about 6,000 years. What events bridge this gap that separates early Cro-Magnon man from the record keeping priests of ancient Sumer? Was the flood or the building of the Tower of Babel among them? And what of legends from other cultures? What about Atlantis and Lemuria and Mu?

We have already seen that early Genesis chapters plainly state the first generations of the Lord's creation were adept in most of the arts of civilization. These included animal husbandry and horticulture, skilled iron and brass work, city planning, ship building and music. Though the Bible does not directly state that the righteous Celestials instructed humans in these arts the apocryphal literature is full of such assertions. In the Secrets of Enoch it tells how Enoch was taken up into each of the ten heavens, and in the last the angel Michael brought him to the Lord. He then commanded Enoch to write down all the "works of heaven, the Earth and sea, and all the elements, and their passings and goings and changes of the stars, the seasons, years, days and hours, the risings of the wind, the number of angels, and the formations of their songs, and all human things ..." It goes on to state that when Enoch was done, after sixty days and nights, he had filled 366 books.

Not only are the Lord and his angels credited with instructing men in the arts of civilization, but the fallen angels are said to have played a part as well. In the section of the Books of Enoch, known as the Book of Watchers, it tells how they, the watchers, or fallen Celestials, taught men to make swords, knives, shields, breastplates, the fabrication of mirrors, and the workmanship of bracelets and ornaments; and the use of paint, the beautifying of the eyebrows, the use of stones of every valuable and select kind so that the world became altered, impiety increased, fornication multiplied, and they transgressed and corrupted all their ways."

Now, though we do not know the source of these traditions, they are clearly reasonable. If the loyal Celestials left a staff behind to look after the fallen creation it is logical their duties would have included instructing humans in arts which would make them useful and religious duties which would preserve them from total depravity. And if the rebellious Celestials were able to share this planet with humans it is also probable they tried to win them over by instructing them in wickedness and arts which would make them allies in rebellion.

PREHISTORIC CIVILIZATION

By putting these hints, given in Genesis and the apocryphal books, together with other non-Semitic legends we can fill in a probable prehistory for the later descendants of the Lord's creation. The nonbiblical stories come from very ancient times and tell of advanced civilizations which existed long before ancient Sumer. One of the best known of these was told by the Greek philosopher, Plato, who asserted that he had knowledge of such a civilization through an acquaintance, Critias.

In the dialogue which bears his name Critias tells the history of a fabulous, lost civilization, Atlantis, which sank beneath the sea. According to Plato's retelling of the conversation the information was given to Critias by Solon, the Athenian lawgiver. He had met a priest of Sais, in the Nile Delta, who told the story which he claimed was contained in sacred archives of the Egyptians. He described Atlantis as an island with magnificent roadways, bridges, a splendid palace and a long canal three hundred feet in width, a hundred feet in depth and almost six miles in length leading up to an inland harbor.

Another of Plato's dialogues, the Timaeus, tells how this island sank beneath the sea in a single day and night in the midst of violent earthquakes and a flood. According to Plato this event took place about 9,500 years before his time, which would place it around 12,000 years ago. Could such a civilization have existed then, and could the cataclysm that allegedly destroyed it have been the same as, or similar to, the one the Bible calls "the flood"? Numerous attempts have been made to locate the site of the "lost Atlantis." Recent deep-sea observations have convinced some archaeologists that it may have been where its mountain tops remain as the present Canary Islands, off the coast of Spain. According to Plato it lay just west of the Straits of Gibraltar which would make this location a possible one. And a giant upheaval centering in the Mediterranean could have involved both this area and the Fertile Crescent at its perimeters.

There are many other legends that tell of lost or sunken civilizations in the remote past. Almost everyone has heard of Lemuria, Mu, Hyperboria and others. Most of them are credited with advanced technologies including monumental architecture, advanced mathematical and astronomical knowledge, control of mysterious energy sources and sometimes flying machines. What are we to make of these stories?

CREATED MAN AS THE BEARER OF ADVANCED CIVILIZATION

Putting together the biblical and pagan legends we arrive at an obvious explanation for filling the gap of prehistory. It suggests that the created homo sapiens became heirs to a Celestially taught civilization. In the millennia following their expulsion from the Garden they migrated throughout the Earth carrying this civilization with them.

As they spread their level of genetic superiority gradually declined because of interbreeding with evolved humans. In the same way their cultural heritage also became fragmented and was eventually lost, perhaps through natural calamities such as those recounted in the Timaeus of Plato, or others which destroyed Pompeii. Yet before this occurred areas to which they migrated became the centers of prehistoric civilizations. These form the factual basis for well known legends such as that of Atlantis.

As cultural dilution and fragmentation continued descendants from these original colonies founded other lesser civilizations. These are the first of which we have direct historical evidence. The Sumerians, the Egyptians, the Indus Valley dwellers, the Chinese, the Druids, the Aztecs and the Mayans were ail probably of this sort.

All of these civilizations show a common mastery of certain kinds of advanced technical knowledge. Because of geography it is difficult to suppose these similarities were due to direct influence on one another.

For example, it seems strange that the Sumerians, the Egyptians and the Mayans, separated by continents and oceans, ail created very similar types of stepped pyramids. And in view of the quite different functions they served it is even harder to explain why they were ail built on similar geometric principles with similar orientations to the stars and solar system. It is also baffling that the ancestors of the Druids, in Great Britain, also built monolithic structures unrelated to pyramids (such as those at Stonehenge) yet followed these same astronomic orientations, as did the builders of stone arrangements at Carnac in France.

Already, during the third millennium B.C., there were many places throughout the ancient world where people shared a common knowledge of cutting, transporting and building with huge blocks of stone. These ranged in size from a ton or two to several hundred tons. They were able, in Sumer, Lebanon, Egypt, North and South America and Easter Island, to move these considerable distances, often many miles, across dense jungles and over mountain ranges. In many places they were lifted to great heights of hundreds of feet, as in the Great Pyramid in Egypt or at Machu Picchu in Peru, where buildings were erected hundreds of feet above the quarries from which their blocks came. Many of these monuments were arranged with such precision they could be used to predict exact times, to the day, of equinoxes, solstices and other astronomical cycles.

The point, of course, is not only that it is astonishing that people of four or five millennia ago could do these things, but even more that we would find them difficult to duplicate today with all the technology of modern engineering. Where did prehistoric men learn such skills and how did they accomplish these results?

As remarkable as these common threads of accomplishment are, other specializations are perhaps even more baffling. These are hard to explain except as fragments from a common seminal culture. It would appear that representatives of the parent culture migrated to different points of the compass carrying with them, in each case, only a part of the original whole.

It is as though some collection of diverse talents in modern times, such as the Princeton Institute for Advanced Study, were to be broken up and its specialists scattered throughout the world. One would carry an advanced knowledge of building and architecture here, another of medicine there and a third of space science and technology elsewhere.

A careful study of these early civilizations shows a similar imbalance of specializations. Each is peculiar for some advanced area of achievement which others do not share and that is unlikely in terms of its own general level of accomplishment

So we find the ancient Mayans and Egyptians had an advanced knowledge of medicine, including surgery and pharmacology, which others did not share. Some, like the inhabitants of Easter Island or the builders of Stonehenge and Carnac, were able to create monumental architecture on a prodigious scale without a highly organized urban lifestyle. Unlike the Egyptians and Babylonians they left no evidence of having developed temple cultures or grid-pattern cities. The Mayans, Egyptians and Babylonians seem to have had a profound knowledge of astronomical cycles, which they used in orienting their pyramids – a knowledge not shown in other centers where monumental architecture with massive pieces of stone was also practiced.

Could these remarkable technical specializations, which lifted certain ancient peoples above their own general level of achievement as well as that of their peers, have been the gift of a superior and otherworldly race?

It is interesting that the myths and legends of the ancient Egyptians, Tibetans, Hindus, Greeks, Aztecs and Mayans all tell of gods coming from the sky to teach humankind the arts of civilized living. These tales contain accounts of what seem to be flying craft, atomic weapons, advanced communications systems and medical miracles.

The ancient Babylonian historian, Berosus, tells of written accounts, going back thousands of years, which credit an animal endowed with reason and a fishlike body (but with human parts beneath and below (could it have worn a space suit?) instructing mankind in letters, sciences and every kind of art. This being, Oannes, is credited, by Berosus, with teaching humans to construct houses, to erect temples, to compile laws and to understand the elements of mathematics and engineering.

Speaking of this and similar stories Carl Sagan noted we do not know where the Sumerians came from. Their language was strange: it had no cognates with any known Indo-European, Semitic or other language, and could only be translated because later people, the Akkadians, compiled extensive Sumerian-Akkadian dictionaries.

In view of this, then, it seems probable that the descendants of the Adamic race were bearers of an advanced extraterrestrial civilization. After centuries of cultural dilution and natural disaster the original centers of this Celestially taught civilization all disappeared.

THE DELUGE

A major factor in this disappearance may have been the Noahic deluge. Scientific criticism of the flood story has generally been based on the assumption that Genesis describes a worldwide deluge. A careful study of the text, however, does not support this view. Though it says the waters covered "the earth," the word for "earth", "erets", can mean either land or the whole Earth. Since the Lord resolved to destroy "man whom I have created" it seems likely that "erets" here means only the Fertile Crescent, the land occupied by the experimental humans in the early accounts of Genesis.

One of the strongest evidences that destructive flooding did occur comes from comparative mythology. As we have already seen flood legends closely resembling the Genesis account have been found among the most widely scattered peoples.

Furthermore, archaeology and geology alike show that massive flooding has occurred, since ancient times, in the Fertile Crescent. And in view of the fault structure at its western end and the delta at its most eastern, it is likely that it has been the scene of severe flooding from time immemorial.

If one of these included the deluge of Genesis it would have been carried by descendants of the Adamic race throughout the world. It is difficult to explain the widespread versions of a flood story on any other basis.

In the Scriptures these descendants are typified by Noah's three sons, Shem, Ham and Japeth. The Bible states that "of them was the whole Earth overspread" (Genesis 9:19). If these speculations are correct it is likely that the descendants of the created race who remained closest to the site of the recreation retained the purest and least fragmented form of the Celestials' civilization.

AFTER THE FLOOD

It is well known that the earliest historical civilization did, in fact, emerge at the eastern end of the Fertile Crescent. It was here that urban civilizations first appeared about 7,000 years ago. We have already commented on the fact that the Sumerians' emergence is unique, among civilizations, in that it seemingly had no development. In the fourth millennium before Christ it appears in the pages of history by what seems to be a sudden leap from stone-age ancestors to full-blown urban status. This includes grid-pattern cities, a highly inflected written language, money, a developed economy, complex and subtle literature, philosophy and art, as well as an advanced knowledge of mathematics and astronomy.

If our speculations are valid it seems likely the Sumerians were the direct lineal descendants of the "unknown ancient modern" who ancestored us all. As the "next of kin" to the "sons of God" they would have preserved much of the material and technical civilization their ancestors had been taught as well as the Celestial religion.

This was not, of course, the popular religion later elaborated by the Babylonians but the patriarchal religion described in Genesis, the religion of Adam and Eve and of Enoch and of Noah. It was this religion which was later carried by Abraham out of Sumer into Canaan where he founded the people to be known as the Hebrews.

In the next chapter we will see how it was that this people was chosen for a special destiny in the redemption of mankind. We will examine the Genesis record to discover how their genetic and cultural purity was preserved through the creation, by the Lord, of a social laboratory-an experiment in righteous living. We will see how their descendants were given the law which embodied the essentials of the Lord's plan for saving his fallen creation.

And I will make of thee a great nation, and I will bless thee, and make thy name great; and thou shalt be a blessing.

– Genesis 12:2

CHAPTER XI

The People and the Law

STARTING OVER AGAIN

Many generations had come and gone since the deluge. In their dispersion the descendants of the flood's survivors had strayed ever further from the Celestials' teaching. Everywhere the Lord saw new signs of the corrupting influence of the fallen Celestials.

He could not afford further delay in setting up his social laboratory. Since the Celestials' Earth base had been removed visits to Earth had been infrequent, but the time for another was now approaching.

The schedule called for a stay of several centuries in the area of the galaxy containing Earth and other potential colonies. During this time the Lord would gather his chosen ones, select a leader and supervise their resettlement. Once they were established in their new land he would give them the law. And, in between times, he could visit other neighboring colonies to confer with melchisedecs and inspect their progress.

The genealogical records and sample data showed the purest strain of his creation was still concentrated near the original garden site as he expected. It had developed an impressive civilization based on the Celestials' training of its ancestors. The Celestial religion had been corrupted almost beyond recognition. It flourished in the great urban centers where its priests ruled the people in an exploitative theocracy.

But here was the genetic material the Lord needed for his "chosen" race. Once a sample had been removed he could renew his covenant with them and begin their training as a "holy" people.

THE PATRIARCHS AND A DELIVERER

Few portions of the Bible have aroused more controversy among historians and other scholars than the chapters and books describing the Lord's next moves. As they stand in Genesis and Exodus the call of Abraham, the saga of his heirs, their exodus from Egypt and the giving of the law to their deliverer, Moses, seem straightforward enough. Countless generations of Jews and Christians have taken them as pure history. And the colorful stories which surround them are the substance which has nourished and inspired innumerable generations of the Lord's chosen people as they struggled for survival.

Taken as a simple narrative their "history" centers on the lives and deeds of a handful of principal actors. The Lord's call comes to Abraham who is dwelling with his family and flocks in Haran. Tough and independent nomads they have migrated from Ur, one of the major cities of Mesopotamia, to this crossroads on the greatest caravan route of the ancient Near East. The Lord's word is short and to the point. "Get thee out of thy country, and from thy kindred and from thy father's house, unto a land I will shew thee" (Genesis 12:1).

Though he is already seventy-five, Abram sets out with his wife Sarai, his orphaned nephew Lot, and his flocks and herds. As the dust of the trail rises around them the promise of the Lord rings in his ears: "I will make of thee a great nation, and I will bless thee, and make thy name great ..." (Genesis 12:2).

Already their course has arched hundreds of miles up through the Tigris and Euphrates valleys. Now it drops southward through Damascus into Canaan. After a sojourn in Egypt, during a famine, Abram and Lot return to Canaan and settle permanently, Lot near Sodom and Abram at Hebron, an unusually fertile region about 20 miles south of Jerusalem.

Here the Lord renews his promise to Abram whom he renames "Abraham." He promises his "seed" will possess the land "forever" and become as numerous as the "dust of the earth" (Genesis 13:15-16). As a token of this new covenant he institutes the rite of circumcision for Abraham and his descendants. He also promises the barren Sarai (whom he renames "Sarah") a son. Soon after this Isaac is born to brighten Abraham's and Sarah's final years.

As the saga unfolds generations pass. Isaac fathers twins, Esau and Jacob. Jacob returns to his grandfather's homeland, "across the river," to find a wife among his Uncle Laban's daughters (Genesis 31:21). He works to pay the bride price for Rachel, whom he loves, but is first compelled to marry her older sister, Leah.

The twelve sons which come from these unions found the twelve tribes of the Lord's people. They are called the "twelve tribes of Israel," because Jacob has also been given this new name by an angel of the Lord with whom he wrestles.

Later Jacob's favorite son is sold into slavery by jealous brothers. This son, Joseph, gains his freedom and rises to power in the land of Egypt. When another famine strikes and his brothers seek refuge in Egypt he forgives them, and the family is reunited.

And with this reunion a large-scale migration of Abraham's descendants begins. For over 400 years Israelites dwell in the land of the Pharaohs. When the Egyptians overthrow their Hyksos invaders a native pharaoh is reestablished on the throne. He and his successor enslave the immigrant Israelites and force them to work on cities and monuments they build to glorify the new dynasty.

Moses, the son of Levite slaves, is born and hidden among the reeds of the Nile to escape a pre-Hitlerian program of genocide. The pharaoh's daughter rescues Moses, and he is reared in the Egyptian court as a prince. As he matures he is disturbed by the mistreatment of the Israelites. Finally, in a fit of rage, he slays a particularly brutal overseer and flees Egypt to save his own life. He goes to live in Midian and marries Zipporah, a priest's daughter. While he is living in Midian the call of the Lord comes to him to deliver his people from Egyptian bondage. He returns to Egypt as a wonder working prophet and calls down God's wrath on a reluctant pharaoh.

The Lord visits a series of plagues on the Egyptians culminating in a dreadful night when he "passes over" the children of the Hebrews but slays the firstborn of all the Egyptian families and flocks.

After this disaster a bereaved pharaoh at last lets the Israelites go. In a mass exodus they miraculously pass through the Red Sea while a pursuing pharaoh, who has changed his mind is drowned along with his army.

Moses leads the Israelites for forty years in the wilderness with the Lord guiding them in a "pillar of a cloud" by day and a "pillar of fire" by night (Exodus 13:21). Finally they are led to Mount Sinai where the Lord gives Moses the commandments and the law.

Such is the Bible's story of how the Lord chose his people. Is it fact or fiction? Is it sacred history or national paranoia? Did God really choose the Jews or have they simply promoted themselves? These and similar questions have provoked endless controversy among scholars and theologians ever since the accounts were first set down.

MYTH AND THE BIBLE

Higher critics have eagerly seized on the seemingly supernatural elements in these stories as evidence of their absurdity--a barren Sarah conceiving at ninety, the miraculous parting of the seas in the Exodus, guidance by a pillar of fire and the commandments, written by the finger of God, on tablets of stone.

Yet, out of the welter of scholarly controversy and popular debate, a solid core of supporting evidence has emerged which argues the essential historical accuracy of the biblical record.

As with other legendary heroes, however, it seems probable their characterizations were based on real lives. Abraham, Sarah and Lot, like Noah and his "sons," may be used, in Genesis, to typify whole populations of migrants. But this does not mean they are unreal. Just as a few outstanding officers or heroic enlisted men are used by historians to create the picture of a battle, so the birth of the Hebrew nation is typified by the deeds of Abraham, Isaac, Jacob and Moses. What they did and felt, what they suffered and achieved, is made to stand for the experiences and accomplishments of the whole group for whom they stand.

Viewed in this way there is good reason for supposing Abraham and Sarah were members of the migrant population historians say did move from northwestern Mesopotamia to Canaan about 4,000 years ago. And though the human-interest items that breathe life into the Bible's stories cannot be documented in the same way, customs and rites, supported by the findings of archaeologists and anthropologists, can tell us much. We know, for instance, that the Genesis characterizations are ones which would have been correct for people in those times and places.

In this way we know Jacob's going to Haran, "across the river," to pick a wife among his Uncle Laban's daughters is how a good son of 4,000 years ago in that part of the world would have behaved. Archaeologists and anthropologists verify that cross-cousin marriages were then, and still are, preferred among Bedouin tribes in the Near and Middle East. And as the daughters of his mother's brother, Rachel and Leah would have been Jacob's cross-cousins. Also the custom of paying a bride price is one which has been practiced in that part of the world for millennia.

Further, research into Egyptian records shows that the Hyksos pharaohs held Canaanite tribes as vassals and allowed them to cross Egypt's borders in times of famine. And historians tell us their amiable and protective policy toward the Israelites changed when the native dynasty was reestablished.

Yet, in spite of such considerations, there is good reason to think the stories of the Hebrew patriarchs and Moses have been embellished by mythic elaborations. Unlike the preflood heroes who are often reduced to little more than genealogical skeletons in Genesis, the lives of the Hebrew culture heroes are fleshed out to an extent mere oral tradition and early record keeping could hardly have provided. It seems probable, on the face of the matter, that these stories have been enlarged and reworked in the process of handing down and retelling. What we know of human nature and the folk process make this inevitable.

Further, studies of these stories by comparative mythologists make it clear they show remarkable parallels with culture hero stories around the world. Yet they tell of events which happened too late to have been spread so widely by diffusion.

So Moses, as a culture hero, follows a well-defined path when his survival is threatened in infancy; he is hidden to preserve his life, is reared by a family not his own and returns to become the leader and deliverer of his people. Variations on this "culture-hero" myth are found throughout the world and in forms which predate the Moses legend by millennia.

Yet, again, this does not mean Moses did not exist. Nor does it imply he was not called by the Lord and did not receive the law in a special revelation.

MYTH AS REDEMPTIVE HISTORY

Modern students of mythology know that myths are true, not in the way that textbooks in history are true but in a deeper and more profound way. Though they may contain embellishments that are contrary to fact, they are like figures of speech. Their truth lies in their hidden revelation rather than their surface detail. Just as it communicates the truth more powerfully to say a man is a "tower of strength" than to describe him as "dependable," so a mythic description evokes commitment and purpose from its hearers which a merely factual narrative cannot. In this sense it is a form of redemptive history and defines for its hearers their deepest values and commitments.

Speaking of this Joseph Campbell, noted scholar of comparative religions, observed that humans need belief in myths, which empower them, creating new civilizations with a beauty and destiny of their own and why, he asks, when people seek something on which to found their lives, do they turn, not to the facts of the world, but to the myths of "immemorial imagination?"

THE JEWS AND REDEMPTIVE HISTORY

And what is it these stories reveal? What is the hidden meaning they conceal amid their trappings of Middle Eastern myth and imagery? The Bible and the identity and survival of the Jews are unanimous on this point-the Jews are a chosen people with a divine calling. Every fragment of the Genesis legends and sagas points up this assertion. By it, and it alone, the "truth" of their biblical history must be judged.

And what is the verdict? Are the Jews God's chosen people? Is the law a redemptive plan given them by divine revelation? The Bible says it is so, and our Space Age interpretation justifies its claim.

Traditional interpretations have strained the credulity and offended the common sense of Jews and Christians alike. Why would a just and benevolent God arbitrarily single out an obscure people for an unfair favoritism? This attitude is cynically reflected in the oft-repeated aphorism, "How odd of God to choose the Jews." Even more, having singled them out and unilaterally imposed a covenant on Abraham's descendants, why would he allow his chosen ones to suffer the exclusions, persecutions and even exterminations which the Jews have undergone? Assimilated Jews, who have rejected their Jewishness, are particularly prone to raise such questions-but so have the faithful. Is it possible to give an enlightened explanation of the idea of a chosen people, a special covenant and the law?

A SPACE-AGE VIEW OF GOD'S "CHOICE"

The starting point in an enlightened understanding of the Lord's "choice" of the Jews, then, is to recognize when he chose them. If our interpretation of the experimental creation is correct it was not when he called Abraham even though the mythic account seems to say this. It was not even earlier when he singled out Abraham's ancestor, Noah, for salvation from the flood. No, the Lord chose those who would become the Jews when he recreated them from an evolved homo sapiens. His choice of them was not a moral or a theological one-it was essentially genetic. The ancestors of Noah and

Abraham were "chosen" by the Lord when he chose to create them. They became his "people" when he designed them to be the people they are.

The later choices, when he covenanted with Noah and Abraham, were not instances of arbitrary favoritism-they were simply recognitions of an inbreeding population that had remained closest to what he originally intended.

THE JEWS AS A "LIVING FOSSIL"

The term "living fossils" is used, by paleontologists, to designate species that have existed through vast ages, while most others have become extinct. During this time they remain virtually unchanged and seemingly extinction-proof.

Earlier, in Chapter VIII, we quoted C. L. Brace and Ashley Montagu, who point out that fossils of the "ancient modern" who ancestored *homo sapiens sapiens* have never been found. And in the strictest sense this is, of course, true.

In another sense, however, there is good reason for believing the Jewish people are "living fossils" of the Lord's experimental creation. For in spite of some miscegenation and assimilation, they have endured as the people of his law. Over millennia, while all the civilizations that were their early contemporaries vanished, they have remained virtually unchanged in their essential culture, without a national identity, without a homeland and without even a common tongue.

Like the coelacanth and ginkgo tree, which have defied the biological laws governing the life of species, the Jews have defied historical laws that govern the life of civilizations.

In this sense, of course, their fossilhood is more figurative than real. There is substantial evidence, however, to support the idea that, as a gene pool, they also show a more literal kind of fossilhood. We have argued the created "ancient modern" was superior to contemporary humanity in intelligence and civilizational achievement. If the Jews represent a fossil survival of this gene type, they too might be expected to show superior capacity for intellectual and civilizational achievements. Is this, in fact, the case? The answer is an undeniable affirmative.

"AND THOU SHALT BE A BLESSING"

One of the most remarkable and inexplicable aspects of Jewish identity is its extraordinary record of intellectual and creative achievement. One has only to examine a roster of eminent men and women in almost any field of intellectual or artistic endeavor to verify that Jews are represented out of all proportion to their numbers.

Since they were first instituted in 1896 by Alfred Nobel, a Swedish chemist, the Nobel prizes have been, perhaps, the world's most prestigious recognition of civilizational achievement. They are awarded annually to the most outstanding contributors in physics, chemistry, medicine, literature and peace. Though Jews constitute only about .3% of the world's population they have received an astonishing 12% of the total of all Nobel prizes ever given; and in Germany alone, in the period preceding World War II, though they made up only 1% of the total German population, they won 50% of all Nobel prizes awarded.

Not only do Jews swell the ranks of eminence out of all proportion to their numbers, but the most sweeping intellectual revolutions in history have, to a remarkable degree, been the work of Jews. Though only one person out of every 300 is a Jew a predominance of Jewish names comes to mind when we think of the great intellectual upheavals that have shaped western civilization and shaken the world-Moses, Jesus, Marx, Freud and Einstein are examples.

The fields of philosophy, religion, science, the arts and philanthropy scintillate with Jewish genius. Sociologists tell us that Jews enter the learned professions more frequently, in proportion to their numbers, than do members of any other ethnic or religious group.

Such statistics inevitably call to mind the Lord's promise to Abraham: "And I will make of thee a great nation, and I will bless thee, and make thy name great; and thou shalt be a blessing ... and in thee shall all families of the Earth be blessed" (Genesis 12:2-3).

In the face of such evidence we are compelled to admit the Lord's promise has been abundantly fulfilled. Wherever Jews have gone, in their worldwide dispersion, they have brought honor and glory to their adopted homelands and bestowed on them the gifts of civilization.

It has been argued by some that Jewish achievement is not the result of genetic superiority but rather of an in-group culture which stresses achievement to an extraordinary degree. And undoubtedly this emphasis is present in the child rearing practices of many Jewish families. Sociologists agree it has been a primary cause of Jewish survival.

THE SOCIAL LABORATORY

This leads us to an inevitable question. Why? Why have Jews survived when all their early contemporaries have disappeared? Why do they excel in business and professional achievements? Why do they swell the ranks of genius and civilizational accomplishment out of all proportion to their numbers?

Is it because, as an inbreeding group in a direct line of descent from the experimental creation, they have retained an unusual amount of their original endowment? Is it, as C. P. Snow has suggested, because they are a "superior genetic pool"?

If our space age interpretation of the creation is correct they are the most direct descendants of the Lord's original experiment. And because they were chosen by him for a unique social experiment they have retained, over the millennia, the isolation and control necessary for maximum reinforcement of their genetic superiority. As those specially selected to spearhead the Lord's redemption of humanity they have remained in a social laboratory throughout the centuries – a social laboratory designed by the Celestials to preserve genetic superiority and reinforce excellence and righteousness in the human gene pool.

A laboratory, in a scientific experiment, can be defined as an isolated and controlled environment in which a scientific objective can be achieved. The isolation and control of the Lord's social laboratory was defined by the rules handed down to Moses – the law.

THE LAW

Scholars have debated the origin of the law. In reality it matters little whether the Lord gave it directly to Moses or it arose in some other manner. Its content is its own proof of Celestial origin. As a legal code it is unrivaled in wisdom and unique in the aims it seeks to accomplish. No other system devised by humanity has equaled its record of endurance, shown its adaptability to all the vicissitudes of the human condition, developed the subtleties and elaborations it has engendered or attempted the range and completeness it possesses.

As an instrument designed to make a people peculiar, separate and holy it has no parallel among other past or present legal systems. No aspect of life, however great or small, escapes its purview. In its historic embrace it has been careful to define standards of barbering, methods for cleansing dishes and utensils, menstrual hygiene, modes of dress, family obligations, business practices, sound nutrition, patterns of work and rest and rituals of worship.

According to Genesis it began with the Ten Commandments written by the finger of the Lord on Mount Sinai. Ultimately, as its revelation unfolded, it culminated in the Torah -the first five books of the Bible: Genesis, Exodus, Leviticus, Numbers and Deuteronomy. According to the Scriptures it is the legislation of Moses inspired by the guidance of the Lord. According to Jewish tradition it embraces 613 commands.

Over the millennia, since it was first given to the chosen people, it has undergone endless analysis, refinement, elaboration and application. Like any other system of laws its own content has been dwarfed by the mountainous structure of rulings and interpretations which have been erected on its foundation. The essence of these has been captured in a monumental work known as the Talmud. The eminent novelist and scholar of Judaism, Herman Wouk, in his book, This Is My God, claims that the Talmud is "the Encyclopedia Britanica and Blackstone of Judaism. Writing of it he calls it a "legal compendium" but like no other. Whereas most of them are "dry as dust" he finds the Talmud "combines" the most careful legal analysis with "illustrative and atmospheric detail" that conjures up "vibrant pictures of Judaism over the centuries."

Yet the heart of the law remains the Torah. And with the Torah we reach the second major artifact which proves the Celestials were here. In the chapter on The Experimental Creation, and earlier, we pointed out that humanity, itself, is the most convincing piece of hard evidence which shows that members of a Celestial civilization once walked the Earth. With our unparalleled strangeness and our unearthly brains we cannot adequately be accounted for by the mechanisms of evolution. Only the assumption that our development was interrupted and drastically improved, within an incredibly short period of time, can offer a sufficient explanation for our philosophical speculations, spiritual strivings, theorizings and creativity.

In the same way the Torah is a second piece of evidence which, on its face, bears the stamp of Celestial origin. We have seen, here and there as our Space Age interpretation has unfolded, that bits of knowledge disclosed in the Scriptures show unmistakable influence of an advanced civilization.

It is as though we are reading some epic or saga, supposedly handed down from the Greeks and Romans, and suddenly come upon a passage stating, "And so Neil Armstrong set foot on the moon." We would, at that point, quite reasonably assume the documents in our hand were not entirely the work of Greek and Roman authors.

In the same way when we suddenly read, in the Psalms or Job, that a "thousand years is as a day" with the Lord, or that "Arcturus with his sons" is "guided" through the heavens, we have evidence that millennia ago Bible writers knew things which we have heretofore believed to be modern discoveries.

In the Torah, we have a blueprint for human living which exhibits precisely the same sort of evidence. Throughout the five books which make up its structure, there is an unending stream of ordinance and counsel proving those who composed it had scientific knowledge surpassing our own in the 21st Century. In its insight into the human condition, its grasp of social psychology, its implied knowledge of biochemistry, nutrition and preventive medicine, it is unrivaled by any other ancient or modern code. The fact that it defines a life style which, alone among those of other ancient civilizations, has survived the ravages of four millennia, including conquest, exile, dispersion and holocaust, suggests there is something special about it.

Scholars have pointed out that many of its laws and prescriptions show parallels with the codes of other Near or Middle Eastern peoples. Some have even suggested that Moses largely borrowed the Ten Commandments of the Decalogue from Hammurabi, an earlier Babylonian lawgiver.

And these parallels do exist. But what these theories minimize, or neglect altogether, is the uniqueness of the law of Moses. Every society which has reached any significant level has had laws for the protection of life and property, for the compensation of the injured by those who injure them, for the punishment of those who threaten it and the protection of those who are innocent of wrongdoing.

Yet most ancient codes, like that of Hammurabi, are forms of class legislation which guarantee special privileges to the rich and powerful and strip those who lack status of basic human rights. Even our own constitution, in its original form, failed to protect the basic human rights of women and slaves. The Torah, on the other hand, gave equality, before the law, to all persons including "foreigners"- over 3,000 years ago.

Few codes, until modern times, have adequately recognized that health and nutrition, as well as a wholesome environment, are responsibilities of the state. Yet the Torah, 3,500 years ago, embodied pure food laws and public health measures which are more enlightened than those enforced by many modern governments, including our own.

The claim that most of these were simply borrowed from surrounding civilizations bas no real plausibility. There is nothing in the records of the ancient. Egyptians or Babylonians that even faintly suggests the extraordinary insight the Torah shows in forbidding foods rich in fat or high in purines. Only since the 20th Century, are biochemists beginning to prove the nutritional link between these dietary imbalances and degenerative diseases such as heart attacks, cancer, diabetes and gout

Early in this century, Sigmund Freud wrote a series of essays attempting to prove the law of Moses, as well as Moses himself, were of purely Egyptian origin. Arguing largely from a psychoanalytic study of comparative mythology, he claimed that circumcision, Abraham's covenantal mark of the chosen people, was borrowed from the Egyptians and was not a part of the original covenant. He argued that Moses was probably an Egyptian priest who had been discredited as a follower of Akhnaton, an heretical pharaoh, who worshipped one god. His religion was swept away, after his death, in a palace revolution. He proposed that Moses had carried this discredited religion into exile, taking a group of rebellious Hebrew slaves with him. Finally he suggested that Moses had imposed the worship of one God and a patchwork of Egyptian legislation on his followers in an attempt to exalt his own ego and perpetuate the immortality of his name.

Apart from the scholarly questions which Freud's views raise (and they have been severely challenged by recent scholarship), such an explanation of the law cannot account for its remarkable scientific insight and endurance. The Egyptian civilization, which he supposed spawned it, has long since disappeared, even though its peoples were not dispersed and have, throughout history, retained a national identity and homeland. How could Moses have extracted anything from it that would explain the unique endurance of the Jews? And, though the Egyptians were remarkably advanced for their times in their knowledge of medicine, surgery and pharmacology, there is no evidence they had a modern understanding of nutrition.

Yet the Torah, in passage after passage, displays the most advanced insights into the relation between diet and health. For example, in Leviticus we read: "Ye shall eat no manner of fat of ox, or of sheep, or of goat. And the fat of the beast that dieth of itself, and the fat of that which is torn with beasts, may be used in any other use: but ye shall in no wise eat of it" (Leviticus 7:23-24).

Not until the last century have laboratory and clinical studies clearly demonstrate the rationale behind this ancient prohibition. Biochemists now know that fats combine with oxygen, both in the bloodstream and outside the body (as with rancid meat), to produce free radicals – a process called "peroxidation." Clinical and experimental studies show these may attack blood vessel walls and genetic material to cause cardiovascular diseases and hasten other chronic diseases of aging.

Further, a high intake of saturated animal fats (the ones forbidden in Leviticus) has been directly linked, in numerous studies, with an increase in the incidence of heart attacks. The best known of these studies is the Framingham, which was sponsored by Boston University Medical Center and followed 5,000 residents of Framingham, Massachusetts, over a twenty five-year period. It showed high blood fat levels increased the risk of heart attack as much as 600%.

While the relation between diet and blood fat is not yet entirely clear numerous studies have recently shown nations having diets low in fat also tend to have significantly lower cardiovascular death rates, less incidence of cancer, less diabetes and joint disease and greater longevity.

These conclusions have become well enough established to win the support of government and other health agencies – 3,500 years after the ancient Hebrews received them in Leviticus. So the Senate Select Committee on Nutrition and Human Needs in the last century recommended a 25% reduction in American consumption of fats. Endorsements of this stand were also given by Gio Gori, of the National Cancer Institute, and David Hegsted, of the Harvard School of Public Health.

How did Moses, or the Hebrews of so long ago, know a high fat intake is a grave hazard to human health? Was it because this law was given to them by Celestials who understood human physiology in the light of a nutritional science more advanced than our own?

And how did the writers of the law know that shellfish can be harmful? What was the insight that prompted the writer of Leviticus to say: "... all that have not fins and scales in the seas, and in the rivers, of all that move in the waters, and of any living thing which is in the waters, they shall be an abomination unto you ..." (Leviticus II:10)? Could Israelites of 3,000 years ago have guessed these forbidden sea animals would be linked, in our time, to increased risk of joint and kidney disease because of a high purine content? Or had a race with higher biochemical wisdom already communicated this discovery to them?

"A SPECIAL PEOPLE"

And what of the remarkable sociological and psychological insights built into the law? Dissenters and assimilators in Judaism often chafe at the restrictiveness of Jewish kosher laws or the awkwardness of sabbath observance in a society which rests and worships on Sunday. And these aspects of the law are indeed irrational to outsiders, and they do make it difficult for Jews to work for, or even socialize with, Gentiles. But that is a part of their point. As the Lord observed to Moses so long ago, "For thou art a holy people unto the Lord thy God: the Lord thy God hath chosen thee to be a special people unto himself ... " (Deuteronomy 7:6).

The ingenuity involved in the Mosaic system of cleanliness and holiness taboos, and of special observances, lies precisely in the fact that it does make it difficult for Jews to work for anyone but Jews, to marry anyone but Jews and to go on vacation or have dinner or to worship with anyone but Jews.

The law is unique in its aim of isolating a people from the possibility of influence or assimilation by outsiders and making them unique and peculiar in their isolation and dedication to a legal code.

Other legal systems aim at equity and justice. The law of Moses includes these but also aims at the higher ideals of righteousness and holiness. To be sure the Jewish people have not always, or perhaps even often, lived up to these unearthly aims. But enough have aimed at them consistently enough so that the chosen people endure today after almost four millennia – a miracle of survival.

Herman Wouk points out that historians and social scientists, in searching for an explanation for the remarkable staying powers of the Jews, converge on the law of Moses as the principal factor. It has created an "institutional system" that has for more than two thousand years, in spite of "all possible adversities", preserved them from assimilation or extinction.

THE LAW AS "SCHOOLMASTER"

Yet, important as its survival value has been to the Jews, Paul, in the New Testament, argues that the law has a wider and higher meaning for the world at large. This value resides in the fact that the law is not just a compilation of rules; it is also a training device whose prescriptions and observances are types and symbols. In its symbolic function the law points to a higher way of life practiced on another world, a way of life which is the foundation of the Celestials' civilization. As such it is intended to disclose ultimate realities and values which lie beyond it. And the highest of these is the Celestial religion. The types and symbols of the law prepare the way for a new revelation of this spiritual heritage which was brought by the Redeemer. So he remarks: "Wherefore the law was our school master to bring us unto Christ, that we might be justified by faith" (Galatians 3:24).

As the stories of the patriarchs and Moses are redemptive history, so the rituals and observances of the law are redemptive symbology. In their ceremonial detail they foreshadow higher Celestial realities which will one day be established on Earth. So the writer of Hebrews remarks: "It was therefore necessary that the patterns of things in the heavens should be purified with these [sacrifices]; but the heavenly things themselves with better sacrifices than these" (Hebrews 9:23). The types and symbols of the law, then, prefigure higher realities of the Celestial religion for which it is a training.

Its demand for covenantal obedience points the way to a living faith which can ultimately fulfill and replace it. Its sacrificial rituals foreshadow the redemptive power of divine cosmic love exemplified in the life and death of the Redeemer. Its feasts and observances imitate the institutions and objectives of the Celestials' civilization which will one day be established on the planet, Earth.

In this sense the law is not just a life style for a "peculiar" people, but a preparation for Celestial citizenship-not only for Jews but for the world at large! Though a great part of its legal structure pertains only to the chosen people, and to certain periods in their development and history, others of its parts have universal relevance and embody the preparation and training the Celestials require of all who aspire to membership in their future utopia.

As we will see, the chosen people continue to occupy a special place in the

Lord's plan and will have a special role at the time of the end in the Celestials' future civilization. Yet in his fulfillment of the law the Redeemer opened up the plan embodied in the law to humanity at large.

In later chapters we will examine how the distinction may be drawn between those requirements that pertain peculiarly to the chosen people and those that were intended for humanity generally. In the final chapter we will examine, in detail, that most unique of all the law's observances, the sabbath. In it we shall discover a hidden meaning which places it at the heart of the Celestials' civilization and makes its observance the highest training for humans aspiring to Celestial citizenship. We will see how the tools of Space Age interpretation can reveal its awesome potential-not just as a religious occasion for rest and worship, but as the very key to the Celestials most prized possession, the secret of immortality!

Before attempting to grasp the ultimate secrets of Celestial civilization, however it will be helpful to take a closer look at some of their more practical achievements. Throughout much of the Bible, and particularly in the books known as "prophetic," a Space Age approach reveals startling similarities between what our own engineers and scientists have produced and what the Celestials revealed to those chosen as the Lord's human messengers. In the chapter which follows we will take a closer look at the hardware of the Celestials' civilization and the light it may throw on one of today's most profound mysteries.

For there is nothing covered that shall not be revealed; neither hid that shall not be known.

– Luke 12:3

CHAPTER XII

Celestials, Prophets and UFO's

In our survey of the civilization of the Celestials in preceding chapters we have seen that robotics play an important part in their domestic life on their own planet and in the furtherance of their colonization efforts throughout their galactic empire. Our own world is no exception as the account of Ezekiel's encounter with a fiery chariot in our chapter on Archeolinguistics showed. Ezekiel's encounter was by no means a singular event. Throughout the Bible, in both the Old and New Testaments, other similar encounters are found which clearly indicate the Celestials maintain an ongoing surveillance and monitoring of the progress of their colonization program here.

THE BIBLE AND SPACE CRAFT

Ezekiel's "chariot" is, perhaps, the best-known example of a spacecraft in the Bible. Numerous exponents of the ancient astronaut theory have seized on it as proof of extraterrestrial visits to Earth. And, in its detail, it is probably the most convincing. Its mention of "wheels" that "lift up" at takeoff and the accompanying noise of its flight "like the noise of great waters" (Ezekiel 2:19, 24), hardly sound like descriptions of a mystical vision. They are much more suggestive of 21st Century space hardware.

Yet Ezekiel's "chariot" is only one of many strange flying objects which appear in the Bible. And along with them we find descriptions of equipment and its usage which is much more suggestive of Space Age technology than of religious symbolism.

An analysis of these would easily require another book in itself. But it will be useful here at least to sample their range. In Old Testament times the spacecraft of the Celestials were so commonly seen they apparently were taken for granted and occasioned little or no excitement. So we find during the time of the Exodus and wilderness experience the children of Israel were led and visited by an object which is variously described as a "pillar of fire" (Exodus 14:24), a "cloud" (Exodus 24:15), a "devouring fire" (Exodus 24:17), and a "cloudy pillar" (Exodus 33:9). On one occasion the book of Exodus reports, "Mount Sinai was altogether on a smoke, because the Lord descended upon it in fire: and the smoke thereof ascended as the smoke of a furnace, and the whole mount quaked greatly" (Exodus 19:18).

Almost five hundred years later the Prophet Elijah is reported to have been carried alive into heaven by a fiery "chariot." Strangely it is suggestive of Ezekiel's craft, for it, too, involved "living creatures" which are described as "horses" by Elijah's companion, Elisha. So II Kings reports: "And it came to pass, as they still went on and talked that, behold, there appeared a chariot of fire and horses of fire, and parted them both asunder; and Elijah went up by a whirlwind into heaven" (II Kings 2:11).

Reacting to this remarkable exit Elisha cried out, "My father, my father, the chariot of Israel, and the horsemen thereof!" (II Kings 2:12). Apparently the Lord's craft was well enough known, by then, that it was commonly recognized as "the chariot of Israel." A little earlier Israel's great King David tells how the Lord "rode upon a cherub, and did fly: and he was seen upon the wings of the wind" (II Samuel 22:11).

Interestingly, "a cherub" is how Ezekiel also .describes the strange "living creatures" with "wings," "arms" and "faces," which made up the helicopter units of his "chariot." So the Lord instructs a technician who is servicing his "chariot": "Go in between the wheels, even under the cherub, and fill thine hand with coals of fire from between the cherubims, and scatter them over the city" (Ezekiel 10:2).

We have already seen that "cherubs" are servomechanisms which can take many forms, including that of flying craft. And the instructions for servicing this "cherub" sound suspiciously like some sort of waste disposal procedure preliminary to refueling.

Other prophets, too, report on flying objects. Isaiah tells how he saw the Lord sitting upon a "throne" which was "high and lifted up." Like Ezekiel's craft a loud, commanding voice issued from it which caused the "posts of the door" to move. And like the Exodus "cloud" it filled the house with "smoke" (Isaiah 6:1, 4). The prophet Zechariah also tells of a "vision" in which he saw a "flying roll," over 30 feet long and 17 feet wide, which had human-like figures "in its midst" that "lifted" it up "between the earth and the heaven." Again they are strangely reminiscent of Ezekiel's man-like helicopter units, though Zechariah describes them as "women", rather than men, with "wings like the wings of a stork" (Zechariah 5:1-9).

Later he tells how he saw "four chariots" come out from "two mountains" that were "mountains of brass" (Zechariah 6:1-3)-a good description for the most common form of "flying saucers." Like Elijah's "fiery chariot" these chariots had "horses" which could be jettisoned and in which pilots, as in David's poetic description, could "ride on the wings of the wind."

This unusually precise description of a mother ship disgorging small craft, or modules, is reminiscent of J. F. Blumrich's conclusion that Ezekiel's chariot was designed to serve as a shuttle between a mother ship and the surface of the Earth.

Finally, in the New Testament, John the Revelator describes a "vision" (probably a televised view) of a command center we have already examined in Chapter VII, Colony Earth. The context of the description makes it clear that the center is not part of a fixed base, but is actually itself a craft remarkably similar to Ezekiel's. Like his chariot it has a central "throne" flanked by four "beasts" with the "faces" of a lion, a calf, a man and an eagle. Like Ezekiel's beasts these have wings; "Seven lamps of fire" burn before its "throne," reminiscent of Ezekiel's "appearance of lamps" which emitted lightning-like flames. A man-like being sits on its throne and "thunderings and voices" come from the "throne." And, like Ezekiel's craft, the command capsule of this "throne" is surrounded by a "rainbow" (Revelation 4:2-8).

It appears that this command center is much larger than Ezekiel's, since it accommodates twenty-four "elders," and it may be housed in a mother spome which is probably the "New Jerusalem," docked on Mazzaroth. The four "beasts" with "eyes and wings" are clearly similar to Ezekiel's "living beings," since they have "faces" that resemble animals and men to these early writers. Yet, as we saw in Chapter II, they apparently contain computers as well as helicopter units. The presence of mechanical arms and leg pods combine to suggest still another function of these ingenious "living creatures." When attached to the main craft they obviously "lift it up," as Zechariah suggested. When jettisoned they can fly independently and serve as modules in which passengers can "ride on the wings of the wind."

But they also have nonflying functions on the ground. When the craft is taxiing, and they are attached, they can collect samples or move obstacles out of the way with their mechanical arms. Their wheels "full of eyes" (as Ezekiel describes them in 1:18) transmit a continuous panorama, by closed-circuit television, of the terrain and obstacles which cannot be seen from the command capsule above.

When they are detached, on the ground, they become independent automata, or robots-the Bible's familiar "cherubim" with wings. Equipped with heads that contain computers and are studded with eyelike sensors, possessing mechanical arms and leg pods, these "likenesses of men" can range out from the craft and perform whatever chores are assigned to them by the commander from the capsule. When it is convenient they walk, and at other times they fly with their wings.

The different animal-like faces they possess are doubtless due to the fact that they are programmed for different functions. The features of a specific face make it easy for controlling Celestials to recognize their programming and capabilities at a glance when they send them out. They may also be the result, in part, of the designs of their different circuits which give different configurations to their "faces." The Bible supports this idea of different types and functions among the "creatures" by calling some "cherubim" and others "seraphim."

Various biblical prophets tell of encounters with these man-like "creatures." So the writer of the book of Daniel tells how he had a "vision" by the River Hiddekel (Tigris), in which he saw a "certain man." Like the familiar cherubim of Ezekiel its "arms and feet" were "like in colour to polished brass." When the creature spoke to him Daniel went into a "deep sleep," but later was awakened when its "hand" touched him and set him "upon my knees and upon the palms of my hands." His comment upon its overall appearance is that it was "like the appearance of a man" (Daniel 0:5-18).

Similarly the Prophet Isaiah tells how, after the doorpost moved and smoke filled the house, a "seraphim" flew to him "having a live coal in his hand, which he had taken with the tongs from off the altar" (Isaiah 6:6). This seraphim had previously "stood" above the "throne" of the Lord which was "high and lifted up" (Isaiah 6:1-2). Apparently the craft here was large enough to straddle the building the writer occupied.

The confusion of these automata with the Celestials themselves, over the centuries, eventually gave rise to the winged angels of medieval art. It is ironic that these mythical representations, which the artists regarded as depicting creatures next to God himself, were actually prompted by mere mechanical contrivances rather than the noble beings that designed them!

Going back to the Scriptures it is evident from passages we have already quoted, and many others found especially in the prophetic books, that their writers were convinced other worldly beings have maintained and continue to maintain a surveillance of our world. In these books they are sometimes referred to as "watchers".

In the book of Daniel we read that "the king saw a watcher and an holy one coming down from heaven ... " (Daniel 4:23). And, again, in Jeremiah, that prophet warns, "publish against Jerusalem, that watchers come from a far country, and give out their voice against ... Judah" (Jeremiah 4:16). The Hebrew words used in these passages are "iyr" and "nâtsar," which refer to guardian beings and carry the meaning of observing and protecting as well as concealment.

In Project Blue Book and other reviews of modern UFO sightings we find a similar conviction among many that surveillance has continued down to our own time. The consensus of evidence on the "hard-core" unexplained UFO cases suggests they are flying craft which follow patterns of intelligent control. Report data indicate their performance exceeds the best man-made aircraft or spacecraft can do. They defy known principles of aerodynamics. They apparently can fly at many times the speed of conventional aircraft; they are capable of right-angle turns or reversals of direction at high speeds and can hover or ascend vertically. In fact, their maneuvers closely resemble those described in Chapter IV by Arthur C. Clarke when he speculates on the behavior of craft employing a "gravity shield" and "inertialess drive".

Evidently, then, the writers of these prophetic books believed Celestials maintain a constant vigilance over the affairs of this world. This idea is also supported by UFO reports coming from a no less prestigious source than the Apollo Space Missions. It was common knowledge, among those closely associated with the Apollo Moon Mission, that our own astronauts were closely monitored while going to and from the moon. Though such reports were not disclosed to the news media, a number of those involved have since made disclosures in articles and books. One of these, Maurice Chatelain, an aerospace engineer who designed and built communication and data processing equipment for the project, comments on these strange events in his book, Our Ancestors Came from Outer Space. He claimed that the Apollo and Gemini flights were followed, both at a distance and sometimes quite closely, by space vehicles of extraterrestrial origin-flying saucers, or UFOs. He states that Walter Schirra, aboard Mercury 8, was the first of the astronauts to use the code name 'Santa Claus' to indicate the presence of flying saucers next to space capsules. He also writes James Lovell, on board the Apollo 8 command module, came out from behind the dark side of the moon and said for everybody to hear: 'We have been informed that Santa Claus does exist.' He writes James McDevitt was the first to photograph an unidentified flying object. He also claims Frank Borman and James Lovell took magnificent photographs of two UFOs following Gemini 7. Finally, when Apollo 11 made the first moon landing on the Sea of Tranquility he reports two UFOs hovered overhead.

In his book Maurice Chatelain also claims Edwin Aldrin took several pictures which were published in the June 1975 issue of Modern People magazine. The magazine did not tell where it got them vaguely hinting at a Japanese source.

That the victorious Celestials, as well as the fallen ones, keep a close surveillance on this planet seems warranted by both the biblical evidence and UFO reports. Indeed, the report data, when viewed as a whole, seem to suggest two different sorts of UFOs. It is almost as though unidentified flying objects are of two totally distinct origins. Some are small, crude and "homemade"' in appearance-obviously short-range craft; others are massive and possess elaborate and refined equipment and accessories-the sort that would be suitable for interstellar travel. Both types seem to avoid human contact for the most part. This would be expected if the victorious Celestials are here primarily to monitor the progress of colony Earth and ensure that the fallen Celestials confine their activities to this region of the galaxy where their rebellion took place.

J. Allen Hynek, one of America's most prestigious astronomers in the last century and consultant to the U.S. Air Force's Project Blue Book, noted, in reviewing that report, that UFO sightings seemed to fall into several groups according to their visual characteristics and size, and the absence or presence of occupants.

He reserves a final category, "close encounters of the third kind," for those sightings in which "animated" occupants are reported to have actually interacted with human observers. Believing them to be "extraterrestrials" the acronym for this word, "E.T.", then became the title for a highly successful science-fantasy film on the subject.

Reports in this category are, however, by no means new. The Bible is full of them as we have already seen. In the second phase of the Celestials' colonization program, when they monitored humans closely, many such "encounters" were reported.

The Prophet Ezekiel has an unusually lengthy and detailed report of going for a visit to a base of the Celestials in the flying craft we studied in chapter II. (Ezekiel 40). Later in the New Testament Jesus has an encounter with a strange lighted object ("a bright cloud" which "overshadowed") while he was gathered with his disciples on a mountain. Two occupants, reported to be "Moses and Elias [Elijah]," descend and converse with him, and he is transfigured-his face shines "as the sun" and his clothes become "white as light" (Matthew 17:1-5 and Mark 9:2-7).

The important point here, however, is that the explanation of UFOs we have offered covers not only remote sightings but more intimate ones, as well. And it covers them all which the "misinterpreted natural phenomena" clearly cannot.

With regard to the fallen Celestials it also explains why a small proportion of close encounters appear to be malevolent. Report literature contains a number of instances in which UFOs or their occupants are claimed to have abducted humans and subjected them to frightening or incapacitating energies and their cars or homes scorched with laser-like beams or perhaps even destroyed. In the latter group is the much debated incident involving Captain Thomas Mantell, an Air Force pilot, whose plane crashed, or was disintegrated, while pursuing a UFO.

And for encounters with craft of both victorious and fallen Celestials the possibility remains that occupants sighted are not Celestials, themselves, but cherubim or seraphim robots with artificial intelligence. This would account for the descriptions given by some contactees, which say occupants lack features or possess anatomical proportions improbable for living creatures.

THE FALLEN CELESTIALS' HEADQUARTERS

One of the most interesting questions still remains to be answered. Since the exiled Celestials need bases, where are they located? Why has the Air Force, or other investigative groups, not tracked them to their lair? Where could a community, or communities, of extraterrestrials hide for centuries? There are, of course, still unexplored areas on the Earth. The most extensive and logical of these would be the depths of the seas. Almost three-fifths of the Earth's surface is underwater, and the depths of the oceans have never been systematically explored.

It would be a simple matter for advanced extraterrestrials to construct a spome on the ocean's floor where they could form unearthly societies and store the equipment and craft of an advanced civilization. This idea acquires added plausibility when we consider that our own scientists are already creating designs for underseas communities. Plans are now underway for building large submerged laboratories where numbers of scientists and technicians could live and work for prolonged periods of time.

If the fallen Celestials have earthly underwater bases, however, it is likely that, with modern technologies of radar, sonar and satellite surveillance some evidence of their existence or of travel to and from them would have been found.

What seems more probable is that habitable bases have been established off the Earth, close enough to make visits and operations involving it a matter of hours or days using their advanced spacecraft. As for sightings of their comings and goings the "unexplained" core of UFO sightings reported in Project Blue Book may include such evidence.

In summing up his final evaluation of Project Blue Book, J. Allen Hynek had this to say concerning its evidence: "We can start with the knowledge that the UFO phenomenon is global, that UFO reports persist in this and other countries despite the Condon Report and the closing of Project Blue Book, and that many small groups of scientifically trained people, especially young scientists, are expressing interest in the subject and dissatisfaction with the manner in which it has been treated in the past." Even more pointedly, a subcommittee set by the prestigious Institute of Aeronautics and Astronautics to study the UFO phenomenon reported: "Taking all evidence which has come to the subcommittee's attention into account, we find it difficult to ignore the small residue of well documented but unexplainable cases which form the hard core of the UFO controversy."

There are moreover official government records now declassified and released under the Freedom of Information Act that show our presidents have had an ongoing involvement in the UFO issue since the end of World War II.

In his book, The President's and UFOs, A Secret History from FDR to Obama, Larry Holcombe, freelance writer and investigator, included photocopies of documents marked "Top Secret" that clearly show a number of presidents over the last three quarters of a century, have been concerned and issued statements concerning investigation into the nature of the UFO phenomenon and its relevance to national security.

Returning to the question of where exiled Celestials might maintain bases off the Earth, "close" enough to allow regular visits, recent evidence produced by NASAs' unmanned missions to our other planets may provide possible answers. Unmanned flybys of both Jupiter and Saturn have revealed that Jupiter's moon Europa, and Saturn's moon, Enceladus, evidently have large subsurface reserves of liquid water. These may harbor life and could house underwater bases.

Advanced extraterrestrials would have little difficulty in establishing underwater bases on these or other moons in our solar system. Travel time to Earth would be as easily accomplished, with spacecraft travelling at a sizeable fraction of the speed of light, as we manage international air travel.

THE FALLEN CELESTIALS' HEADQUARTERS

For both victorious and fallen Celestials the purpose of visits to Earth would probably be both information gathering and aid or harm to its human populations. In carrying out such missions, like out own intelligence agents, they would at times assume "human" covers and identities in order to move freely in achieving their objectives.

We have already seen, in chapter V, that the Old Testament gives several accounts of people encountering "angels" who mistake them for humans until they do something that reveals their extraterrestrial origin. Abraham and Lot entertain "angels" mistaking them for ordinary travelers (Gen. 19:2). Jacob wrestles with another whom he mistakes for an ordinary intruder. (Gen. 32:24-30) In the New Testament the author of the book of Hebrews admonishes readers to "be not forgetful to entertain strangers for thereby some have entertained angels unawares". (Hebrews 13:2)

Obviously such anecdotal accounts cannot be taken as prima facie evidence that Celestials have walked among us. There is however one case of an alleged wonder worker that stands out above all others, for whom an extraterrestrial origin and mission has been and still is claimed. In the next chapter we will consider the accounts and archeolinguistic import of texts that support this claim.

> For I know that my redeemer liveth, and that he shall stand at the latter day upon the Earth ...

> – Job 19:25

CHAPTER XIII

The Redeemer

In 1742, George Frederick Handel set Job's immortal confession of living faith to immortal music. Opening the concluding part of the great oratorio, "I know that my redeemer liveth" rises to spiritual heights that are almost Celestial in their elevation.

Speaking of Handel's magnificent achievement one modern critic observed: "... the opening sections of 'Messiah' are already touched with radiance. Only a composer drunk with inspiration could proceed from this point to ever higher levels of greatness."

Yet the artistic tributes to the carpenter of Nazareth are dwarfed by the sheer impact of his existence and its consequences. There are some who question his reality. Even his most devoted chroniclers did not agree entirely about his deeds and sayings.

The records of his life indicate he had little or no formal education; he never married or had a family; his only job skill was rough carpentry; he never owned a home or a decent wardrobe; his ministry scarcely carried him beyond the region where he was born; he was never appointed to a political post or office; and he died at thirty-three, a convicted criminal, by the most hideous form of capital punishment the ancient world could devise.

Yet more books have been written about him than any other man who ever lived. His name is probably more widely known than that of any other human being. His followers today number in the hundreds of millions. That most famous of world conquerors, Napoleon, had this to say about his existence: "Alexander, Caesar, Charlemagne, and myself founded empires; but on what foundations did we rest the creations of our genius? Upon force. Jesus Christ founded an empire upon love; and at this hour millions of men would die for him."

THE PROBLEM

Over 60,000 books on Jesus are said to have been written in the 19th century alone. The literary flood has swollen since. Most of these have been concerned with establishing the facts of his life or the meaning of his message. Yet they have arrived at no consensus. Scholars and followers alike cannot agree on what Jesus did or believed or taught.

The problem lies in the records of his life. Like Noah and Abraham and Moses he is a legendary hero. He exists, like them, not in the pages of scholarly history, but in the redemptive prophecies and legends of the Bible-and in the living faith of his followers. Unlike them the Scriptures and his followers credit him with a unique mission and identity. This claim is simply, and starkly, that he was, and is, God!

Of course, many religions, and even some political systems, claim their founders, or leaders, were gods. Some have even regarded them as being immortal, and, when they proved they were not, reinstated them by proclaiming they had risen from the dead.

But the religion founded by the historical Jesus and his followers is different. It proclaims a resurrected Jesus, the Christ, as living in the world today, through the invisible church of his followers. The ancient rivals of his church, the mystery religions, Mithraism, Gnosticism have all disappeared. Their leaders and gods, resurrected or otherwise are no longer followed or worshipped.

But the Christ of the resurrection continues in the lives of his followers who live in and through him. So the Apostle Paul eloquently expresses this mystical insight of the indwelling Christ, "...I live; yet not I, but Christ liveth in me: and the life which I now live in the flesh I live by the faith of the Son of God, who loved me, and gave himself for me" (Galatians 2:20). And again, more poetically and with sublime simplicity, this former archenemy of Christianity confesses, "For to me to live is Christ ..." (Philippians 1:21). How did a man as obscure as Jesus achieve such a hold on the hearts and minds of men and women throughout the ages? The problem is without a historic parallel.

THE HISTORICAL RECORD

The record of Jesus' life is contained in the first five books of the New Testament, the four gospels and the Acts of the Apostles. The writers are held, by tradition, to have been disciples-Matthew, Mark, Luke and John, the Beloved. Luke is generally also credited with authorship of Acts. He undoubtedly speaks for all the writers when he says their purpose was "to set forth in order a declaration of those things which are most surely believed among us" (Luke 1:1).

His declaration makes it clear that in the gospel record, once again, as all through the Bible, we are dealing with redemptive history, not just the usual textbook variety. It was not the purpose of the writers simply to give a factual narrative of events. They selected and arranged and interpreted the facts for the purpose of emphasizing their redemptive message. As a result there are differences of emphasis, minor discrepancies and doctrinal divergences, which distinguish these several accounts.

There is a general agreement that the four gospels achieved their earliest written form in the last third of the first century. Mark is thought to be the oldest (about 70 A.D.) and John the last (probably 95 A.D.). Matthew and Luke are believed to have borrowed heavily from Mark. Because these three gospels share many incidents in common they are called the synoptic gospels (from the Greek, "seen together"). John, on the other hand, omits the parables contained in the other gospels and presents Jesus and his teaching in a more philosophical and mystical light.

THE LIFE OF JESUS

Since these records are somewhat divergent in detail and point of view, and may have passed through many hands, some New Testament scholars seriously doubt their accuracy. This is especially so where the accounts show strong parallels to the myths of other cultures or to "types" and "symbols" which are supposed to foreshadow them in the Old Testament. Elaborate parallels of this sort suggest literary tampering. Some have even gone so far as to argue that this prevents our knowing anything for sure about the historical Jesus.

Yet, we must once again remember that the weight of present-day scholarship is against this position. As we have already seen, culture heroes are usually developed out of the lives of real people. As Abraham and Moses were probably real, so, even more, is it likely the gospels disclose a real Jesus. For Jesus is much nearer our own time, and the picture we get of him is accordingly more detailed and vivid. And in its vividness and psychological probability it carries a conviction of truth.

Besides, secular history is not silent concerning Jesus as it is for Abraham and Moses. Historians and social critics of his day, or soon after, speak of him-Pliny, Tacitus, Suetonius, the Jewish historian Josephus, and even the Talmud. And, significantly, even those most opposed to Christianity did not question his existence or his centrality to the new faith.

The narrative of the gospels is simply told. An angel appears to Mary who is "espoused" to Joseph. The angel tells her she will conceive of the "Holy Ghost." In due time she becomes pregnant, though still a virgin, according to the custom of the day which required a waiting period before consummating marriage. She and Joseph journey to Bethlehem, from Nazareth, for a census count. While there Jesus is born (probably in the year 6 b.c.).

Herod, the king, hears his throne is endangered by a new born "king." He orders the death of newborn infants, and Joseph and Mary flee to Egypt with their child. After Herod's death they return to Nazareth where Jesus is apprenticed to Joseph and learns the carpenter's trade. Apparently he also studies the law, for at twelve he is examined in the Temple at Jerusalem, where his parents are celebrating Passover and astounds its teachers with his knowledge.

His later youth is unchronicled until he appears at the River Jordan, in his thirtieth year, to be baptized by his cousin, John the Baptist. He undergoes a profound spiritual experience, withdraws for forty days of solitude and meditation, then begins his ministry.

He gathers a group of twelve disciples about him and begins a career of teaching and healing which extends from Galilee to Judea. He preaches in synagogues proclaiming the coming kingdom of God. He heals the sick, exorcises evil spirits and even raises the dead. He walks on water, feeds 5,000 with a few loaves and fish and proclaims an unworldly ethic in the Sermon on the Mount. Yet his tolerance of sinners, his outspoken manner and his popularity, antagonize the influential pharisees. A later Herod hears of his teaching and miracles and fearing he is the Messiah or John the Baptist returned to life plots with the leaders of the pharisees to kill him.

Jesus flees with his disciples to Judea. After preaching there for several months he makes a final visit to Jerusalem for Passover. He is given a hero's welcome by the common people. A large procession accompanies him to the Temple, where he cleanses it of sacrilege by overturning the tables of money changers and driving out the vendors of sacrificial animals.

On the eve of the Passover Jesus celebrates Seder with his disciples. Afterward he retires to the Garden of Gethsemen where he is arrested. He is tried before the Sanhedrin, the Jewish high court, and convicted of blasphemy for claiming he is the son of God. Since the Sanhedrin cannot carry out the death penalty they bring him before the Roman governor, Pilate, who extracts an admission from him that he is "a King." With this evidence of treason to Caesar Pilate sentences Jesus to die by crucifixion. The order is carried out and he dies an agonized death on the cross.

On the following Sunday morning a group of women who have been close to him come to his tomb to pay their last respects. The stone is rolled away and a person who is nearby says, "Be not affrighted: Ye seek Jesus of Nazareth, which was crucified: he is risen; he is not here: behold the place where they laid him" (Mark 16:6).

Afterward Jesus appears to his close friend, Mary Magdalene, and the disciples. He commissions them to "preach the gospel to every creature" (Mark 16:15) and shortly after ascends into "heaven." Such, in essence, is the gospel story, with some variations from one gospel to another.

Only Matthew and Luke give infancy stories, and Luke does not mention the flight to Egypt. Only Luke deals with Jesus' later youth. John, as we said before, omits the parables which form such an important part of Jesus' teaching in the synoptic gospels. When it comes to the great central event of Christianity, the resurrection, there are the usual divergences one expects when several witnesses are reporting an emotionally charged event. Matthew says an "angel" rolled the stone away and spoke to all the women who came to the tomb (Matthew 28:2-5). Mark says it was a "young man" who actually sat in the tomb and spoke to them '(Mark 16:5). Luke says "two men" in "shining garments" addressed the women (Luke 24:4-7), and John says it was "two angels" who spoke to Mary alone (John 20:12-13).

Yet, in its main outlines, the story is remarkably consistent considering it was set down nearly half a century, or more, after the events and by at least four different writers of diverse backgrounds. The picture of Jesus and his followers is extraordinarily vivid. And it rings true psychologically. A clever novelist might have created some of the habits and mannerisms and motivations of the principal characters, even including Jesus. But four different writers could hardly have achieved the consistent and fleshed-out portraits that emerge. They have the feel of reality about them. And historians and archaeologists have verified that many of the background circumstances and events recounted are actual or characteristic for that time.

THE "GOOD NEWS"

From this story the apostolic church gathered its central articles of faith-- the redemptive message. This was the gospel they preached-the "good news." It focused on the three pivotal events of Jesus' life-his birth, his death and his resurrection. In his birth they proclaimed God became man-"the Word was made flesh, and dwelt among us" (John 1:14). In his death they proclaimed he atoned for the sins of the world: "But God commendeth his love toward us, in that, while we were yet sinners, Christ died for us" (Romans 5:8) . And in his resurrection they proclaimed he conquered death so that we all might have eternal life: "our Saviour Jesus Christ . . .hath abolished death, and hath brought life and immortality" (II Timothy 1:10). This was the good news that sustained the early church through savage suppressions and incredible persecutions. It is the faith on which it has endured for 2,000 years.

Are its claims valid? Do they proclaim historic fact, or are they outmoded mythology? This question has been a growing concern in Christian theology of the last two centuries. With the advance of science and the rise of higher criticism of the Bible increasing numbers of Christians have come to question the fundamental beliefs on which historic Christianity was built.

Speaking for many of them, the German theologian, Rudolf Bultmann, expressed the central problem of modern faith. He wrote that the gospel story is "incredible". It is no longer believable for modern men and women whose knowledge compels them to reject a New Testament view of the world.

The solution to this problem, Bultmann believes, is to "demythologize" the good news. Unlike earlier higher critics he was not willing to dismiss the whole gospel record as the superstitions of a bygone age. Rather, he felt that underneath its surface incredibilities lay a core of genuine revelation. This can be disclosed, he claimed, by removing the mythic "envelope" that surrounds it.

"DEMYTHOLOGIZING" DEMYTHOLOGIZED

The difference between our Space Age view of Jesus and Bultmann's lies in what is to be taken as mythic. We have no desire to minimize the value and the contributions of recent New Testament scholarship. And it has successfully shown that the gospel record emerged by stages and from a variety of sources. And there can be little doubt that in the process the remembered deeds and sayings of Jesus underwent some reworking and even mythic elaboration.

But this does not mean the gospel story, as a whole, is a "mythological envelope." Nor does it mean its cardinal claims are "incredible," or that modern men and women can no longer hold a New Testament view of the world."

The problem with Bultmann's program of "demythologizing" is that it rests, itself, on a mythic worldview - the view of late Nineteenth Century scientific materialism. And what Bultmann failed to realize was that, even before he wrote Kerygma and Myth, this worldview had already been refuted by developments in Twentieth Century science. Bultmann's judgment that the New Testament view of the world was obsolete was made from the perspective of his own worldview which, itself, had become obsolete.

For Twentieth Century discoveries in physics, astronomy, medicine and psychology have thoroughly invalidated his assumptions that the incarnation, the resurrection, extraterrestrial civilizations and the advent of Celestials to our world are "incredible."

In spite of the obsolescence of the worldview of mechanistic materialism, or "naturalism" as it is often called, it persists as a bedrock assumption on the part of many liberal and skeptical historians of religion and theologians. A recent publication, How Jesus Became God, by Bart D. Ehrman, a professor of religious history at the University of North Carolina, is typical of this trend.

Like Bultmann he starts off with the assumption that Jesus was simply a "lower class Jewish preacher" from a rural Galilean "backwater." Despite this unpromising beginning he was then "exalted": by credulous followers, to the status of "God". This status was then secured for history by fictitious miracle myths invented by the obscure gospel writers of the New Testament.

To establish this claim he then points out that the claims made for Jesus were by no means unique. Claims of messiahship were rife among the discontented Jewish population of the time under harsh and oppressive Roman rule.

Under the heading "A Remarkable Life" he then points out that Apollonius of Tyana, who, like Jesus, was claimed by his followers to have had a divinely induced birth also had an itinerant ministry of healing, casting out demons, raising the dead and, after his death, ascending into heaven.

Further he points out, Apollonius was only one of many such false messiahs of the time for whom similar claims were made. Why then, he asks, should we give any more credence to the claims of the gospel writers than to those made for these other "messiahs", particularly since they are all incredible from an enlightened scientific viewpoint today.

In fact, he implies, there is more reason to believe the claims made about Apollonius than those about Jesus, since his chronicler was a well known Pythagorean philosopher, Philostratus, and his following was greater among the Roman elite.

Yet Apollonius is largely unknown today, as Professor Ehrman himself admits, while Jesus can reasonably be claimed to be the most widely known and most renowned person who ever lived.

One could probably walk the streets of almost any major city in the world today and question the first hundred persons met without finding one who had ever heard of Apollonius of Tyana. On the other hand, if they were asked, it is doubtful if even one could be found who had not heard of Jesus.

Professor Ehrman's argument is that it was the naive credulity of his followers, and the mythic "exaltation" created by the gospel writers that account for his millions of followers today. This fails to explain, however, why millions would die for him today, as Napolean observed, or why millions have already been willing to die for his cause over the centuries.

As an explanation of how Jesus came to be worshipped as "God" Professor Ehrman's argument is a total failure. The obscurity he attributes to Jesus himself; the fact that his first followers were among the poorest and most dispossessed in Roman society; the fact that the gospel writers identities are in question even today - all should have resulted in his memory being more completely obliterated than many of the other "messiahs" of his time. Yet just the opposite occurred.

The miracle of his life and its impact on history and the world can only be explained by admitting that something about his identity sets him apart from any other person who ever lived. Viewed in this light the claim of the gospels that he was of an otherworldly origin takes on a unique plausibility - a plausibility that is consistent with the Space Age worldview that is emerging in 21st Century science and that is supported by an archeolinguistic analysis of the gospel record.

RECOVERING THE JESUS OF HISTORY

Yet other theologians have been much more optimistic about knowing the real Jesus. So Bernhard Anderson, commenting on recent New Testament criticism, argues we are not driven to skepticism about the historical Jesus. We face the same problem in dealing with Socrates who left no writings and is known only by his impact on others. The fragments of oral tradition incorporated in the texts are invaluable for they give vivid glimpses of Jesus in action, "small tableaux" of his ministry. From them we can reconstruct much of his career and essential aspects of his message.

So it is that, once again, our Space Age approach to the Bible offers a prospect of bringing new light to bear on ancient truths. By focusing on the language of the texts, and those "glimpses" and "small tableaux" of which Bernhard Anderson speaks, we have discovered a new perspective on the historical Jesus.

And in this perspective he emerges not as the First-Century cult leader and magician some recent scholars have made him out to be. Nor does he fit the portrait of Nineteenth-Century higher critics who saw him as a psychotic with fixed delusions of messiahship and divinity. He does not even fit the sympathetic portrayal of Albert Schweitzer, who attempted his rescue from Nineteenth Century higher criticism.

He emerges as more than the good man and great teacher who reasonably, though mistakenly, believed he would fulfill the messianic expectations of his age.

Surprisingly he is recovered much as he appeared to the apostles and those who proclaimed the "good news" in the early church. He appears simply and plausibly as the Lord's promised Redeemer.

IS THE "GOOD NEWS" SCIENTIFICALLY PLAUSIBLE?

We have already seen, in our opening chapters, that modern "miracles" such as teleportation, resurrection and even immortality are already being predicted for our own future by scientific futurologists. We have also seen that archeolinguistic analysis of Scripture indicates celestials had already mastered these technologies when the scriptures were written.

If these things are so they mean the "good news", the incarnation, the miracles of Jesus' ministry, the resurrection, his ascent into heaven and his ultimate return in the clouds, are not incredible. In themselves they are perfectly credible if we attribute them to a civilization far more advanced than our own. What made them incredible to Bultmann is that the gospels seem to claim them for a First-Century carpenter in an insignificant outpost of the Roman Empire.

But if Jesus was not just an obscure human carpenter-if he was an advanced extraterrestrial sent on an undercover mission to Earth-then all the things Bultmann finds incredible about his life must be reconsidered.

It would be logical and necessary that he would be "landed" on Earth in a way that would give him a believable "cover." And by being born into a human family of a human mother he would have the most perfect "cover" possible. No one could reasonably question his humanity. It would also be probable he would exhibit advanced knowledge and powers that would seem "supernatural" to his contemporaries and "mythological" to modern critics.

The only thing that is improbable in the gospel record, if he was a Celestial, is his death. We will consider the remarkable reasons for it later in this chapter. We will only note here that it requires some extraordinary explanation. For if he were a Celestial he could surely have avoided it, or those who sent him could have rescued him from it.

Once it occurred, however, his resurrection would be a matter of course, as would his removal from our world when his mission was finished and it would be likely it would be by some sort of advanced technology that seemed "miraculous" to his followers and still seems so to conservative biblical literalists today. A Space Age view of his ascension, however, offers the possibility of teleportations as the means by which it was accomplished.

In our chapter, How To Take Over the World, we cited Professor Michio Kaku's observation that, since we have already teleported photons and atoms, nothing, in principle would prevent the teleportation of people in the future. We also referred to Arthur C. Clark's *Profiles of the Future*. In it he proposes that, since we can send sounds and images around the world at the speed of light, it is reasonable to believe that in the future we will be able to teleport "solid objects - even 'men'" in the same way. Summing up his argument he states his belief that in our future we will be able to "move from pole to pole within the throb of a single heartbeat"

If the Celestial's civilization is millions of years in advance of our own then the teleportation of Jesus , when his mission was accomplished, would be a matter of course and would appear to his First Century followers as it is reported in the New Testament gospels.

All of these things would follow as a matter of course and would in no way be incredible if Jesus were a Celestial. The real issue, then, is not the wonders and miracles that surround Jesus' life. It is the nature of Jesus himself. Is there any real evidence that he was not just a simple First Century carpenter, but was rather an undercover extraterrestrial?

WAS JESUS A CELESTIAL?

The evidence, if there is any, would have to lie in the gospel records, for these are all we know of Jesus. Yet they could not be the gospel claims themselves, for, as we have seen, these are not scientifically or historically verifiable.

What then would do? The only convincing evidence would be statements or claims, made in the records, which involve modern scientific knowledge. If the gospels make claims about Jesus or his message which involve modern scientific discoveries, then the very content of the statements would be evidence. Even if what was claimed could not be proved the very fact that it was claimed would be evidence of extraterrestrial intervention into the narratives. Do the records contain any knowledge of this sort? We believe the answer is yes. The evidence is of two sorts. One concerns Jesus' birth; the other concerns his message.

"VIRGIN BIRTH" AND CLONING

The key to the mystery of Jesus' birth lies in certain statements he made about himself. These are found in the Gospel of John. The occasion is one of the most touching in all the gospels. The disciples are gathered in Jerusalem for their final Passover with Jesus. He has commended them to humility and has urged them to love one another. After washing their feet as a demonstration of humility and love, he tells them that the time has come for him to leave them. He assures them he is going to his father's "house" to prepare a place for them. Philip, one of the first Jesus had called to his circle and a leader, says, "Lord, shew us the Father ... " and Jesus replies, "Have I been so long time with you, and yet hast thou not known me, Philip? he that hath seen me hath seen the Father; and how sayest thou then, Shew us the Father?" (John 14:8-9). Earlier he also tells them, "I and my Father are one" (John 10:30), and still again, "the Father is in me, and I in him" (John 10:38).

On the surface these seem to be extraordinary statements. If Jesus is just saying he is his father's representative, why would he tell Philip that to see him is to see the father? The point of his remarks here seems to be that he looks exactly like his father. And who was his father-Joseph?

Both Matthew and Luke agree that Mary was a virgin and that Jesus was conceived by a nonhuman father, through the agency of the "Holy Ghost" (Matthew 1:18, Luke 1:35). Could such an extraordinary statement be true?

In the mid-1960s, John Gurdon, a biologist at Oxford University, succeeded in reproducing frogs using one parent only. The technique he used is called "cloning." It involves using the genetic material of a single parent, rather than the sexual method of combining genetic material from two parents. The technical name for nonsexual reproduction is "monogenesis," and cloning is one sort of monogenesis.

The gospel writer John tells us that Jesus was the "only begotten" son of God (John 3:16). The Greek word he uses for "only begotten" is monogenes – the same word from which the English word "monogenesis" comes. Could it be that Jesus was the monogenetic son of Jehovah, rather than the son of a human father? This is clearly the claim the gospels make.

HOW TO TELL A CLONE

The significant evidence of cloning is that the offspring is an identical twin to its parent. Since a single parent is used, the offspring's genetic type can only come from that parent. It must therefore be an exact duplicate of the parent-an identical twin except for age!

Now let's consider again the extraordinary statements John attributes to Jesus. He says that if you have seen him you have seen his father. He says he and his father are "one." He says his father is in him, and he is in his father.

Is there anything these statements could mean other than that Jesus is a duplicate of his father-a look-alike who has an identical constitution? If this is what they mean, then Jesus is saying, in effect, that he is a clone of Jehovah-a claim that fits extraordinarily well with what Matthew and Luke have to say about his conception.

For a virgin can give birth to a clone. And she can do so without "knowing a man," as Luke has Mary claim. And even though we can't verify the claims of Matthew and Luke, the question remains, how did they know about cloning? How did they know a virgin could give birth without "knowing" a man? And how did John know a son could be an identical twin to his father? Until John Gurdon's experiments it had never happened before – or had it? Did Celestials solve the problem of human cloning long before the First Century A.D.? And did they use some form of information bearing radiant energy which "overshadowed" Mary, as Luke claims (Luke 1:35), to impose Jehovah's DNA blueprint on the genetic material of her ovum? The Greek word used for "overshadow" is "episkiazo" and has the meaning of "a haze of brilliancy."

If they did then Jesus was indeed a clone of Jehovah-his identical twin. And the extraordinary statements he made about himself then make sense. As the clone of Jehovah he was, as the writer of Hebrews puts it, "the express image of his person" (Hebrews I:3)-the literal, biological "Son of the Lord God." The mystery of the incarnation–God become human–is solved. Jesus was a [h]e of extraterrestrial origin. He was, in fact, a Celestial!

And being a Celestial, sent on a mission to Earth, the extraordinary claims [of] the "good news" then fall into place. His unusual birth, his preciosity as a child debating scriptural doctrine with elders in the temple, his gifts of healing, his alleged paranormal abilities – all these would make sense if he were programmed at conception with prepared learning imposed on his genome for his undercover mission. These could be reinforced or added on to in his contact with a UFO on the Mount of Transfiguration. His resurrection, his ascension–all are predictable and make good scientific sense. Yet one fact in the "good news" remains which does not fit. This is Jesus' death. An examination of the gospel record shows it cannot be accounted for by the mere fact that Jesus was a Celestial. Quite the contrary. For, if he were a Celestial we would expect him to have escaped death or to have been rescued. Why, then, did he die?

JESUS' MISSION

To understand this unexpected turn of events we must now examine the reason for Jesus' mission. As we pointed out in Chapter VII, Colony Earth, it had two objectives. The first was to live among men and women to teach them about the Celestial's coming kingdom and to exemplify the way of life the Celestials require for citizenship in it. In short he was to teach, in as pure a form as possible, the Celestials' own religion. The second was to form a church which would carry this "good news" throughout the world.

And what was this religion he was to exemplify? As we have seen it centered on the Celestials' discovery and use of the ultimate Creative Power of the cosmos as the basis for their moral, spiritual and even material civilization.

They had long ago recognized that the ultimate Creative Power is a kind of conscious energy which, as Sir James Jeans put it, has "something in common with our own individual minds." They knew it underlies both mind and matter and is the directing and controlling force in the universe. They called this cosmic intelligence, or power, the "Holy Spirit."

Long before Jesus' birth they learned how to open up their lives to its influence and guidance. They called this experience the "baptism of the Spirit." Once they had received this indwelling "Spirit" it guided their individual and communal life with the same cosmic intelligence with which it directs the course of biological and cosmic creation. Further, it conferred powers on them which we would call "paranormal." By means of it they could accomplish feats of telepathy, clairvoyance, healing, resurrection, control of material objects and even the neutralizing of "laws" of nature, such as gravity. The most important discovery they made about it was that it had something in common with our own human experience of "love." That is to say, it is not just cosmic intelligence, or "logos," it is a cosmic force for good, for fulfillment, for healing and for progress and elevation. It is the creative and constructive and organizing force of the universe.

sus' mission to bring the gift of the Holy Spirit to humanity. To
s so far above their current level of development that the work
ried out by human prophets and teachers. The abortive attempt to
Garden had left a fragmentary knowledge which had been carried,
is of the Adamic race, throughout the world. Something of it was
sed in many religious traditions. In Taoist and Buddhist cultures it was
ca... ki. Hindu yogis knew it as prana. Polynesians called it mana, North
American Iroquois called it orenda, and Ituri pygmies called it megbe.

But these fragmented versions of the original Celestial teaching produced
uncertain results. Training in its use was long and arduous, and only those who
were especially adept and persistent ordinarily experienced a genuine "baptism,"
or acquired paranormal powers which they could use for good.

Jesus' assignment was to use his gifts for teaching and his development as an
adept to explain and demonstrate the gifts of the Spirit to humanity. By exhortations
and parables, adjusted to their level of understanding, he would teach humans the
use of cosmic love and its place in the coming "Kingdom of God:" By a ministry
of healing, therapy of character disorders (exorcism) and good works he would
exemplify the power of Cosmic Love.

And he would gather around him a special band of followers whom he would
initiate into the "baptism of the Spirit." They would form the nucleus for his
"church" which would carry the "good news" to the world.

Yet all of this would leave the outcome uncertain. Jehovah had tried the first
phase of his plan already, with his people and the law, and the outcome had been
less than encouraging. Humanity, even those closest to his original design, had
proved a corrupt and undependable lot. What was needed was some ultimate
demonstration of cosmic love and its redemptive powers which would become a
supreme symbol to this unpredictable race for all time.

THE ATONEMENT

So it was decided Jesus must die. The mystery of the atonement has eluded
theologians and apologists since the foundation of Christianity. The early apostles
attempted to explain it in terms of the Judaism they knew. Some used the metaphors
of temple worship and spoke of Jesus as a worthy "sacrifice" sufficient to appease
the wrath of a condemning Deity. Others used the language of the law and spoke
of a "redemption price" necessary to buy back humanity's edenic state. Neither
seems very logical or morally acceptable to the modern mind. How could a just
God require the death of an innocent person, especially his own son, before he
would forgive his fallen heirs? What could the death of an innocent person have
to do with buying back favor for the guilty? Yet with a Space Age interpretation of
the atonement the true reasons behind Jesus' death become clear.

As humanity's moral and spiritual exemplar he was the representative of the
ultimate Creative Power—a son not only of his biological father, Jehovah, but a
"son" of the highest creative and governing power of the Universe. As he was the

biological incarnation of Jehovah, so he was the revelational incarnation of the Logos-Divine Love.

His death, an innocent person, would therefore be the supreme act of love. If he died, not of illness or accident but deliberately, his death would be the ultimate expression and example of the love he taught. Nothing else would do equally well. If he died, when he could have escaped, because he persisted in carrying out his ministry of love, and justifying it by his credentials as the "son of God," the point would be ultimately made for all time.

And it was. The terror and passion of the atonement have gripped the hearts and minds of men and women as no other event in human history has done. The incomprehensible love that would impel an innocent man, a Celestial, to live among degraded humans, to sacrifice every human comfort and pleasure to his mission and finally to die by a hideous form of capital punishment has gripped human imagination as no other event in history. It has inspired supreme works of poetry, of music and of art. It impelled a handful of followers to proclaim the "good news" in the face of savage persecutions, until they had convinced half the world. Ultimately the Roman Empire itself bowed to the carpenter of Nazareth and embraced the religion he founded. Through the ages the cross has remained the symbol of all that is highest and best for untold millions of men and women. Jesus' act of redemptive love fully vindicated his mission. Since Golgotha he is known throughout the world as the Redeemer.

JESUS' MESSAGE

Two aspects of Jesus' ministry further show an unearthly strangeness. One is his mode of ministering—his attitudes and outlook; the other is what he taught.

Nothing is more indicative of Jesus' unworldly background than his attitude toward death. To most men and women death is that "last, great, final enemy." To Jesus it seemingly had little of that meaning or finality. This is brought out very forcibly in John's account of the resurrection of Lazarus.

Jesus had been preaching on the eastern side of the Jordan near the place where he was baptized by John. A messenger came from his closest friends in Bethany, not far from Jerusalem. The two sisters, Martha and Mary, and their brother Lazarus, provided the nearest thing to a home Jesus had in his wandering ministry. Martha tended his physical needs and showed exceeding concern for his comfort and rest. Mary, the younger, found a special place in Jesus' affection. Without fully understanding his unusual nature and mission she, with rare intuition and insight, grasped his loneliness and sense of isolation. She supplied the sympathy and small attentions which a woman's understanding can give a man whose vocation requires dedication and self-denial. Lazarus he loved as a brother.

The word tells him Lazarus is gravely ill. It urges him to come at once. Because his ministry is not yet finished, and reasoning that the illness is probably not as serious as they fear, he lingers two days before starting for Bethany. When his disciples ask him about the delay he assures them it will all work out "for the glory of God, that the son of God might be glorified thereby."

"LAZARUS, COME FORTH"

When he finally arrives in Bethany Lazarus has been dead four days. Martha meets him desolated with grief. He comforts her assuring her, "Thy brother shall rise again." She replies, "I know that he shall rise again in the resurrection at the last day." Jesus reassures her with one of the most famous utterances in all the gospels: "I am the resurrection, and the life: he that believeth in me, though he were dead, yet shall he live."

By that time Mary has arrived. She falls at his feet, prostrated by her anguish, and cries out, "Lord, if thou hadst been here, my brother had not died." At this Jesus undergoes a strange alteration. Before he has been composed and sure of his ability to handle the situation.

Now he suddenly groans "in the spirit," and is for the first time "troubled." Suddenly he breaks down and weeps uncontrollably. Continuing to groan he moves to the grave which is in a cave. Requesting that the stone be moved away he calls out, "Lazarus, come forth." And the dead man, "bound hand and foot with grave clothes," appears (John 11: 1-44).

What caused Jesus' sudden change? The only obvious explanation is that until his confrontation with Mary, he had looked on the whole affair from the Celestial point of view. Death was no problem. Resurrection could easily take care of it. It would be an opportunity to help the friends he loved and to reveal his heavenly father's power at the same time.

Now suddenly, because of his special empathy for Mary, her appearance confronts him with the human point of view -a point of view essentially foreign to him. He is compelled to look at death in terms of the desolation and suffering it has brought to those he loves for four agonizing days. For the first time he experiences the grief and hopelessness they have had to endure because of his delay. Only then does he look at death in the normal, human way, and, sharing their suffering and bereavement, he groans and is overcome with weeping.

This unearthliness of attitude and outlook is frequently found all through Jesus' ministry. In his priorities of concern in his career, in his attitudes and behavior at his trial and crucifixion and in his sense of mission and message an otherworldly outlook prevails. It is most evident of all in his ethic.

"MY KINGDOM IS NOT OF THIS WORLD"

The ethic of Jesus has been a subject for unending debate. Some take it for granted that it is the ethic of Christianity. Others doubt that much of Jesus' outlook and spirit survives in the church he founded. Critics point to the contrast between the simplicity of Jesus' life and the message, pomp and panoply of his church with its sectarian division and dogmatic pretensions. How, they ask, can followers of Jesus believe the Sermon on the Mount and erect pretentious churches and cathedrals? How can they support institutions that exploit the poor and racial minorities? Why are they uncharitable toward fellow Christians who have different interpretations of his teachings? Why have they condoned force and violence and ask God's blessing on their "right" side in most wars? Perhaps this is why George Bernard Shaw once said that Christianity is probably a good idea, but "it is hard to tell, since no one has ever tried it."

Yet, throughout history there have been those who have earnestly tried to live the ethic of Jesus. Some have even pushed it to its extremes and used it as a tool of social change and revolution. And where they have it has changed the course of the world.

Indeed, no more revolutionary doctrine has ever been taught. In its unworldly approach to social relations and worldly aspirations it strikes at the heart of all that is corruptive and abusive in human living. More than this it proposes an unearthly method for healing human hurts and woes for it urges us to curb those natural and instinctive responses we inherit from ancestors who followed the law of the jungle.

THE ETHIC OF JESUS

The ethic of Jesus says: "Blessed are the poor in spirit: for theirs is the kingdom of heaven.... Blessed are the meek: for they shall inherit the earth.... Blessed are the peacemakers: for they shall be called the children of God.... Blessed are ye, when men shall revile you, and persecute you, and shall say all manner of evil against you falsely, for my sake" (Matthew 5:3-11).

In the same vein Jesus advised his disciples: "Bless them that curse you, and pray for them which despitefully use you. And unto him that smiteth thee on the one cheek offer also the other; and him that taketh away thy cloak forbid not to take thy coat also" (Luke 6:28-29).

The unearthliness of these teachings lies precisely in that they run counter to everything that is encoded in our evolutionary heritage; they run counter to everything that is institutionalized in our society, and they run counter to our philosophy of worldly success.

Recognizing the unearthliness of his outlook on human relations and his concept of community Jesus observed: "My kingdom is not of this world: if my kingdom were of this world, then would my servants fight ... but now is my kingdom not from hence" (John 18:36). And in this utterance Jesus put his finger on what is strangest in his teaching. It is his attitude toward the handling of evil in the world.

No part of his teaching has been more disparaged than his advocacy of nonviolence in the face of evil. Philosophers have ridiculed it as a morality of weaklings. Pacifists who have tried to follow it have been branded cowards or imprisoned as felons.

Yet when it has been tried it has renovated societies and overturned empires. Early Christians walked unresisting to martyrs' deaths in the arenas of ancient Rome. Yet in the end the mighty Roman Empire knelt at the cross and embraced the faith of the founder it had crucified almost three centuries earlier.

Mahatma Gandhi's followers fell unresisting under the lathis of the native policemen who enforced Britain's Salt Act. Speaking of their sacrifice newsmen wrote, "Hour after hour stretchers carried back a stream of inert bleeding bodies." Yet in the end the little holy man who inspired them was invited to negotiate with the empire's viceroy, and Britain relinquished her control of 350 million Indians.

In their civil-rights struggle, Martin Luther King, Jr., locked arms with black and white men and women singing "We Shall Overcome". They continued marching, as many lay bleeding on the streets and languished in jails. Yet in the end segregation in schools and buses was ended, and civil-rights legislation was enacted.

Speaking of the difficulty of living up to Jesus' precepts King wrote: "It is not simple to adopt the credo that moral force has as much strength and virtue as the capacity to return a physical blow; or that to refrain from hitting back requires more will and bravery than the automatic reflexes of defense. But he went on to comment, "The argument that nonviolence is a coward's refuge lost its force as their heroic and often perilous acts uttered their wordless but convincing rebuttal ..."

JESUS AND LAW

It is not just Jesus' precept of nonviolence, but the tenor of his whole ethic that goes against the grain of human nature. The beatitudes are a litany of unearthly ideals. Blessedness lies in poverty of spirit, in meekness, in pacifism, and in being persecuted and reviled in a good cause. Giving is better than receiving. Loving one's enemies is nobler and more effective than fighting them.

Human legal and ethical systems are based on the worldly ideals of equity and justice-getting what one deserves. The penal codes of most civilized nations rest on some form of the lex talionis – the "law of the claw." An eye for an eye; a tooth for a tooth. Let the punishment fit the crime." Even Hillel, one of the greatest teachers of the Judaic law, summed up its essence as a negative form of the golden rule. "What is hateful to thee, do not to thy neighbor." But Jesus viewed the law differently and so fulfilled it, for he stated the same rule in its positive form: "... whatsoever ye would that men should do to you, do ye even so to them: for this is the law and the prophets" (Matthew 7:12).

Jesus was not interested in mere equity or justice-his guiding principle was love. Love does not ask what is deserved but what it can give. So Jesus says: "And whosoever shall compel thee to go a mile, go with him twain.... Ye have heard that it hath been said, Thou shalt love thy neighbor, and hate thine enemy. But I say unto you, Love your enemies, bless them that curse you, do good to them that hate you, and pray for them which despitefully use you ..." (Matthew 5:41, 43-44)

And in teaching this law of love Jesus transcended human ideals of justice and revealed his Celestial nature. Only the son of Divine and Cosmic Love would have the audacity to urge his followers, "Be ye therefore perfect, even as your Father which is in heaven is perfect" (Matthew 5:48).

What are we to make of such teaching? Even if we grant the value of these ideals how is it humanly possible to live up to them? Jesus' answer was the one he gave to Nicodemus.

"YE MUST BE BORN AGAIN"

According to John, Nicodemus was an administrator of the Jews who came secretly to Jesus, by night, for spiritual counsel. Jesus responded with one of his most famous injunctions: "Verily, verily, I say unto thee, Except a man be born again, he cannot see the kingdom of God." Nicodemus, astonished, asked him, "How can a man be born when he is old? Can he enter a second time into his mother's womb, and be born?" Jesus answered, "Verily, verily, I say unto thee, Except a man be born of water and of the Spirit, he cannot enter into the kingdom of God" (John 3:1-5). And with this strange interchange, at the outset of John's Gospel, we come to the central purpose of Jesus' mission on Earth—the bringing of the baptism of the Spirit to humanity.

The first birth by "water", the breaking of the amniotic sac in childbirth, leaves humans with a nature incapable of living up to Jesus' ideals. Without spiritual transformation we cannot live up to the Celestials' requirements for citizenship in their coming "kingdom." The second birth, the birth of the Spirit, accomplishes the needed transformation. Jesus taught that by surrendering one's life to the indwelling of the Holy Spirit, and accepting its regeneration and guidance, humans could be restored to the possibility of righteousness and love.

NEW BIRTH AND JESUS' "BAPTISM"

Like Nicodemus many people find the idea of being "born again" incredible. Some reject it as completely absurd, and others see it as some sort of bogus mysticism.

Now research into depth psychology and parapsychology throws new light on this ancient teaching. What exactly was Jesus talking about? Some have supposed his "baptism" was water baptism. Yet speaking of the charge that Jesus baptized more followers than John the Baptist, John says, "Jesus himself baptized not." (John 4:2). He adds that only Jesus' disciples baptized.

Morton Smith, a New Testament scholar, has speculated that Jesus' baptism was a secret magical rite in which he used hypnosis to induce possession-like states in hysterical or schizophrenic disciples. He has even suggested that Jesus induced hallucinations of literal ascent into the "kingdom of God" in his followers.

Yet fifty days after Jesus' death, at Pentecost, over 3,000 people are reported, by Luke, to have received this same baptism of the Spirit. Jesus himself was no longer present, and no cult leader or "magician" was there to take his place as a hypnotist. Further, the phenomena of Pentecost, which we will examine in the next chapter, are not those typical of hypnosis. Nor is it likely that 3,000 hysterics or schizophrenics would have assembled by chance. Twelve might be collected, over a period of time, by one charismatic cult leader, but 3,000, at one time and in one place and by coincidence, never!

Yet there can be little doubt that the "baptism of the Holy Ghost", reported in the book of Acts at Pentecost, is the same "baptism" Jesus practiced. It was his own cousin, John the Baptist, who told his followers, "I indeed baptize you with water unto repentance: but he that cometh after me is mightier than I ... he shall baptize you with the Holy Ghost, and with fire" (Matthew 3:11). We shall have more to say about this peculiar association of "fire" with the baptism of the Holy Spirit in the chapter that follows. But the point here is that Jesus' "baptism" was evidently the same "birth by the Spirit" which he recommended to Nicodemus and the "baptism of the Holy Ghost" which was experienced by 3,000 at Pentecost.

THE NEW BIRTH AND CONVERSION

To many people today the term "born again" is associated with images of skid row rescue missions, sawdust trails, and Bible Belt revivalism. In spite of the fact that many entertainment celebrities and national leaders claim "born again" religious experiences, the impression persists that spiritual rebirth is not quite respectable. In many ways this is strange since some of the world's greatest spiritual teachers have received their calling and inspiration in dramatic "rebirth" experiences. Among them were Moses, the Buddha, the Apostle Paul and St. Augustine.

Perhaps a part of the problem lies in what Christopher Frye called the "domestication of the enormous miracle"—the making of something that is sacred and special into what is commonplace and trivial. There has been a confusion over conversion, as a psychological phenomenon, with spiritual rebirth, to which it sometimes leads.

While many religious "conversions" produce beneficial and lasting changes in converts, others are of short duration and produce little evidence of a genuine growth in moral and spiritual sensitivity. As a result controversy has developed, among believers, concerning the value of religious conversion. Conservative, evangelical protestants continue to feel it is the only valid entree into the religious life. Liberal Protestants, most Catholics and Jews question its long-range benefits. They feel true spiritual development comes about gradually by searching, study, prayer and instruction.

A SPACE AGE VIEW OF THE NEW BIRTH

With the insights of Space Age psychology Jesus' teaching can now be set in a clearer light. What mattered for Jesus was that the individual undergoes a spiritual transformation -a rebirth. The "birth of the Spirit" brings this about.

Genuine spiritual rebirth often produces profound changes in our beliefs, attitudes and behavior. For some people these are achieved by a conscious process of study, work, self-examination and seeking. Their progress is gradual, and they experience it as spiritual awakening or growth. For others, especially those who are deeply conflicted about spiritual matters, changes may be largely unconscious or even denied. Only when their conflict becomes overwhelming do they admit

Heaven is not reached by a single bound -
But we built the ladder by which we rise
From the lowly earth to the vaulted skies

the other side of their "divided self," and acknowledge it in a sudden "decision", or compulsion, to reform. As in the case of the Apostle Paul it may be the result of some crisis experience such as his Damascus road encounter with what he believed to be the risen Christ. Or it may be a near death experience or loss of relationship, position or possessions.

William James, America's founding psychologist and researcher in the field of religion and paranormal phenomena recognized this divide among religious believers in their spiritual development. In his classic Varieties of Religious Experience he cites examples and gives case studies of what he terms "once born" and "twice born" souls. The former are often born into religious family environments and feel themselves to be religious from the time of their earliest memories. They see their religious development as paralleling development of other traits such as physical and intellectual capabilities. They reach religious maturity gradually and never consciously undergo a "crisis" which suddenly transforms their present life to a different one.

The "twice born" often have little or no exposure to religious training in their early life or rebel against what training they have had. They are conflicted and find themselves to be torn between two opposing ways of life.

Writing of his own conversion Paul, as an arch prosecutor of Christians, describes what William James called a "divided self" that preceded his Damascus Road experience. So in the Epistle to the Romans he wrote: "For that which I do I allow not; for what I would , that do I not, but what I hate, that do I. . .For I delight in the law of God after the inward man. But I see another law in my members warring against the law of my mind . . . O wretched man that I am: who shall deliver me from the body of this death."

As a Pharisee brought up in the strictest observance of Jewish law he began his career of prosecutions with such zeal that he overreached the inherent justice and mercy of Judaism and became a fanatic zealot. But he was also a man of genuine concern for others and their courage in suffering for their beliefs undoubtably troubled this side of his nature leading to a crisis on his way to Damascus. Suddenly and unexpectedly a blinding light knocked him off his horse, and he heard a voice challenging him. "Saul, Saul, why persecutest thou me?" (Acts 9:1-8)

The experience left him blinded for several days and, on recovering, he rechanneled his zeal and became the greatest promoter and missionary of Christianity the early Christian world had known and eventually its martyr.

Writing of his post-Damascus road state in one of the New Testament's most famous perorations he concludes: "There is therefore now no condemnation to them which are in Christ Jesus, who walk not after the flesh, but after the Spirit. For the law of the spirit of life in Christ Jesus hath made me free from the law of sin and death . . .who then shall separate us from the love of Christ? shall tribulation, or distress, or persecution, or famine, or nakedness, or peril, or sword . . . Nay, in all these things we are more than conquerors through him that loved us. For I am persuaded, that neither death, nor life, nor angels, nor principalities, nor powers, nor things present, nor things to come, nor height, nor depth, nor any other creature, shall be able to separate us from the love of God, which is in Christ Jesus our Lord." (Romans 8: 1-39)

Conversion is a psychological phenomenon, not confined to religion. People are often converted from one political persuasion to another, or from social conservatism to a liberal or even radical and revolutionary outlook. In Charles Dickens, A Christmas Carol, Scrooge is converted from being a miserly misanthrope into a warm hearted philanthropist as a result of three "visitations" or nightmares on Christmas Eve. The requirement for spiritual rebirth, then, is a transformation or baptism of the Spirit that redirects life energies toward righteousness and love, whether it comes gradually or by a sudden epiphany, or "conversion" experience, is immaterial.

To undergo this baptism it is not necessary to join any particular church, or to espouse some particular faith or body of doctrine. There have been righteous men and women in most cultures throughout the ages. To be sure the support of a community devoted to spiritual living can be a great aid in accomplishing spiritual rebirth and in promoting those guidelines and way of life required for Celestial citizenship.

In the chapter which follows we will examine what Jesus meant by the "Spirit" and its "baptism" more closely from the viewpoint of a Space Age interpretation of the Bible.

And there appeared unto them cloven tongues like as of fire, and
it sat upon each of them. And they were all filled with the Holy
Ghost ...

– Acts 2:3-4

CHAPTER XIV

PENTECOST AND BIOCOSMIC ENERGY

Fifty days had passed since Jesus celebrated his last Passover with the
disciples. In the interim they had plumbed the depths of despair and reached the
peaks of joy. Jesus, their leader, had been arrested, tried and crucified. One of their
number, his betrayer, had committed suicide. In the terror of those events they had
been scattered by the impact of the tragedy and its aftermath. John, the Beloved,
had taken Mary, the mother of Jesus, to a place of safety and retirement. Peter,
stricken with grief and overwhelmed with shame at his denial of Jesus, had gone
into seclusion. Others of the disciples had fled the city. The women who visited the
tomb on resurrection morning had remained close by but had lost touch with the
disciples.

Then the incredible had happened. The women were the first to know of it
before dawn on Resurrection Sunday. The tomb was empty. A stranger, or strangers,
told them Jesus had risen. Soon after he appeared to Mary Magdalene and still later
to two followers on the road to Emmaus about four miles outside Jerusalem. Still
later he appeared to the assembled eleven and allowed them to see and feel his
wounds.

Now, seven weeks later, they were all assembled together for the first time
since those momentous events. The gathering included the disciples, family and
friends of Jesus and most of his other close followers-about 120 in all. They had
collected, probably in the same upper room where he celebrated his last Passover,
to share the summer festival, Shavuos, the feast of Pentecost. And though they did
not yet know it they were also about to celebrate the founding of Christianity.

Luke tells the story in the book of Acts. In the opening chapter he repeats the account of Jesus' ascension, taken up into a "cloud" which received him out of their sight (Acts 1:9). Just before he is "taken up" the bewildered disciples ask if he will now finally assume his role as Messiah: "Lord, wilt thou at this time restore again the kingdom to Israel?" Jesus responds cryptically that it is not for them "to know the times or the seasons." Seeing their disappointment he then adds: "But ye shall receive power, after that the Holy Ghost is come upon you: and ye shall be witnesses unto me both in Jerusalem, and in all Judaea, and in Samaria, and unto the uttermost part of the earth" (Acts 1:6-8).

Now the time for the fulfillment of that promise had arrived. Luke moves swiftly to the central event in the second chapter. "And when the day of Pentecost was fully come they were all with one accord in one place. And suddenly there came a sound from heaven as of a rushing mighty wind, and it filled all the house where they were sitting. And there appeared unto them cloven tongues like as of fire, and it sat upon each of them. And they were all filled with the Holy Ghost, and began to speak with other tongues, as the Spirit gave them utterance" (Acts 2:1-4).

With these words Luke lifts the curtain on the strangest, but most portentous, part of the entire gospel story. For in this aftermath to the life of Jesus he introduces the principal actor in the drama—Jesus' Cosmic "Father," the Holy Spirit. Throughout the four gospels Jesus speaks of his "Spirit," and in the Gospel of John he speaks of him as a "Comforter" who will watch over and guide the disciples when he is gone.

THE "THIRD PERSON" OF THE TRINITY

In the first centuries of the church early theologians had trouble identifying this "Spirit," or "Comforter." Was it a person separate from Jesus and his Father? Or was it just an aspect of one or the other? Were they also just aspects of one another?

Didn't Jesus say he and his Father were "one," and didn't he refer to the "Comforter" as his "Spirit"? Perhaps they were all one in some mysterious way. Yet Jesus also spoke of them as though each had a separate identity and a distinct role.

At first a variety of opinions prevailed on this question. Eventually those favoring the three-in-one view won out. The doctrine of the Trinity was established as the correct one by church edict, and other views were declared to be heresies.

This stopped most of the argument, but the problem remained. The church had spoken. There were three persons in one-but how? Philosophers took over where theologians left off and tried to provide explanations to account for the mystery.

In the meantime ordinary believers, who had difficulty following both theological disputes and philosophical explanations, were formulating their own ideas. Jesus they could understand. After all, he was incarnated-a man. Of course, there were no photographs and the gospels didn't give a physical description, but church artists filled the gap. The familiar bearded figure-the "pale Galilean" of Swinburne's poem-was beginning to take on a standard artistic expression.

God the Father was another problem. Not until Michelangelo would he, too, become the heroic, bearded Semite of the "Creation". Until then he remained a shadowy sort of superhuman king, Jesus' "Father," who bore an uncertain resemblance to the Old Testament Jehovah.

The Holy Spirit remained, however, wholly "without form and void." The Scriptures gave no hint as to his, or its, appearance. Some artists were content to picture it as a dove descending on Jesus at his baptism. Others made it just a beam of light-a sort of off-stage spot highlighting dramatic events in the New Testament.

The fact that prayers and salutations were never addressed to him, or it, in the Scriptures increased the difficulty. God, the Father, was often addressed as "Our Father." Jesus was addressed as "Lord." But no one, including Jesus himself, ever seemed to address the Holy Spirit directly.

When the King James version appeared and used the expression the "Holy Ghost," things looked more hopeful. But hope faded as the language of the translation fell into disuse. Today, the term is of no help at all. A ghost is just something in a white sheet left over from a dead person. It doesn't seem a very appropriate label for the third person of the Trinity.

A PROBLEM OF SEMANTICS

Why has the Holy Spirit been such a problem in Christian art and theology? Why, as one of the principal actors in the New Testament, has he, or she, or it, remained so nebulous and insubstantial especially since the baptism of the Holy Spirit was the central event in Jesus' teaching and in the early church? Why did the gospel writers and Jesus leave the agent, whose "baptism" qualifies us for admission into the kingdom of God, in a semantic limbo?

The answer to this question is again one of the major discoveries of our Space Age interpretation of the Bible. To our surprise it has rescued the Holy Spirit from the obscurity into which Christian theology had let it fall and restored it to the central role it played in the thinking of Jesus and the apostles.

As we have implied a great deal of theology's neglect of the Holy Spirit seems to be due to a semantic dilemma. The language used to describe it does not fit the theological notions early churchmen had about it. It was easier to ignore the whole matter than to revise their thinking.

DESCRIBING THE INDESCRIBABLE

The Greek term used for Holy "Ghost," in Luke's account of Pentecost, is "pneuma". This literally means a "breath" or "wind"-a moving current of air. But the figurative use is clearly the one intended in Luke, and this is abstracted from the action of breath or wind. It suggests a power or "spirit." Like the wind, the Holy Ghost is an invisible "power." Further, the figurative use of pneuma also carries the meanings of "life" and "mind." This invisible power has something in common with our own lives and minds-it is an intelligent, vital principle.

The English word "ghost" is totally misleading, for it suggests a sort of astral double-the theological "soul." So early modern Protestants were misled by the King James translators into thinking of the Holy Ghost as a sort of soul of Jesus and God-a "soul" they shared, since they were "one."

When the King James translation says a human "gave up the ghost," however, "ghost" is used for a different Greek word, "ekpneo". Clearly the "Holy Ghost" is not the immortal soul of Jesus or God, nor is it their apparition, in spite of some modern theologians who insist both Jesus and God are dead.

One other Greek word is used in the New Testament for the Holy Spirit. It is the word "parakletos", and it is used only in John's Gospel. It means simply an "intercessor". For this reason the Holy Spirit is sometimes called the "Paraclete." John uses the term when Jesus tells his disciples he will send the "Paraclete" to take his place and comfort them. So he says to them, "But when the Comforter is come, whom I will send unto you from the Father, even the Spirit of truth, which proceedeth from the Father, he shall testify of me ... " (John 15:26). And again he tells them the Comforter will "teach you all things, and bring all things to your remembrance, whatsoever I have said unto you" (John 14:26).

Putting these meanings together, we arrive at a very abstract notion. The Holy Spirit is an invisible power. It has the qualities of life and mind and, as a "comforter," can teach all things and "bring to remembrance" the teachings of Jesus-which were principally those of love. *NB*

CONCEIVING THE INCONCEIVABLE

Four words stand out, then, in these characterizations of the Holy Spirit-power, life, truth and love. And remembering that it is principally John who gives us these attributes, we are drawn back to the opening verses of his gospel. In these he says: "In the beginning was the Word, and the Word was with God, and the Word was God.... All things were made by him ... In him was life; and the life was the light of men.... And the Word was made flesh, and dwelt among us ... " (John 1:1-4, 14).

The Greek word translated "Word" in these passages is "logos"-a term which almost defies translation into English. Though it is often translated "word" or "thought," it has a much broader meaning in Greek. This use is indicated by its frequent addition, as a suffix, at the end of scientific terms. So we get geology (geologos), a systematic knowledge of the Earth; biology (bio-logos), a systematic knowledge of life; and psychology (psyche-logos), a systematic knowledge of mind.

Some New Testament scholars believe John was influenced, in his use of logos, by the Greek philosophy of stoicism. The stoics used logos to mean the ultimate reason which underlies all things and explains all existence. So he tells us (speaking of the "Word") : "All things were made by him; and without him was not anything made that was made" (John 1:3).

Bible scholars have generally understood John's "Word" to be Christ. As the Cosmic Christ he was "made flesh" and "dwelt among us." Jesus' pre-existence of his own birth in Bethlehem is assumed to be that of the Cosmic Christ.

Yet Paul tells us that this Christ "dwells" within him and that he lives through this Christ, and Jesus said he would send the "Comforter" for just these purposes. If these things are so then John's Word and the Cosmic Christ and the Comforter are all one and the same.

THE HOLY SPIRIT AS ULTIMATE CREATIVE ENERGY

So we come to a startling conclusion. The Holy Spirit is not the pale shadow of the other two full-bodied members of the Trinity. It is the principal actor. John says it made the world. Jesus said it was his Spirit which existed before him and would replace him, after his departure, in the hearts and minds of his followers.

Granting this, then, the Holy Spirit is the being whom we have called "God, the Creator," in our chapter In The Beginning. The Holy Spirit is the Divine Logos, the Cosmic Christ, the Word, the ultimate Creative Power. And as we said in Chapter VI, it is at the very least a person and a God. It is, in fact, the God beyond all gods- the God worshipped by the Celestials, themselves, including Jehovah and Jesus. They are divine to the extent that they express its power, and we become "sons and daughters" of God through its "baptism."

This is why Jesus speaks of it as his "Spirit" (power), for it was the source of all his power. The miracles attributed to him in the gospels were performed by means of it. And this is why Jesus speaks of it as the "Spirit" (or power) of his Father, Jehovah. By means of it the Lord God performed the wonders attributed to him in the Old Testament. It is the universal mind Sir James Jeans referred to when he wrote of the "Mind in which the atoms, from which our minds have grown, exist as thoughts."

Yet it is more than cosmic mind or intelligence. It is also Cosmic Power. It is that mysterious being which underlies the mind stuff and other entities of the physical world, and of which they both are manifestations. Its relation to them is the link which astronomer V. A. Firsoff sought when he spoke of a "modulus of transformation" which could relate mind and matter and transform one into the other."

It is the "consciousness" Professor Goswami writes of in his previously cited book, "The Self-Aware Universe, How Consciousness Creates Matter". And throughout centuries it has been experienced as on a continuum with, and inclusive of, our own individual minds. This is reported, not only by professed mystics, but by religious believers of all faiths and even many of our greatest scientists.

Among those who are called "new atheists", however, there has been an ongoing effort to promote the idea that atheism is a logical necessity for those who truly understand what science has proved. Because of this they argue those who have experienced and believe they have a personal relationship with an ultimate creative intelligence are suffering from a malfunction of their brains. So one of the leaders in this effort, Richard Dawkins, a Professor of Public Understanding of Science at Oxford University, wrote a book entitled "The God Delusion" in which he attempts to defend this claim.

In view of the fact that repeated surveys have shown the distribution of believers, agnostics and atheists to be about the same for scientists as for the general college educated population the claim that atheism is the only logical conclusion consistent with a proper understanding of science and its practice is clearly wrong. We have already seen in the chapter, In The Beginning, that any claims about what may or may not have existed and operated before our present universe came into being is not scientific but unsubstantiated speculation. This is underscored when a historical survey of believing scientists is made as it reveals many of the greatest scientists have been, or are, believers.

For example Isaac Newton, who fathered the rise of modern science with his co-invention of calculus and formulation of the laws of gravity and motion, was a firm believer in God and spent almost as much of his time trying to formulate a system for understanding the Bible as he did for formulating a system of laws for understanding nature.

Other major scientists who have contributed in important ways to our present understanding and mastery of the world, were, or are, observant practitioners of religion. Among them we have George Lamaitre, a Catholic priest, who first proposed the big bang theory as the origin of the universe. Another Catholic priest was Teilhard de Chardin, a world famous paleontologist, who contributed to the field of anthropology by helping expose the Piltdown man hoax.

Among other more recent scientists who are believers and eminent in their fields we have Arno Penzias, Noble Laureate, co-discoverer of the cosmic background radiation that enabled accurate dating of the big bang; Isadore Rabi, discoverer of nuclear magnetic resonance (of MRI importance), and Chairman of the Atomic Energy Commission; Nobel Laureate, Joseph Taylor, who discovered rapidly rotating stars and, perhaps, of widest public recognition, Francis Collins, M.D., Ph.D., leader of the Human Genome Project and Director of the National Institutes of Health. He also had an academic career as professor of internal medicine and genetics at the University of Michigan. Among his many honors are the Biotechnology Heritage Award, the National Medal of Science Award, and the Presidential Medal of Freedom. All of these accomplishments seem even more unlikely when we consider them in light of Professor Dawkin's declaration that all who believe in, or believe they have had direct experience of, God are delusional. In Dr. Collin's case he started out as one of the new atheists, and, like the apostle Paul, underwent a conversion to Christianity as an adult. His present religious belief and experience are a central part of his life as a highly accomplished scientist, and he has continued to receive the highest honors from both the scientific community and his nation.

Since Professor Dawkins believes a thorough understanding of modern science logically compels one to atheism, the work and beliefs of the scientists we have mentioned, and of many others who could be mentioned, clearly refutes his belief and is so opposed to the facts that it could be called the "Dawkins delusion".

Ancient spiritual disciplines recognized this cosmic consciousness as *chi* or *ki* or *prana*. Modern researchers in paraphysics and parapsychology have suggested it is identical with what they call "bioplasmic" or "biocosmic" energy. Because it underlies and interfuses and directs and controls all things it is that Being of which Wordsworth wrote in the Lines Written a Few Miles Above Tintern Abbey. It is that "presence" which "disturbed" him with the joy

> Of elevated thoughts; a sense sublime
> Of something far more deeply interfused,
> Whose dwelling is the light of setting suns,
> And the round ocean and the living air,
> And the blue sky, and in the mind of man;
> A motion and a spirit, that impels
> All thinking things, all objects of all thought,
> And rolls through all things.

Could it also be that same power which entered like "rushing wind" and baptized those gathered in the upper room at Pentecost? That it was a physical, as well as a spiritual, power is testified by the fact that Luke says it appeared as "cloven tongues like as of fire." In fact, Luke's statement is reminiscent of John the Baptist's announcement that one would follow him who would baptize "with the Holy Ghost and with fire" (Matthew 3:11). It also calls to mind Jesus' own statement that he came "to send fire on the Earth" (Luke 12:49). New Testament scholars often assumed both John and Jesus were using "fire" in a figurative sense to mean a rekindling of religious fervor, but the Greek term, "pur", means "lightning" and could also suggest an energy form similar to electricity.

This raises an interesting question. Could the Holy Spirit manifest itself in a physical, as well as a purely spiritual, form? If it is the ultimate Power which underlies both mind and matter might its "baptism," or uses, not result in physical as well as psychic manifestations? If so, Luke's statement about the sound of "rushing wind" and "tongues of flame" would begin to make more sense.

THE HOLY SPIRIT AND KIRLIAN AURAS

Modern physics recognize a fourth state of matter in addition to the traditional three. Besides solids, liquids and gases there are plasmas. In ancient Greek philosophy this division, was also recognized. The first three states were represented by Earth, water and air. The fourth was known as fire!

New Testament scholars believe Greek scientific and philosophical ideas influenced the gospel writers. Did they call the energy manifestations of Spirit baptism "fire" because they were influenced by Greek philosophy? If they did it may be that what Luke described at Pentecost was some kind of plasma phenomenon.

Modern paraphysical research has developed a technique for investigating plasmas that surround many objects. The technique is called Kirlian photography. It is photography which uses high voltage electricity rather than light to expose photographic plates. It shows plasmas surrounding material objects as energy halos. These are particularly active around living objects and are therefore often referred to as "bioplasmic" or "biocosmic."

Principal centers for Kirlian research have been the Soviet Union and UCLA's Neuropsychiatric Institute, under the supervision of Dr. Thelma Moss. Kirlian photographs of living objects, such as a leaf or a person's hand, show flame-like emissions of light which are reminiscent of the "cloven tongues like as of fire" described by Luke and "halos" medieval painters sometimes showed around the heads of saints.

Two journalists in the last Century, who surveyed Kirlian research in the Soviet Union, described a photographed leaf as being surrounded by colored flares coming out of the leaf. The colors were different for every item ... but a living leaf gave off a multicolored aura.

While some scientists have suggested that the halos are due to electrical phenomena connected with the process itself, a leading Soviet researcher, Victor Inushin, claims, the light visible in Kirlian pictures is caused by bioplasma and not the electrical state of the organism.

Kirlian photography suggests, then, that all material objects, including living things, have energy halos which can be enhanced by invasion of outside energy. The halos resemble cloven tongues of fire."

Luke suggests that those gathered at Pentecost also exhibited halos which became visible when they were invaded by the Holy Spirit. These, too, resembled cloven tongues of fire. Could the phenomena, in both cases, be the same? Psychic researchers have investigated sensitives who claim they see energy auras surrounding people. Some claim to diagnose diseases and emotional states from the colors and forms of patients' auras.

Dr. Shafica Karagulla, a neuropsychiatrist formerly associated with Wilder Penfield at Montreal University, is one of these researchers. She told of a sensitive who saw people's auras as a "vital energy body or field" like a "sparkling web of light beams." From these she diagnosed diseases. Evaluating her diagnoses, Dr. Karagulla said, she can see the physical organs of the body and any pathological functions. She had not studied medicine or physiology, and often her descriptions were those one would expect of a layman, but they were accurate and easily translate into medical terms. Medical diagnosis proved that the sensitive was often correct and accurate in what she described.

Other psychics seem to heal diseases by touching afflicted areas of the body or even mentally concentrating on the diseased part. Kirlian photographs show that healers' auras diminish after healing and that patients' auras increase. So Dr. Thelma Moss reported on one study at UCLA in which a healer treated twelve patients for three months. In each case the healer's corona grew smaller after treatment while the patients' grew larger and brighter. Similar photographs of a nonhealer, used as a control, failed to show such changes.

The gospel writer and physician, Luke, tells of a similar observation. The healer was Jesus. A woman who had an "issue of blood" for twelve years came to him while he was on his way to heal another patient. As Luke tells it, she "had spent all her living upon physicians, neither could be healed of any." Approaching Jesus, she "came behind him, and touched the border of his garment: and immediately her issue of blood stanched. And Jesus said, Who touched me? When all denied, Peter and they that were with him said, Master, the multitude throng thee and press thee, and sayest thou, Who touched me? And Jesus said, Somebody hath touched me: for I perceive that virtue is gone out of me" (Luke 8:43-46). The word Jesus used for "virtue" here is "dunamis", which means "miraculous power" or force.)

PENTECOST AND THE PARANORMAL

In the light of these various findings and experiences it seems likely, then, that those gathered in the upper room at Pentecost underwent some sort of change of energy state as an effect of their baptism. The result was an outbreak of paranormal phenomena similar to those investigated by modern researchers.

Luke continues the story in Acts. As the "cloven tongues like as of fire" sat upon their heads they were all "filled with the Holy Ghost." (Acts 2:3) Luke makes the natural assumption that the settlings of the "tongues" caused the "filling." From our preceding discussion of energy auras it seems more likely that the "filling" with the Spirit caused the auras to increase. And whether they increased to the point of normal visibility, or whether those filled became psychically sensitive and saw otherwise invisible auras, is not clear. It seems probable that, like Dr. Karagulla's sensitive, they saw auras which "unbaptized" people would not have seen.)

"OTHER TONGUES"

In any event, upon being filled they "began to speak with other tongues, as the Spirit gave them utterance" (Acts 2:4). Some New Testament critics have assumed the "tongue speaking" at Pentecost was a kind of hysterical dislocation of speech behavior-babbling, or what is technically called "glossolalia." So Morton Smith, one of these critics, speaks of post-Pentecostal spirit baptism as involving "incomprehensible cries – a common symptom of schizophrenia."

And while some later instances of "speaking in tongues" in the New Testament do involve glossolalia, the "unknown" or "angelic tongue" of Paul, Luke makes it clear that this was not what occurred at Pentecost. Rather, the phenomenon here was xenoglossy. This is the ability to understand, or use, a foreign human language which the speaker or hearer has never studied.)

Writing of this Luke says, "And there were dwelling at Jerusalem Jews, devout men, out of every nation under heaven. Now when this was noised abroad, the multitude came together, and were confounded, because that every man heard them speak in his own language. And they were all amazed and marveled, saying one to another, Behold, are not all these which speak Galileans? And how hear we every man in our own tongue, wherein we were born?" (Acts 2:5-8).

At first it might seem that this story of a polyglot group all understanding a single language is just another tall tale. And so it might be dismissed were it not that xenoglossy has occurred in modern times under well-documented conditions – often in connection with baptism of the Spirit. John H. Sherrill, a journalist and staff member of Guideposts, tells of an interview he had with Harold Bredesen, an ordained minister of the First Reformed Church, Mount Vernon, New York. The Reverend Mr. Bredesen had experienced the gift of xenoglossy on several occasions. Sherrill reports one in which Bredesen was praying outside a mountain cabin where he was in retreat. Suddenly there was "the most beautiful outpouring of vowels and consonants and also some strange guttural syllables. I could not recognize any of it. It was as though I were listening to a foreign language, except that it was coming out of my mouth." Dumbfounded, Bredesen rushed down the mountain and encountered an old man sitting in front of his cabin. Still speaking, the minister paused, and the old man answered, talking rapidly in a language Bredesen didn't know. When it became obvious Bredesen could not understand the old man said, "How can you speak Polish but not understand it?" "I was speaking in Polish?" The man laughed, "Of course it was Polish." Bredesen reported that, as far as he knew, he had never before heard the language. On another occasion he stated he spoke old Arabic to the daughter of an Egyptologist who understood him, although he, himself, could not understand what he said.

Controlled and well-documented cases of xenoglossy have also been reported by the British Society for Psychical Research in connection with spiritualistic seances. In his book, The Life Beyond Death, Arthur Ford tells of one of the best known of these. Four different mediums, all independently, gave alleged communications from F. W. H. Myers, a classical Greek scholar and the deceased founder of the society. The messages included lengthy quotations from Homer's Iliad, in classical Greek, which none of the mediums had studied. Each medium received a separate part of the message, though they were on different continents and in different seances and unknown to each other. Separate parts of the complete quotation were reported to the Society where someone else coordinated or cross referenced them, into complete quotations. An account of these "cross correspondences" was reported in the Proceedings of the British Society. They said Myers claimed to have devised these "cross correspondences" to prove his survival of bodily death.

Tongue speaking continued to be an important part of apostolic Christianity. The Apostle Paul, speaking of his own involvement, wrote, "I thank my God I speak with tongues more than ye all." (I Corinthians 14:18) This extraordinary man, who authored nearly a third of the New Testament, has overshadowed all subsequent Christian thinkers. As the most outstanding Christian theologian of his age and perhaps of all time his word on tongue speaking carried, and still carries, great weight. He approved of glossolalia but laid down strict rules for its use. He stipulated that when it occurred in public there should be translators present. Otherwise, he stated, he preferred that the unknown, or "angelic" tongue (I Corinthians 13:1) be practiced privately where, he implied, it had value as a mode of prayer or praise to God. So he says, "If any man speak in an unknown tongue, let it be by two, or at the most by three, and that by course; and let one interpret. But if there be no interpreter, let him keep silence in the church; and let him speak to himself, and to God" (I Corinthians 14:27-28).

SPIRITUAL OUTPOURING

The outbreak of xenoglossy at Pentecost did not end the paranormal manifestations, however. The crowd which it attracted had swelled until over three thousand were now collected outside the upper room. The eleven gathered in front of them and Peter, as their spokesman, explained their strange behavior to the crowd, many of whom were ridiculing those baptized. He assured his listeners they were "not drunken, as ye suppose" but had undergone the outpouring of God's Spirit which had been prophesied by the Old Testament Prophet, Joel. He then went on to announce the resurrection of Jesus and to proclaim him the Christ. He ended his sermon by urging them to repent and accept the baptism of the Spirit themselves. A rugged Galilean fisherman, Peter, was not noted for his oratory or brilliance. The little band of followers had turned to him, after Jesus' ascension, as their natural leader primarily because of his generous and loyal nature and his sheer worth as a human being.

His effect on his audience was therefore another paranormal event of that day. Luke reports that virtually the entire assembly of 3,000 underwent the birth of the Spirit and became loyal members of the first Christian fellowship in Jerusalem (Acts 2:14--42).

HEALING

One more remarkable event marked the day. As with modern healers, the invasion of the Spirit and the aural manifestations signaled an increase in healing ability. As John and Peter left the gathering and walked toward the temple for prayers they were detained by a beggar who had been born a cripple, unable to walk. He was daily carried to and from the temple area where he begged. Seeing Peter and John he asked for alms. Luke then dramatically proceeds: "And Peter, fastening his eyes upon him with John, said, Look on us. And he gave heed unto them, expecting to receive something of them. Then Peter said, Silver and gold have I none; but such as I have I give thee: In the name of Jesus Christ of Nazareth rise up and walk. And he took him by the right hand, and lifted him up: and immediately his feet and ankle bones received strength. And he leaping up stood, and walked, and entered with them into the temple, walking, and leaping, and praising God" (Acts 3:I-8).

THE HOLY SPIRIT AND MODERN PHYSICS

What are we to make of Luke's account of Pentecost? The episodes it narrates can be duplicated and topped many times throughout the entire Bible. "Fire" from heaven, auras, "outpourings" of the spirit, psychic healings – even resurrections and levitations – are reported in both the Old and New Testaments. Are they just the superstitions of a bygone age or mythic elaborations of the folk process? If they are, then why do modern psychic researchers, many psychologists, physicists and medical doctors, report similar happenings in modern times? Why have some of the same events reported in Jesus' healing ministry and at Pentecost been duplicated, under laboratory conditions, at UCLA's Neuropsychiatric Institute, and Stanford's Research Institute and at Duke University? Are the "tongues of fire" at Pentecost really less believable than Thelma Moss' Kirlian auras? Is Peter's healing of the lame man less believable than those of modern psychic healers who have been investigated by teams of medical doctors, recorded on motion-picture film and subjected to Kirlian photography?

Are these modern counterparts superstitions and myths also? They have been monitored by some of the most sophisticated scientists in the world. And they have been recorded on graph paper and photographic film which are not subject to the folk process or mythic elaboration.

In taking a Space Age look at the Bible it is necessary to realize that the Space Age has brought more than the exploration of space and computer technology. It has also brought a revolution in our worldview.

The scientific materialism of the last century has become obsolete. Relativity theory and quantum physics have given us a new worldview. In this view we see the world not as a collection of hard, impenetrable atoms organized into mechanical systems. It has rather become a continuous energy field in which the principal agents are events-not objects.

We still perceive the world as consisting of objects of course – tables, chairs, people, etc. But physics tells us these objects are really energy complexes in continuous flux and inseparable from one another. Speaking of this, Fritjof Capra, a University of California physicist, has explained that the universe is experienced as a dynamic whole always including the observer. In this experience the traditional concepts of space and time, of isolated objects, and of cause and effect change much of their meaning.

In this new worldview energy, not matter, has become the basic reality. Energy events, not objects, are the "things" that make it up. Change, not permanence, is the real state of affairs, and everything is related to and interacts with every other. Given this new kind of worldview, the miracles of the Bible and the paranormal events of modern psychic research are no longer unbelievable. If our body is just an energy complex it stands to reason that a disruption of its energy flow may produce illness. And if it does it also stands to reason that a sudden influx of energy may restore its balance and as suddenly heal it.

And if everything is interrelated to everything else it also stands to reason that a healer's touch may transfer energy to an ailing patient. In fact, if mind and matter are related, then merely thinking of the ailing organ may cause a transfer of energy to that organ. Modern physics opens up vistas of interrelatedness in the world which were not suspected before the coming of the quantum physics and the Space Age.

THE HOLY SPIRIT AS LOGOS

As the ultimate Creative Power underlying both mind and matter the Holy Spirit has the qualities of both. It is manifest in matter as energy. As mind it manifests itself as organizing tendency and order in the universe.

In this latter aspect it is appropriately called "Spirit" or cosmic intelligence. And as cosmic intelligence it not only thinks the "atoms from which our minds have grown," as Sir James Jeans, wrote it thinks the atoms of the cosmos as well. Every conceivable actuality is preconceived in it as possibility; every thought as concept. This is why psychics can access information that is not mediated through the normal senses and to which they have had no previous exposure.

As the "Spirit of truth" it can instruct us in other areas as well. It can heal our bodies because it contains the cosmic blueprints from which they were made. It can heal our minds and characters because they pre-existed in it as thoughts. It can bring wholeness in social relationships because it is cosmic love. And because it embodies the psychic elements of both male and female identity it can lift human love to the heights of mutuality overcoming sexist bias and exploitation in true psychic union.

Its restoration to the head of the Trinity is a needed corrective in traditional Christianity. As the union of both masculine and feminine principles it is a counterbalance to sexist views of the Deity.

THE "GIFTS" OF THE SPIRIT

When people open their lives up to the baptism of the Spirit they become channels for directing it outward toward others. When they do, Jesus and the apostles taught, they can use it to accomplish supernormal and paranormal feats. These are the "gifts of the Spirit" Paul speaks of when he says, "For to one is given by the Spirit the word of wisdom; to another the word of knowledge ... To another faith ... to another the gifts of healing ...To another the working of miracles; to another prophecy ... to another divers kinds of tongues ..." (I Corinthians 12:8-10).

Through these they who are baptized in the Spirit minister to the world around them. So Jesus and Paul taught. So the mystics of the ages have taught. Speaking of the Spirit's indwelling as "passive energy," Father William Johnson observes that this activity of the Spirit transcends all measurable energy. It can be found in group prayer or can exist between two persons, usually a master and disciple. And in ministering with these gifts sons and daughters of God prepare the world for the coming of "kingdom of God".

THE HOLY SPIRIT AND THE KINGDOM OF GOD

No teaching was more frequently repeated, throughout Jesus' ministry, than the teaching of the coming kingdom of God. Christian theologians have puzzled over its meaning throughout the centuries. The early apostolic church saw it as the earthly, visible kingdom established by Jesus' physical return-the "parousia," or second coming, which Bultmann finds incredible. Recent scholars have tended to give it a more figurative meaning-the kingdom of God's invisible church of believers-those baptized of the Spirit.

Our space age interpretation of this central teaching suggests that both views are correct as we have already pointed out. The Cosmic Spirit does rule, in the invisible church of those who follow the way, whatever their creed or culture. Saints and mystics of all ages and every nation belong to this church. Men and women of simple faith who "hunger and thirst" after righteousness, as Jesus put it, belong to this church. And through it the world prepares and moves forward toward the heritage that will be brought by the Celestials when they return.

Members of this invisible church are the beachhead of that Celestial civilization that will make God's kingdom visible on Earth. Its citizens will be made up of the redeemed of all ages who have helped carry forward this work.

RULES FOR MEMBERSHIP

The rules for membership in this church are much simpler than for any earthly church or faith. It is not necessary to learn a catechism or undergo a ritual. Attendance is perpetual wherever you are. The code of conduct is simple-whatever you choose to do with the Spirit's guidance. There are no elders or deacons. There is no creed-or rather there are as many as humanity has devised; for the Celestials' original teaching has found its way, to some degree and in some form, in many faiths, and the Spirit is everywhere to inform and guide.

There are just two simple requirements, and Peter summed them up in his sermon at Pentecost: "Repent, and be baptized" (Acts 2:38). Translated into modern terms this means simply, (1) reject what is unrighteous in your life and, so far as you can, try to undo any wrong you have done; (2) accept the guidance of the Holy Spirit and follow it to the best of your ability. If you do you will receive its baptism and guidance. And in receiving it you will find what else you need to know and given the strength to live up to it.

These are the rules for membership in the invisible church and for celestial citizenship in God's kingdom. The key to fulfillment of these rules is the birth of the Spirit, for as Blake said, "It is the cosmos to those who know the way and chaos to those who lose it. It is Ariadne's thread whose windings create the world and yet enable us to unravel it-or ravel it. I give you the end of the Golden String. Only wind it into a ball. It will lead you in at Heaven's Gate built in Jerusalem's wall."

And there shall be no night there; and they need no candle, neither light of the sun; for the Lord God giveth them light: and they shall reign for ever and ever.

-Revelation 22:5

CHAPTER XV

THEY'RE COMING BACK!

The invention of computers and birth of the information age in the last century has generated speculation that, in time, electronic money will replace metallic and paper currency and bring about a worldwide common market.

Today we take it for granted that salaries can be paid by electronic deposit, commercial credit extended in the same way, and a large part of all purchases made with credit or debit cards. A recent article on the emerging global economy reminded us of a passage in the thirteenth chapter of Revelation where John the Revelator predicts that at the time of the end, the whole world will be brought under the control of a "beast." In this case the word for "beast" is "therion"- a "wild animal." Many New Testament scholars believe this to be John's metaphor for a ruthless and dangerous world leader.

John then says his "image" will be made to "live" and "speak"-a reasonably good description of television. And everywhere men and women will be compelled to "worship" his image-a worldwide dictatorship exercising control through the mass media.

He goes on to say that under his regime all men "both small and great, rich and poor, free and bond" will receive a "mark" in "their right hand, or in their foreheads ...". Further, he states that "no man might buy or sell, save he that had the mark, or the name of the beast, or the number of .his name" (Revelation 13:15-17). This is the mysterious "mark of the beast" which has loomed large in the imagination of Christians since John's fearful prophecy was first penned.

TOMORROW'S NEWS 2,000 YEARS AGO

As we read John's account we once again marveled at how exactly some of the prophecies of the Bible anticipate the developments of today. Like pieces in a jigsaw puzzle things we had read or heard began to fall into place. A recent suggestion that the energy crisis and Middle East oil situation might bring about the formation of a worldwide common market under a director who would have unprecedented powers. Recent proposals that all personal data – Social Security, IRS, FBI, military, police, motor vehicle, and business and credit-be merged into a single system accessed by a simple code have been made.

If these things should be done, John's vision of the future would become actuality. A worldwide common market could, with modern communications technology, control the economic activities of every man, woman and child on the planet. People could not buy or sell without a number given them by the "beast." Superimposed over the forehead on a "mug shot," or the right hand on a handprint, it would be an infallible proof of identity. Unable to buy food, shelter, transportation or communications without identification, people could be controlled by economic restriction as they have never been controlled by the cruder techniques of old-fashioned police states. The "mark of the beast" would be the most coercive and frightening method of totalitarian control ever devised!

It would be impossible to buy a hot dog, feed a parking meter, purchase a tank of gas, ride a bus, enter a theater, or make a phone call without leaving a permanent record of the transaction in the computer's memory bank. And anyone, knowing the access code, could get the time and place of the act, along with your identification and personal history, by simply entering a code.

PROPHECY AND THE BIBLE

John's vision of a coming world dictatorship is only one of a number of forecasts the Bible makes for the time of the end. Many of these, as we saw in Chapter III, have already been fulfilled, suggesting that the time of the Celestials' return is at hand. Others, like that concerning the "mark of the beast," are already being predicted by our own scientists for the near future. How was it possible for Bible writers, twenty to twenty-five centuries ago, to foresee the present with such accuracy? Is it mere coincidence? Or is foretelling the future genuinely possible? Once again recent research in physics and parapsychology seems to provide an answer. Before looking at this, however, it will be helpful to see why traditional answers given in the heyday of higher criticism are unsatisfactory.

"IT'S JUST COINCIDENCE"

Many critics have insisted that fulfillment of biblical prophecies is an illusion. Certain that foretelling the future is impossible they have fallen back on two stock explanations for every seemingly valid case of prophecy. One is that the prophecy is so vaguely worded we cannot determine its exact meaning. As a result it can be arbitrarily interpreted to fit events which happen later.)

(2) The other is that, though specific, it refers to events which happened before the Bible received its final form. So, it is claimed, the particular prophecy was written into the record by later copyists or editors after the facts it is supposed to foretell.

Unfortunately for the critics, neither of these explanations can account for the crucial prophecy which sets the timetable for the Celestials' return. As we saw in Chapter III, both the Prophet Ezekiel and Jesus forecast the return of the Jews to Israel after a dispersion "among the nations." This event, the founding of the State of Israel, is so unlikely, after a 1900- year dispersion, that coincidence can be ruled out as a possible explanation.) *Ignores Jewish perpetual attachment to location in Palestine*

Some critics have suggested the prophecies of Israel's rebirth refer to one, or more, of the Jews' various returns from exile that occurred before the Bible received its final form. While this could apply to Ezekiel's prophecy, though his phrase, "in the latter years" (Ezekiel 38:8), is standard Hebrew phraseology for the time of the end, it can in no way account for Jesus' prophecy. There has been only one return from dispersion among "the nations" since Jesus' time, and that occurred 1,900 years after the gospels received their final form. Jesus' prophecy of the "fig tree" (a traditional emblem of Isreal) putting forth "its leaves" once again, just before the time of the end, seems to be an unambiguous reference to the rebirth of Israel (Matthew 24:32). And its occurrence in 1948 makes it impossible that these words could have been put into Jesus' mouth after the event had already taken place.

1. (Clearly, then, we have in this prophecy a genuine forecast, across almost 2,000 years, of an event so specific, dramatic and unlikely there can be little reasonable doubt its occurrence was a fulfillment of prophecy.) ? !

PROPHECY IN THE LABORATORY

How can this be? Genuine prophecy seems so contrary to common sense and what has been taken to be "scientific" that most Bible scholars have been inclined to write these prophecies off as vague references whose meaning can no longer be recovered.

Yet, in many cases they are not vague, and their meaning is quite specific. It just happens to be a meaning which is difficult for skeptical scholars to accept. Once again a Space Age interpretation of Bible prophecy puts a wholly new light on the matter. If the prophets were just human fortune tellers, acting on their own initiative, then their remarkable accuracy would be incomprehensible. We would no more expect it of them than we would of tea-leaf readers, crystal-ball gazers or palmists.

But if these prophecies come from a civilization that knew, in their time, more than we now know, then their accuracy becomes more understandable. For our own psychic researchers are studying people who can foretell the future in the laboratory. This skill, called precognition, has been widely investigated under the most stringent controls.

Helmut Schmidt, J. B. Rhine's successor at Duke University and a brilliant research physicist, had remarkable success with subjects foretelling the occurrence of atomic events that normally defy prediction. His experiments involved guessing the order in which lamps were lighted by the target impact of subatomic particles-a process that is theoretically unpredictable. Summarizing his success, Arthur Koestler, in his book "The Roots of Coincidence" points out that the odds against the results some of his subjects obtained are "ten thousand million against one." In attempting to explain Schmidt's success, Koestler theorizes that the old idea that coming events cast their shadow before them is true even in the field of subatomic physics. He cites quantum physicists, such as University of London's Professor D. Bohm, who believe future events send out "feelers" which foreshadow them in the present. He also cites Cambridge mathematician, Adrian Dobbs, who believes future events try out tentatively all the potentialities out of which one actually emerges." Koestler's point is that psychics, like those Helmut Schmidt tested, seem to be able to detect these "feelers" and use them to predict future events they foreshadow.

THE CELESTIALS AND PROPHECY

If the Celestials have mastered the uses of psychic power, as we earlier suggested, their prediction of present-day developments thousands of years ago may have involved a similar method. It is also possible, of course, that they can predict complex social phenomena, such as the rebirth of Israel, by ordinary techniques of scientific prediction, much as our own scientists can predict eclipses or the weather. Though these involve the unpredictable elements of human decision and behavior they are no more indeterminate than the subatomic events predicted by Helmut Schmidt's subjects.

With advanced mathematical and data-processing techniques they could doubtless measure and interrelate the more complex causes of historical events as easily as our own scientists can predict the trajectory of a missile or space probe. And this might be possible even for events thousands of years in the future. In the same way our own scientists can predict the coming of comets or the dates of eclipses thousands of years before they occur. As we will see later in this chapter, they may even have machines, similar to television receivers, which can translate the "feelers" of future events, or the analysis of their causes, into video forecasts. These machines would be similar to "time machines" envisioned by our own science-fantasy writers which could enable us literally to see the future. It is even possible, according to Einstein's theory of relativity, that they can time travel into the future and witness its events first hand.

Of all the prophecies in the Bible none is more often or emphatically asserted than the promise of the Celestials' return to Earth. And throughout the ages, no problem has preoccupied conservative Christians, who believe in that return, more than the time of its occurrence. Over the centuries they have continued to echo the disciples' query: "Tell us, when shall these things be? And what shall be the sign of thy coming, and of the end of the world?" (Matthew 24:3).

Jesus' answer was unambiguous. "But of that day and hour knoweth no man, no, not the angels of heaven, but my Father only" (Matthew 24:36). Yet in spite of Jesus' assurance on this matter a favorite pastime, for students of the Bible's apocalyptic books, has been the attempt to deduce a day and an hour. The apostles expected Christ's return during their own lifetime. Almost every generation of Christians since has produced some who have been convinced they would live to see the ultimate event. Numerous dates have been set in the past-the last day of the year 1000; October of 1844; September of 1936. Needless to say the fateful event failed to materialize on any of them.

The logic that prompted their selections was various. The year 1000 seemed destined to some, because it ended the first millennium following the birth of Jesus. Others seized on the cryptic reference to 2,300 days in the Book of Daniel and matched it with an equal number of years calculated from the rebuilding of Solomon's Temple (Daniel 8:14 and 9:25). Pyramidologists arrived at the 1936 date because the number of inches in the passageway leading to the King's Chamber suggested it, if one let an inch equal a year and reckoned from the birth of Christ. Why God would have left cryptograms in which a year is disguised as a day, or an inch, they did not bother to explain, but the failure of the advent to follow their timetables was evident to believers and skeptics alike.

In the end we are driven back to Jesus' declaration that "of that day and hour knoweth no man ... " Yet he did not say that an approximate time could not be determined. In fact he, himself, gave one very specific clue. And if we assume his Celestial origin-argued in Chapter XIII, he, as the son of Jehovah who alone knows, should have been able to pinpoint an approximate time.

"EVEN AT THE DOORS"

Jesus' clue is given in the book of Matthew shortly after he assures his disciples that the exact date and hour cannot be known. He links it to his famous prophecy concerning the restoration of Israel. Speaking of that event he says: "Now learn a parable of the fig tree; When his branch is yet tender, and putteth forth leaves, ye know that summer is nigh: So likewise ye, when ye shall see all these things, know that it is near, even at the doors. Verily I say unto you, This generation shall not pass, till all these things be fulfilled" (Matthew 24:32-34).

We have already pointed out that the fig tree is a historical emblem of national Israel. It "put forth leaves," for the first time since Jesus' day, when the new State of Israel was born in 1948. Jesus' clue to the time of his return is given in his assurance that the "generation" which witnessed this event should "not pass" until the rest of his prophecy had been fulfilled. And what was the rest of his prophecy? It is given in a verse immediately preceding. So he says, "And then shall appear the sign of the Son of man in heaven: and then shall all the tribes of the Earth mourn, and they shall see the Son of man coming in the clouds of heaven with power and great glory" (Matthew 24:30).

Taking Jesus literally, it is evident he means the Celestials' return will occur during the lifetime of those witnessing the founding of the State of Israel. Since the maximum human lifespan is only a little more than a century this suggests that the Celestial's return will occur in our present century. We must not forget, however, Jesus's caution that no man knoweth "that day and that hour"which in the light of past misinterpretation of other passages leaves open to question the accuracy of this interpretation, as well.

THE APOCALYPTIC PUZZLE

Though Jesus declared that the day and hour of the Celestials' return cannot be known, the temptation to narrow the time as much as possible has always been irresistible to believers. And to those who are tempted, the clues in the Bible are an endless maze. Principally they are found in the prophetic books-Jeremiah, Isaiah, Ezekiel, Zechariah and others. Especially they are found in the two great apocalypses-the books of Daniel and Revelation. An apocalypse is a prophetic writing that predicts an end of things which is near, swift and cataclysmic. Both Daniel and Revelation make such predictions.

Scholars are undecided about the authorship of both books. They generally regard Daniel as a literary hero invented by the unknown author of his apocalypse. The book is usually dated around 165 B.C., though it tells of a time 400 years earlier. Critics therefore feel the fulfillment of many of its prophecies was due to their being written in after the facts.

Revelation was written toward the end of the first century A.D by an unknown author who simply called himself John. He wrote from the Isle of Patmos, in the Sporades, where he had been exiled-a common fate for stubborn Christians who held out against the emperor worship reestablished under Domitian.

Both apocalypses were written in times of persecution to rally the spirits of their author's contemporaries. Both seek to show that deliverance is near. Daniel prophesied it through a Messiah who would reestablish Israel's earthly kingdom. John sees an end of suffering through the return of Christ to set up a millennial paradise on Earth.

In both works these joyful events are preceded by dreadful upheavals that purge the Earth of evil and prepare for the triumph of righteousness and peace. The books are fraught with an unending succession of heavenly portents, natural catastrophes, wars and judgments. The actors in these dramas are a strange and nightmarish assortment of beasts with multiple heads, weird zoological hybrids, malevolent anti-christs, false prophets and dragons.

Through the centuries Jews and Christians have tried to fit these strange symbols to events and personalities of their own times. And though these speculations have all been refuted by the failure of the world to come to an end, certain beliefs about the last days have emerged and remained. They are still taken today, by conservative Christians, as the core meaning of the Bible's prophetic books.

Now, as we stand on the threshhold of our own Space Age we must ask, once again, whether anything can be extracted from the Bible's prophetic and apocalyptic maze. Does it throw any genuine light on the happenings of today, and can it give any identifiable signs by which we can verify that ours is the time of the Celestials' return?

"SIGNS OF THE TIMES"

We have already seen that John's vision of a coming world dictatorship seems to bear on the coming use of electronic money. And both Ezekiel and Jesus appear to have predicted the founding of the State of Israel.

Could it not be, then, that amid the tangle of what Bultmann called "apocalyptic myth" the Bible contains a solid core of Celestial information? Just as the gospels reveal Bernhard Anderson's "vivid glimpses" and "small tableaux" of Jesus' life, in spite of mythic elaboration, may it not also be that the prophetic writings afford genuine insight into the last days and the end, itself?

In Chapter X, The Bible and History, we pointed out that the times of Daniel's and Revelation's compositions was one in which old oral traditions and forgotten writings were being rediscovered. Their incorporation into the apocryphal and canonical books of that period makes it likely these works include much that is genuine Celestial information. The problem, however, is to separate the wheat from the chaff.

As we saw some critics have tried to distinguish the genuine sayings and deeds of Jesus and his disciples from later additions to the gospel record. In the same way our Space Age interpretation provides a key for separating what is Celestially inspired, in the prophetic and apocalyptic traditions which have come down to us, from what was contributed by the times and circumstances of its writers.

In looking for the prophetic core which genuinely applies to our own age we should be guided by the logic of the Space Age interpretation itself. If the conclusions it draws about the Bible's meanings are valid then those conclusions will imply certain things about the time of the end. Using these we can construct a Space-Age scenario for the end of our present world.

And using this scenario as a guide we can then search for prophetic scriptures which seem to support it. If we find them their coincidence with our independent conclusions will be evidence that they are genuine prophetic insights. By this method, then, we may be able, as Jesus put it, to "discern the signs of the times" (Matthew 16:3).

A SPACE AGE APOCALYPSE

Two assumptions stand out, in our Space Age interpretation of the Bible, which set the stage for an apocalyptic ending of our world. One is the idea that we are soon to be invaded by highly advanced extraterrestrials who will establish a world order of peace and righteousness. The other is that our region of the galaxy is a prison for rebellious Celestials who exist in force and have duplicated and stored Celestial technology in undercover bases.

Given these two ideas, a cataclysmic end to our present world is inevitable.

The logic of the situation requires that the return of the Celestials will be marked by sudden and worldwide catastrophe. Let us see why this is so.

We earlier quoted Jesus' remark that Satan is the "Prince of this world." Since Satan and his followers were expelled for their attempted revolt and disruption of the Celestial's colonization plan their activities have been confined to Earth's region of the galaxy.

Since they have short-range spacecraft, and, in all probability, some military hardware, the logic of the situation dictates that they will make a final, all-out effort at retaining possession of their domain. Even if Satan believes he is doomed to failure, his pride, and the fact that he has nothing to lose, would demand some kind of last-ditch stand.

What form will his campaign take? Our premises dictate certain moves. The first of these would be recruiting whatever help is possible from human allies. Since the rebels are outnumbered by the victorious Celestials their only hope would be in increasing their strength.

Their approach to the problem would probably involve an undercover strategy. Humans would be used to front for the fallen Celestials. A puppet leader would probably be chosen, along with aides, who would be directed by Satan. With Satan's superior knowledge and skill the puppet's rise to world power would be assured. Taking advantage of global problems (such as the energy crisis, economic disruptions, and inflation), the building of a world dictatorship would be accomplished through economic, rather than military or political, means. Nations would voluntarily enter a common market under the control of Satan's puppet leader who would seem to have the solution to their problems.

Once his power was established this leader would form an international police force to "keep the peace." He would probably also establish himself as leader of a state philosophico-religious system to provide sanction for his power and to extend his control over his followers.

Taking advantage of the current revival of interest in religion and the occult he would use biocosmic energy to perform miracles. He would probably also employ the traditional device of leader worship to achieve a fanatical following and unquestioning support. Satan's interest in perverting everything basic to the Celestials' civilization makes this course a probable one.

When the Celestials' return is imminent (and Satan would be familiar with the "signs of the times") the puppet dictator would be directed to launch a "preventive war" against the nations that have refused to join his common market. The politics of energy and the Middle East power alignment make this area the likely theater of action, and Israel would be the most probable target for attack. With Jerusalem at its center, it would be the headquarters for the returning Celestials. Any successful resistance to their return would make seizure of this site a first military objective.

The actual return of the Celestials would almost certainly be marked by space warfare and nuclear holocaust. The fallen Celestials would put whatever spacecraft they have into the air to disrupt the takeover. The puppet leader and his army would move on the prospective landing site at Jerusalem. Since the returning Celestials have the advantage of superior numbers and technology the result would be inevitable. Satan's army would be destroyed in the field by nuclear weapons or artificially triggered natural disasters. His spacecraft would be destroyed in the air by missiles launched from the Celestial's space city as it lands. Modules would be sent out from it to pursue survivors of the holocaust. These they would methodically destroy. Satan and his followers would probably be imprisoned on some planetary or satellite base near Earth. There they would remain until the end of the probationary millennium when a general judgment would be set up to separate those qualified for Celestial citizenship from others who have failed to meet the requirements. At that time a final disposition would be made of the rebellious Celestials, as well.

Knowing what we do of the Celestials, victorious and fallen, this scenario seems to describe the most probable course of events at the time of the end. Does Bible prophecy support it? It most assuredly does. Let's examine the prophetic and apocalyptic scriptures which offer support.

"A TIME OF TROUBLE"

The stage for the final drama is set in the last chapter of the Book of Daniel. Speaking of the time of the end, its writer says: "... and there shall be a time of trouble, such as never was since there was a nation even to that same time: and at that time thy people shall be delivered, every one that shall be found written in the book. And many of them that sleep in the dust of the earth shall awake, some to everlasting life, and some to shame and everlasting contempt. And they that be wise shall shine as the brightness of the firmament; and they that turn many to righteousness, as the stars for ever and ever" (Daniel 12:1-3).

The events that characterize this "time of trouble" are described in Revelation. John the Revelator tells how a door is "opened in heaven", and he ascends apparently into one of the Celestials' spacecraft. A voice says to him: "Come up hither, and I will shew thee things which must be hereafter" (Revelation 4:1). His preview is apparently seen on a type of video forecaster, a time machine, such as we described earlier in the chapter. He sees a "sea of glass mingled with fire" (Revelation 15:2) a remarkable first-century description of a television screen, and his vision unfolds. Satan, the dragon, raises up a world leader-the "beast" or "anti-Christ." "And I stood upon the sand of the sea, and saw a beast rise up out of the sea ..." (the reference here is apparently to a "sea of glass", a television screen, not a watery ocean as traditional scholarship has supposed). "... and the dragon gave him his power, and his seat, and great authority.... And they worshipped the dragon which gave power unto the beast: and they worshipped the beast, saying, Who is like unto the beast? who is able to make war with him? ... And it was given unto him to make war with the saints, and to overcome them: and power was given him over all kindred, and tongues, and nations" (Revelation 13:1-2, 4, 7).

John goes on to tell how this beast is represented by another beast later called the "false prophet." Apparently he is the high priest of the state religion the Antichrist will found, for he "doeth great wonders", so that he maketh fire to come down from heaven on the earth in the sight of men, and deceiveth them that dwell on the earth ..." (Revelation 13:13-14).

He it is who "gives life" to the "image" of the beast and causes it to "speak" (Revelation 13:15). Apparently he functions as minister of propaganda, as well, and uses the television medium to maintain and enhance the beast's power. He is also the one who causes "both small and great, rich and poor, free and bond" to receive the "mark" in their hands or foreheads-the fearful "mark of the beast" whose number is "Six hundred threescore and six"-666! Without it people can neither buy nor sell, and by means of it the antichrist is able to maintain a fearful grip on the lives of men and women everywhere. Those who refuse his mark and worship are put to death.

John then goes on to tell how the dragon and false prophet cooperate to raise a huge army. Working through representatives, fallen Celestials, or "demons", they "go forth unto the kings of the earth, and of the whole world, to gather them to the battle of the great day of God Almighty" (Revelation 16:14).

They gather near Jerusalem at Armageddon-the Plain of Migeddo. And there are "voices, and thunders, and lightnings," and "a great earthquake, such as was not since men were upon the earth," so that "every island fled away, and the mountains were not found." Finally "a great hail" falls on men "out of heaven" (Revelation 16:18, 20-21). The degree of the carnage is indicated when John tells us an "angel thrust in his sickle into the earth, and gathered the vine of the earth, and cast it into the great winepress of the wrath of God ... and blood came out of the winepress, even unto the horse bridles, by the space of a thousand and six hundred furlongs" (Revelation 14:19-20).

With this conclusion to the abortive "Battle of Armageddon" the Celestials land. As they touch down Satan's aerial army is blasted out of the sky like falling stars, and the smoke of nuclear holocaust darkens the sun and dims the moon to a reddish hue. John's account rises in a crescendo of apocalyptic terror: "And I looked, and behold a pale horse: and his name that sat on him was Death, and Hell followed with him... and, lo, there was a great earthquake; and the sun became black as sackcloth of hair, and the moon became as blood; And the stars of heaven fell unto the earth, even as a fig tree casteth her untimely figs, when she is shaken of a mighty wind" (Revelation 6:8, 12-13).

"FALL ON US"

The mop up operation is described in scarcely less dramatic terms. John sees a "white horse" in heaven and "he that sat upon him was called Faithful and True ... His eyes were as a flame of fire, and on his head were many crowns ..." (one of the computerized robots with which we are already familiar). The "armies which were in heaven" follow him on "white horses" (Revelation 19:11-12, 14). Like the robot of our opening scenario a "sharp sword" goes "out of his mouth" so that he can "smite the nations" (Revelation 19:15).

As John tells it, "kings of the earth, and the great men, and the rich men, and the chief captains, and the mighty men, and every bondman, and every free man" will hide themselves in the dens and in the rocks of the mountains." And they will call out to the rocks, "Fall on us, and hide us from the face of him that sitteth on the throne" (Revelation 6:15-16).

In the end the "beast" and false prophet, along with the survivors of their army, are consumed with "fire" (Revelation 19:20). Satan is "bound" for a "thousand years" (Revelation 20:2), after which he and the then resurrected unrighteous will be judged and consigned to the limbo of cosmic memories forever.

With the destruction of Satan's forces and his own imprisonment, peace descends. John's vision continues as the "sea of glass" reveals "them that had gotten the victory over the beast, and over his image ... and over the number of his name ..." They stood "on the sea of glass" (an appropriate description of video images) "having the harps of God" and singing, "Great and marvelous are thy works, Lord God Almighty; just and true are thy ways, thou King of saints" (Revelation 15:2-3). And so, with John's vision, we come full circle back to our opening scenario.

THE COUNTDOWN BEGINS

If we have interpreted the time table correctly, as suggested by the fig tree parable, the countdown for the Celestial's return may already have begun. Are diplomats already working out the coalitions that prepare the way for a coming world dictatorship? Is John's fearful antichrist already quietly preparing for the prophesied role he is soon to assume, unsuspected by those around him?

Do today's newscaster tell us that the countdown has already begun? Certainly we live in an age that fits Daniel's description of the "time of the end"-a time when "many shall run to and fro, and knowledge shall be increased" (Daniel 2:4). Also it is "a time of trouble" (Daniel 12:1) which invites desperate remedies.

The energy crisis looms as a problem without historic parallel. Because of it world tension has been focused on the Middle East. The rebirth of Israel, which Daniel and Jesus prophesied for the time of the end, has made it the key to this explosive situation. Many analysts of world affairs believe a full-scale outbreak of Arab-Israeli hostilities could trigger worldwide conflict.

In the meantime, international problems of unemployment, inflation and unstable currency are forcing nations to form economic alliances that look toward world government. Chief among these is the European Common Market, the emergence of a global economy and the expanding role of the United Nations which numerous economic and political analysts see as pointing towards a coming world government. Taken together with diminishing resources, climate change and the growing threat of international terrorism it seems to many that a world government, with powers of enforcement, may be the only way to deal successfully with the crises now facing our planet.

If these events are signs of the times, predicted in Daniel and Revelation, then the countdown to the Celestial's return has already begun. It is a countdown which would take us through a world-wide economic dictatorship to the brink of global disaster prevented only by the return of the Celestials.

Apart from biblical prophecy and the "signs of the times" there is one other piece of supportive evidence which adds weight to our conclusion that the return of the Celestials is impending. This evidence comes from astronomy.

We have already seen that biblical etymology points to a planet of Arcturus as the Celestials' headquarters or a way station. We have further seen how space science dictates that space missions are launched according to schedules requiring the closest approach of the launching site and the target.

Since planets move around their suns, and suns, or stars, approach and recede from one another, ideal times for launching missions occur infrequently. When a launch site and its target are in closest approach, a "launch window" is said to be open. It is then that a mission can be completed in minimum time and with the least cost and effort.

Astronomers agree that the Celestials' site,—Arcturus, is now at its closest approach to the Earth in the last 500,000 years. Its present rate of approach, at about 3 miles per second, has brought it to within 38.3 light-years of our own sun. The time for launching a major mission to Earth has never been better in recent geological times. Further, Arcturus will remain virtually at this distance during the next few thousand years, when the establishment of a new colony might require a succession of follow-up missions.

If Celestials, using Arcturus as a base, did visit our Earth thousands of years ago; if they continued periodic visits in recent historic times; if they now plan a large-scale migration, and if they will continue to transport large numbers of personnel and equipment over the next few thousand years then the positioning of Arcturus has, is and will continue to be ideal for their plan of colonization!

The most extraordinary thing about these facts is that we only discovered them after we had deduced, from independent biblical evidence, that a possible planetary system of Arcturus may harbor a base for their opperations in this part of our galazy. The remarkableness of this unsuspected coincidence can be better appreciated by examining the accompanying diagram. It shows that the timing and extent of Arcturus' launch window, in relation to our sun, almost ideally fit colonization requirements.

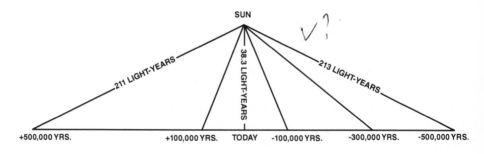

The launch window is open. Arcturus is now at its closest point of approach to Earth.

"HEAVEN AT LAST"

And with the establishment of Earth as an actual Celestial colony, humanity's age-old dream of heaven will come true! Unlike traditional conceptions of heaven, however, the real Heaven will be here and now. It will not exist as some never never land in the sky-a realm of white-robed spirits playing on harps. Our Heaven will be this colony of the Celestials' empire, the planet Earth-our own terra firma. For within hours, after their landing, the incredible technology of the Celestials will have transformed our planet into "a new Earth" serving also as "Heaven"(II Peter 3:13).

An Earthly and visible Kingdom of God will replace the invisible church of Christ, whose members will now be its citizens. They will make up "a great multitude, which no man could number, of all nations, and kindreds, and people, and tongues" (Revelation 7:9). And in special roles of leadership, among those redeemed, will be representatives of the chosen people who will be rewarded for the millennia of persecution and suffering they have undergone in carrying out their special role in the redemption of humanity. These outstandingly faithful and righteous Jews will, at the time of the end, realize the fulfillment of their own hopes for a deliverer and messiah. For Jesus, as the melchisedec of this world, ruling from their capitol city, will fulfill their own ancient prophecies for a restoration of the kingdom at the time of the end.

And at last these leaders, and the numberless others of their people who have been faithful to the covenant, will realize Isaiah's great promise: "And the ransomed of the Lord shall return, and come to Zion with songs and everlasting joy upon their heads: they shall obtain joy and gladness, and sorrow and sighing shall flee away" (Isaiah 35:10).

Then, throughout the Earth, that "great multitude which no man could number", living and resurrected; of "all nations, and kindreds, and people, and tongues"-will begin a life of utopian splendor. As John the Revelator says, "They shall hunger no more, neither thirst anymore; neither shall the sun light on them, nor any heat. For the Lamb which is in the midst of the throne shall feed them, and shall lead them unto living fountains of waters; and God shall wipe away all tears from their eyes" (Revelation 7:16-17).

WHAT IT WILL BE LIKE

Because it is beyond earthly experience, the idea of heavenly life has always eluded those who try to describe it. Ministers and writers who talk about it usually resort to homely analogies or hackneyed phrases lifted from the Scriptures. The agenda seldom ventures beyond walking streets of gold, playing on harps or singing around the throne of God. Understandably many people feel this doesn't add up to a very interesting lifestyle.

Now that our own Space Age has arrived we should be able to do a better job of picturing life in an advanced, extraterrestrial civilization even though, as the apostle Paul, assures us, "Eye hath not seen, nor ear heard, neither have entered into the heart of man, the things which God hath prepared for them that love him. (I Cor. 2:9). But, examined under the lens of archeolingusitics we have found the scriptures give sufficient clues to form some conception of what it may be like.

WHERE IS THE STING?

In breaking away from past notions that are too earthbound or hackneyed we should concentrate on points of difference. And, without doubt, the major point of difference between human and Celestial life is their ability to halt aging and extend life indefinitely. In his version of how they will employ this incredible technology on their return to Earth the Apostle Paul wrote, "death will be swallowed up in victory." 1 Cor 15:54. For immortal life is what most distinguishes Celestials from humans and heaven from Earth.

According to the Bible, the transition from mortality to immortality will start here on Earth, as the Celestials' return. It will occur with the mass resurrection of the righteous of all ages. With their restoration to life the work of humanity's greatest enemy, death, will be neutralized at a stroke. As the Apostle Paul so eloquently puts it, death will be "swallowed up in victory" "Oh death where is thy sting, Oh grave, where is thy victory?" (I Corinthians 15:54+55).

We saw, in Chapter IV, that individual resurrection might be accomplished by a mechanical replicator. Mass resurrection, however, would obviously require a different technology.

At first it may seem impossible that any technology could resurrect millions, or billions, of humans. And even if this were possible where could the resurrected be accommodated? How could these multitudes of past ages find a place in a world that is already overcrowded with the living?

The answer may be found in new ideas which are coming out of quantum physics and astrobiology. In the case of mass resurrection the solution may be in the fact that we live in a two-level universe. As we saw, earlier in this chapter, quantum physicists, such as Professor Bohm, believe the things and events we call actualities are preceded by potentialities that exist as precursors. In the last chapter this same idea was expressed in a different way when we said the Holy Spirit, or Universal Mind, contains the ideas of all that becomes actual including ourselves. As Sir James Jeans put it, "it is the universal mind in which atoms, giving rise to our own minds, exist as thoughts."

But if this is true, then it must also be a record of all that has been, for when actualities cease to be they must return to possibilities in this eternal Logos. Ancient religious teachings have held that such cosmic records exist. Esoteric traditions speak of them as "Akashic records." The Bible speaks of a "Book of Life." If the Logos, or energy field of the universe, does retain a record of all that has been, including people, then these records would be blueprints from which the dead could be reconstructed. An energizing force applied to the information patterns of the dead would become a resurrecting energy. By irradiating the Earth with it, as they landed, returning Celestials could bring about mass resurrection, and death could truly be overcome at a stroke!

RESURRECTION AND QUANTUM PHYSICS

Modern quantum physics views things and events, including ourselves, in a way which supports this explanation of resurrection. For it "things" are nothing but energy frames (or "information patterns") on which energy events, sub atomic particles, are temporarily hung.

In this view a living person is not unlike a television image. A television receiver creates a moving image out of luminescent particles embedded in its screen. In the same way a living person is created by an energy pattern whose form is clothed with subatomic particles like a television image in 3D.

The blueprint for the television image is an information pattern imposed, by the broadcasting station, on the electromagnetic field that surrounds the Earth. The blueprint for a person is an information pattern that is contained in the biocosmic energy field that is the universe.

And just as a television image can be recreated again and again, from a videotape or CD, so, in theory, could people, no longer living, be recreated, from cosmic records of their former existence.

Resurrection, in this sense, would simply be a repetition of the process which brought the person into being in the first place. An information pattern, or energy frame, that is clothed once more, with the particles-or bits of energy -which characterized that person during his, or her, original lifetime.

"I AM NOT YET ASCENDED"

The resurrection of Jesus, as told in the gospels, suggests that a resurrection energy was employed for him, for Matthew tells us that "many bodies of the saints which slept" near Jesus' tomb arose, and "came out of the graves after his resurrection ..." (Matthew 27:52-53). This suggests that a resurrection energy was used which was powerful enough to inadvertently resurrect others buried nearby.

Later, when he first appeared to Mary Magdalene on resurrection morning, Jesus warned her, "Touch me not; for I am not yet ascended to my Father" (John 20:17). The context makes it clear that Jesus was not referring to his ascension into heaven here, for eight days later he allowed Thomas to probe him freely, although that ascension had not yet occurred. The Greek word "anabaino", translated as "ascend," means "to grow up from a base." It precisely describes the "clothing" of an energy frame with particles which quantum physics tells us is necessary for the actualization of an object. Jesus was evidently telling Mary he was not yet fully actualized. His state was apparently an intermediate one, something like that of an apparition, which some parapsychologists believe may be a partial materialization of a cosmic record. Had Mary touched him she would probably have been frightened by his shadowy insubstantiality.

Jesus' appearance, while not yet "ascended," is reminiscent of the "phantom leaf" phenomenon in Kirlian photography. Researchers have found that a leaf cut in half will, under proper conditions, show a Kirlian aura that is intact. Even though half the particles that "clothe" it have been removed, the energy frame, on which they were hung, still remains unaltered and shows on the photographic plate. Like Jesus, the cut portion of the leaf still appears, though it is no longer "ascended."

If our inferences from quantum physics are correct we, too, have "phantoms" which continue even after bodily life has ended. Their occasional partial "ascensions" may be the explanations for apparitions or hauntings, so some parapsychologists believe. Their accidental invasion into the minds and bodies of living persons may also account for seeming instances of reincarnation and for certain types of possession as well as phenomena of exorcism. As fragments of Koestler's "Cosmic Mind", these "phantoms", are the basis for what theologians call the "soul." And they are the Celestials' blueprint for resurrection.

By tuning resurrection energy to the "frequency" of the righteous they could accomplish a selective resurrection much as a television receiver can selectively tune in one channel signal from the many around it. And just as the receiver can create images from that signal alone, so the Celestials can apparently resurrect all the righteous of a planet (or the "saints" around Jesus' tomb as Matthew recounts).

This resurrection force is, in all probability, a concentrated form of biocosmic energy. And just as psychic healers radiate it more strongly while healing, so those who are supercharged with it may be able to bring about resurrection by their mere presence-as Jesus is reported to have done with Lazarus.

"MANY MANSIONS"

The analogy of television may also explain how the Celestials handle the housing problem on planets where they have accomplished mass resurrection. A television receiver does not have to be near the broadcasting station to create an image on its screen. The information which it uses for producing the image is broadcast everywhere within its range. In the same way our cosmic records may be broadcast throughout the cosmos. If this is so, we could be resurrected wherever the resurrection force is focused.

The resurrected dead of crowded worlds like our own could simply be resurrected on other worlds. In this way people of past generations, or ages, could be kept together until they had been reoriented to living in a futuristic society. Afterward, new citizens of the Celestials' empire could probably move freely, or even select worlds on which they wished to live.

OVERCOMING AGING AND DEATH

Here on Earth the ravages of aging and untimely death too often cut short the work of our greatest leaders and people of genius. Those who try to carry on their work are deprived of the training and guidance they could have given.

Only a civilization in which life spans of centuries, or even millennia, are possible could provide the continuity of effort and progress needed, to carry out the governance of an empire stretching over thousands of light years' distance. Is there anything on our present frontiers of life extension research, or predictions by our futurologists, that would support the Bibles' claim that Celestials on another world far older than ours already enjoy such lifespans? And is there any evidence suggesting we might be able to achieve similar lifespans ourselves? A "yes" answer for both questions is suggested when we consider recent developments in anti-aging research.

In the past the usual argument given against the possibility of extending human life indefinitely has been that living on for centuries or millennia is impossible, because it would violate a fundamental law of nature. This law, known as the second law of thermodynamics, states that all closed material systems that do work must eventually wear out and run down. It is commonly believed to apply not only to everyday mechanical devices such as engines, clocks and computers, but to the largest material systems we know such as our solar system, galaxies, and the universe itself. Those offering this argument also assume it applies to systems that are alive such as viruses, bacteria, plants and animals including ourselves.

In assuming this, however, it is often forgotten that the second law of thermodynamics only applies to systems that are closed. No material system is truly closed so long as new matter and sources of energy can be introduced into it.

Proof of this can be found in one of the mechanical devices most common in our everyday lives, the automobile. While it ordinarily has an operating span of a decade or two, and most are traded in before that, we occasionally hear or read of cars that have been driven for half a million miles or more. Even more remarkable are the many cars that exist in showroom condition seven or eight decades after their original manufacture.

Most of us have visited shopping malls or plazas where antique car shows are in progress and have examined cars from the forties and thirties, or even twenties, of the last century still looking as though they had just been driven off the showroom floor. Even more amazing, perhaps, is to pull alongside one of them being driven at modern freeway speeds among cars seven or eight decades newer.

These experiences prove that aging and wear of a complex mechanical device can be reversed and its operation restored to optimal efficiency indefinitely so long as needed parts and repair technologies are available to accomplish it. Theoretically there is no limit to how long such renewal can be kept up. If needed parts can be salvaged or remanufactured and required repair technologies are available. cars made anytime during the last century could still be operating with like new efficiency hundreds or even thousands of years in the future.

If this is possible for non-living material systems, such as cars, would it not also be possible for living material systems such as extraterrestrials or humans here on Earth?

GENETICS AND IMMORTALITY

In the closing decade of the last century a series of brilliantly designed experiments, here and abroad, made it clear that indefinite extension of human life is possible, and these experimental results point the way toward a method for achieving it. In the process speculation about anti-aging science has moved from the state of fiction and futurology to respectable scientific research.

What microbiologists and gerontologists have established can be summed up briefly. First, immortality, defined not as inability to die but as the ability to live on indefinitely when necessary conditions of life are maintained, is already a part of our genetic make-up. Some of our cells, known as reproductive, already possess immortality, as we have defined it. Other somatic, or bodily, cells have genetically limited lifespans.

In sexual reproduction the union of male sperm and female ovum produces a "zygote" cell that begins dividing into two, four, eight, and higher multiples. In this process it becomes a human embryo. Its earliest stage consists of cells known as stem cells, which have the ability to become every kind of tissue that is needed to build a new human being. Its cells are therefore called "pluripotent", (capable of becoming any of the tissues composing the human body). The new individual that results can then pass on genes inherited from his or her parents to his or her children, and they, in turn, eventually repeat the process. In this way, though the individuals die, the germline transmitted through sexual reproduction goes on over generations. This ensures immortality, as we have defined it, not for the individual, but for the species. So though humans usually die within the span of a century, homo sapiens, as a species, has lived on for a quarter of a million years, or more, and will continue to do so indefinitely.

Through understanding this process anti-aging researchers came to realize, in the last half of the 20th Century, that conditional immortality for individuals should be possible, too, if we can discover a way to introduce pluripotent stem cells into their aging organs or turn their somatic cells back to a pluripotent stage.

Working towards this goal anti-aging researchers, here and abroad, tried various approaches. Some harvested cells from aborted embryos and transplanted them into experimental animals or humans. Others tried removing somatic cells and subjecting them, in culture, to unusual environments to see if this might trigger their return to a pluripotent state.

In early 2014 we read of an experiment in which two researchers, Charles Vicanti of the United States, and Shinga Yamanaka of Japan, succeeded in turning back the aging clocks of human somatic cells to an "induced pluripotent state." They did this by subjecting them, in culture, to a sublethal acidic environment for half an hour. On receiving the history of this late 20th Century research we were reminded of a grid Vivianne had developed more than three decades earlier dealing with immortality. It was the Vacanti, Yamanaka experiment that reminded us of this grid and focused our attention on one of its key words, "Shabbat"

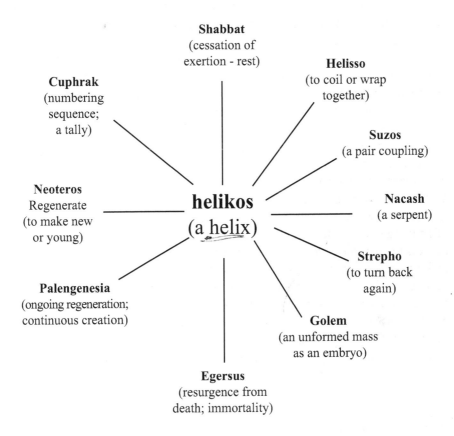

Shabbat
(cessation of
exertion - rest)

Helisso
(to coil or wrap
together)

Cuphrak
(numbering
sequence;
a tally)

Suzos
(a pair coupling)

Neoteros
Regenerate
(to make new
or young)

helikos
(a helix)

Nacash
(a serpent)

Strepho
(to turn back
again)

Palengenesia
(ongoing regeneration;
continuous creation)

Golem
(an unformed mass
as an embryo)

Egersus
(resurgence from
death; immortality)

Vivianne's archeolinguistic analysis of roots and cognates in these Herbrew and Greek words made it clear they contained clues to a methodology employed by our Celestial ancestors to suspend aging and prolong life indefinitely. These clues lay in semantic parallels between their roots and cognates and our current research dealing with halting and even reversing aging and extending the lifespans of experimental animals and ultimately humans.

Two key terms in the grid that coincided with, or paralleled, what modern microbiological research has found are, first, "helikos" (a helix) which is, of course, the structural form of the DNA in our genome. This helical structure, suggested by "helisso" (to roll or coil together), and "suzos" (a pair as in the twin coiled strands of the helix) encode the blueprint for every bodily organ.

Her journey through this semantic grid was an interesting one. It began with "the tree that is in the midst of the garden" - the tree of life. It led, by infrequent excursions into the Hebrew and multitudinous ones in the Greek (immortality is a peripheral idea in Judaism, but a central one in Christianity) to the idea of a center, a core or a matrix. This matrix, "built up from a base" by "pairing" or "coupling" in a "centrifugal" fashion, seemed a confirmation of Vivianne's intuition that the "tree of life" might be a mythic reference to the DNA helix. This reference to a thing "paired" and "coiled" aptly catches the visual configuration of the coiled strands of DNA and is reminiscent of the caduceus - the winged staff with a pair of serpents coiled around it. In the Old Testament Moses lifts up a brazen serpent on a staff to dispel a plague among the children of Israel. From the Greeks to our own day the caduceus has been the emblem of medicine and healing. How is it that cultures so different as the Hebrew and Greek both arrived at the notion that health and life are associated with a helical structure coiled about a matrix? Could it have been a mythic survival of Celestial knowledge infused into our racial consciousness by a primordial extraterrestrial contact?

These Greek terms of the grid come from passages in the New Testament dealing with the idea of immortality. Hebrew terms from the Old Testament such as "cuphrak" and "golem" also have root meanings and cognates which point to microbiological information we regard as 20th and 21st Century discoveries. In some cases whole passages are suggestive of such contemporary scientific knowledge. So we read in Psalm 139, "I will praise thee, for I am fearfully and wonderfully made. Thine eyes did see my substance yet being imperfect, and in thy book all my members were written, which in continuance were fashioned when as yet there was none of them." (Ps 139: 15-16)

If we paraphrase this passage with Watson's and Crick's 20th century discoveries in mind it is plausible to read "genome" for "yet imperfect substance" and "DNA code" for "all the written members". The "continuous fashioning" of what is encoded would then logically be the developmental process that culminates in birth.

Turning again to the grid other significant terms are "cuphrak" (numbering, a tally) suggesting gene sequencing of DNA making up the genome; "strepho" (turning back) and "golem" (resulting in an unformed mass as in the early embryonic state); "palengenesia" (signifying an ongoing process of regeneration and renewal); "neoteros" (denoting return to a youthful state) and "egersus" (resurgence from dying and renewal of life).

Modern scholarship has shown the Psalms were written over a period of several centuries and were principally the work of court poets. The unknown author of this Psalm attributed his work to his king, David, according to the custom of the time.

The literary genius and depth of insight into the human condition, and the spiritual elevation of his song/poems have made them some of the best known and frequently read, recited, or sung of all the collection. They give him a place with such other literary immortals as Dante and Milton, whose greatest works were based on biblical themes.

The one word that is left, "Shabbat," seems too different to be related to the rest, yet has cognates that link it with them. To our surprise archeolinguistic analysis revealed that an elaborate web of Sabbath rituals lies at the very core of the Celestials' methodology for maintaining immortality.

THE SABBATH AND IMMORTALITY

Having been reared in traditional Christian homes we were both, of course, familiar with the idea of sabbath observance as a weekly religious obligation. It is included as one of the Ten Commandments in the Old Testament and is generally regarded, among Jews and Christians, as a day of rest from occupational labor, business conduct and strenuous physical activity. In addition its principal rite is held to be temple or church attendance. With Christians, this is often followed by feasting, family gathering, social visitation and recreational excursions. As such it is a cultural feature of religious life.

The idea that it might also have a different but equally important purpose of halting aging and prolonging life came from the anti-aging immortality grid as a total surprise. And of all the terms in the grid "Shabbat" was the one that provided the most specific information concerning the Celestials' methodology for maintaining immortality.

To begin, the word, itself, has, as its primary root meaning, to desist from exertion or to rest. Taken seriously and to its full import this means not just abstaining from occupational work or business activities but reducing all the body's functions to a minimal level approximating that of sleep. In sleep our conscious awareness shuts down, decision making and planning stops, and bodily action is reduced to automatic functions such as heart beat and breathing and to occasional turning to rest every part of the body. In accord with this "Shabbat" has cognate links to repose and sleep.

The Celestial's weekly 24-hour Sabbath, then, not only involves abstaining from occupational work and usual leisure activities but even from the basic life support activity of eating which imposes work on the digestive system. A 24-hour fast then is also an essential part of the Celestial's Sabbath. Taken together these abstentions permit the life energy saved to be redirected into regenerating tissues that have been depleted by the wear and tear of the preceding week.

Of course, the normal capacity for eight hours of daily sleep has evolved in our species to repair the wear and tear we accumulate during the other sixteen hours. In infancy we sleep much more, because a great deal of our life energy goes into creating new cells for growth. Toward the end of life people often sleep and nap much more, because the mechanisms of repair succumb to aging, and it requires more time to restore the body for the day ahead.

Even during the prime of life, however, the usual seven to nine hours of nightly sleep fails to keep the body in a steady state of efficiency, and its gradual decline manifests itself in the process we call aging. Many of our repair biorhythms are set to a seven-day cycle (for example minor injuries). For this reason many people have set aside a weekly day of rest to catch up on what nightly rest cannot accomplish. This has been arrived at in many cultures around the world. Where it is practiced, however, it is insufficient to offset the gradual decline of bodily functions.

It follows from these facts that if this customary seventh day of rest could be observed as twenty four hours of the kind of rest we normally achieve in sleep, with all life energies not needed for sustaining life used for repair and regeneration, it would slow, or even reverse, many aspects of aging. This does actually occur in cases of serious illness or injury where total bed rest, often involving continuous dozing or coma, combined with intravenous feeding, are the means of saving almost all life energy for repair and restoration as a means of preventing death.

The inclusion of fasting in the Sabbath forces the body to turn for energy to fat reserves in the cells and flushes out wastes left over from normal metabolism. This produces a more acidic state in the body, precisely the condition Vacanti and Yamanaka found turned cultured somatic cells back to an embryonic, pluripotent state.

If a general increase in acidity of the body has a similar affect on somatic cells, in situ, then the 24-hour fast could well be the most potent anti-aging factor in the entire regimen of the Celestials' sabbath. It would be a principal factor in the renewal of aging tissues and maintaining an ageless continuance of life.

Further contemporary anti-aging research has shown that calorie restriction, which a fast accomplishes, is also one of the most promising ways to extend lifespan in experimental animals, and evidence is mounting that it does the same in humans.

One recent 2012 study of calorie restriction in rhesus monkeys, conducted by University of Wisconsin scientists, showed calorie restricted dieting by adult monkeys produced a sharp reduction in age related mortality. A non-restricted control group had a 2.9 times greater rate of death from the same causes.

Archeolingustic analysis of Bible texts relating to health and life extension make even stronger claims for fasting. Writing of the value of fasting another Hebrew prophet, poet, and author of the last part of the book of Isaiah declares, "Is this not the fast that I have chosen? To loose the bands of wickedness, to undo the heavy burdens, and . . .to let the oppressed go free. Then shall thy light break forth as the morning, and thine health shall spring forth speedily . . .and thou shalt be like a watered garden and like a spring of water, whose waters fail not." (Is: 58:6-11)

In the next verse he goes on and adds "and they that shall be of thee shall build up the old waste places: thou shalt raise up the foundation of many generations and thou shalt be called the repairer of the breech." (Is: 12-13) On the other hand, Sabbath keeping as it is generally practiced by Judeo-Christian believers, does not achieve these two necessary conditions of total rest and avoidance of food intake for twenty-four hours. Bible texts relating to immortality do suggest, however, that the Celestials weekly Sabbath observance accomplishes both goals, and, as a weekly protocol, is the first of three ceremonial regimens that form the web of "Sabbath rituals" we referred to earlier.

The second ritual ceremony is a monthly Sabbath, or Sabbath "moon," which is more elaborate. Biblical references to it lead, etymologically, to root meanings relating it to the tree of life in the midst of God's paradise. Chief among these are the ideas of being "coiled," "wrapped," a "matrix" and even a "helix." Such a cluster of meanings inevitably involves the image of Watson's and Crick's model of the DNA helix-two intertwined strands "coiled" or "wrapped" around a "matrix." This cluster of meanings makes it evident that in addition to continuous regeneration of organs by turning their cells back to a pluripotent state in a weekly day of rest something more is needed to halt the aging process. This is the ongoing editing of the cellular DNA, itself, which is subject to breakage, transpositions of chromosomes, and activation of aging genes as cellular reproduction is repeated. This monthly protocol seems to involve some form of nucleic acid editing therapy combined with elaborate cleansing and detoxification procedures. So we read again in Isaiah—"And it shall come to pass, that from one new moon to another, and from one Sabbath to another, shall all flesh come to worship before me ..." (Isaiah 66:23). And John the Revelator tells us that the tree of life, in the Celestials' holy city, yields its fruit "every month." Its "leaves," he says, are for the "healing of the nations" (Revelation 22:2). And again Ezekiel speaks of a holy city with a tree "whose leaf shall not fade." It brings forth "new fruit according to his months" and its leaf is "for medicine" (Ezekiel 47:12). These references to a "fruit" (which we have already seen) may mean nucleic acids) that heals, restores and renews makes it clear that the new-moon Sabbath is a rejuvenation ritual. Even at our own early level of research we have a new technology known as "gene editing" (or "crispr",) being developed at London's Frances Crick Institute, University of California at Berkeley, Harvard University, and elsewhere which promises to revolutionize healing and enable reversal of aging. In fact Professor George Church, of Harvard Medical School, has already used crispr to reverse aging in mice and predicts it will accomplish age reversal in humans within the next five years. It seems likely the "fruit" mentioned here is a more advanced form of delivery for a gene editing technology.

The third ritual is a periodic, empire-wide holy day emphasizing fundamental spiritual values of the Celestials. It is pictured impressively in the book of Revelation as penned by a first century mystic known only as John. He portrays it as he envisions it will be celebrated on the return of the Celestials; described in apocalyptic symbolism and imagery that make an awe-inspiring climax to the Bible's final book.

So he writes "and behold, and I heard the voice of many . . .and the number of them was ten thousand times ten thousand and thousands of thousands. And every creature which is in heaven, and on the earth, and under the earth, and such as in them heard I , saying blessing and honour and glory, and power be unto him that siteth upon the throne and unto the Lamb forever and ever." (Rev 5:11 and 13) In its entirety this texture of Sabbath rituals defines a life style that programs aging therapy and provides biological, social and spiritual supports for maintaining immortality.

"A CROWN OF LIFE"

One other step is essential to ensuring immortality. This is the prevention of disease, for disease, even more than aging, can lead directly to death. The Bible makes numerous references to a device called the "crown of life." So James assures those who endure temptation that they will receive "the crown of life, which the Lord hath promised to them that love him" (James 1:12). John the Revelator also tells how the "first and the last" says, "be thou faithful unto death, and I will give thee a crown of life" (Revelation 2:8, 10) Evidently this is more than a figurative reference to immortal life, itself, for its etymology leads, not to the idea of eternality, but to moderation, or balance.

Specialists in preventive medicine are coming increasingly to recognize that disease is not a natural state of affairs in the human body. It gains a foothold only when the body's normal functions and defenses are lacking or interrupted. The maintenance of these functions and defenses implies a vital balance-a balance biologists call "homeostasis." As long as perfect homeostasis is maintained, disease processes cannot establish themselves. So one leader in preventive medicine observes: "When all organs are working in harmony, the body machinery is in balance and we have perfect health."

The "crown of life" appears, then, to be a type of biofeedback device which is worn on the head to regulate homeostasis. By monitoring the body and sending appropriate input to the brain it signals release of neurotransmitters, enzymes and hormones for maintaining a steady state of homeostasis – a state in which disease cannot gain a foothold. Our own medical technologies have accomplished significant first steps in this direction with pacemakers and devices to monitor and transdermally deliver biologicals and medications as needed to maintain healthy bodily function.

"I DON'T WANT TO LIVE FOREVER"

To some the idea of immortality is a doubtful boon. They remember the nightmare state of advanced aging described by Shakespeare as "sans teeth, sans eyes, sans taste, sans everything" and say, "No thank you!" Some even pretend to prefer the hedonistic philosophy that glorifies mortality. "Live fast, die young, and make a beautiful corpse" is their motto.

Yet, in the deepest recesses of the human mind lurks a yearning for immortality which will not be denied. It expresses itself in our clinging to life, in our cult of youth and in our need to live on through children, achievements and fame.

Early in the last century the novelist James Hilton captured people's imagination with his story of Shangri-La, the quiet Asiatic Eden just beyond the lost horizon. There monks lived to be hundreds of years old, and princesses remained beautiful young maidens into their nineties.

The Bible tells us a Shangri-La far exceeding the fantasies of James Hilton will come to Earth with the return of the Celestials. It will offer youth and conditional immortality to everyone who meets its citizenship requirements. Those who don't want to live forever will not be forced to do so. But to all who relish the prospect of unending youth and life it extends the invitation with which John the Revelator closes the Bible: "... the Spirit and the bride say, Come. And let him that heareth say, Come. And let him that is athirst come. And whosoever will, let him take the water of life freely" (Revelation 22:17).

And to newly adopted citizens of the Celestials' earthly Shangri-La this invitation will offer limitless vistas of enjoyment, adventure and achievement. For

them the passing centuries and millennia will not bring enfeeblen
They will realize the dreams most of us have had about what we w
own dreams may suggest a sampling of the lifestyles that would be
this heritage of conditional immortality becomes a reality.)

We would start by spending a few centuries visiting all the be
on Earth we have never had a chance to see. We could sightsee ar.
play in all the capitals and resorts we've read about and never visited.   we
find someplace specially interesting we could stay awhile and enjoy their cuisine,
participate in their customs, rituals and amenities and in between these excursions
there would be an almost unending range of things we could do at home; campus
or online learning, artistic and athletic avocations, recreational hobbies or even
taking up entirely new careers we have always dreamed of.

Social life could be carried on with our favorite people from the past or newly
acquainted contemporaries or by inviting, for reunions and celebrating holidays,
relatives from our whole family tree. We could enhance our spiritual life by
visiting interplanetary centers of worship, participating in their rituals, sharing
their celebrations and volunteering for their outreach missions and charities. And
for those with more adventurous natures, challenges could be found in climbing
some splendorous peak on a distant earth-like exoplanet or sailing an exotically
beautiful sea in some out-of-the-way corner of the galaxy.

In fact, whenever we begin to imagine all the things we might do in a celestially
provided future it seems we would only be able to make a beginning of it during
the first 10,000 years. But that wouldn't really matter since conditional immortality
provides an open-ended life span that could far exceed that. As a familiar old hymn
from our childhoods so aptly puts it, "we'll have a grand homecoming week the
first 10,000 years!" *"when we've been there 10,000 years*
bright shining as the sun ...." →

WE GO CELESTIAL!

And with the Celestials' homecoming to Earth the future of this planet will be
merged with their own timeless destiny. An unending reign of peace, justice and
righteousness will begin. Those who have proved themselves "heirs according to
the promise" will receive full citizenship in the Celestials' intergalactic federation.
As Celestial heirs they will live out their heritage of immortality through endless
eons of time.

And as they begin that glorious homecoming week they may well lift their
voices in another hymn, remembered from pre-Celestial days, to the Redeemer
who made it all possible:

And have the bright, immensities
Received our risen Lord,
Where light years frame the Pleiades, and point Orion's sword? Do
flaming suns his footsteps trace, through corridors sublime, The Lord of
interstellar space and conqueror of time?

EPILOGUE

This is the story of our Celestial heritage as told in the Bible. Its reality is supported by a variety of evidences – evidences from such widely scattered fields as astrobiology, etymology, genetics, quantum physics, parapsychology and futurology.

It may be objected that we have not proved our case – that these "evidences" establish only a tissue of possibilities or, at best, probabilities. To such objections we can only point out that the ultimate "truths" men and women live by have never been a matter of proof. We cannot prove that all men were created equal or endowed, by their Creator, with "certain unalienable rights." We cannot prove that peace is better than war or freedom than slavery. These are matters of moral commitment and living faith.

So it is with our Space Age interpretation of ancient religious "truths." For some our 21st Century view of the Bible's challenge and promises may open eyes of faith which other interpretations have left closed. If it does its effort will be vindicated. For living faith needs no proof. It brings with it the substance which "proof" seeks.

I do not need to prove to myself that I exist if I already do exist. I do not need to prove that the Spirit exists if, with the Apostle Paul, I can say, it "liveth in me." And if it does dwell in me it is not necessary to prove a heritage of eternal life is possible. As Jesus pointed out, he that believeth already "hath everlasting life." Living faith, not proof, then is the goal of valid interpretation. And if our Space Age interpretation is to be vindicated it will not be by evidence but by the living faith of those it inspires. Like the writer of Hebrews they will understand that sublime paradox which affirms that "... faith is the substance of things hoped for, the evidence of things not seen."

APPENDIX:

CALCULATIONS FOR
"A THOUSAND YEARS
IS AS A DAY."

THE EQUATION IS $T_A = \dfrac{T_B}{\sqrt{1 - \dfrac{V^2}{C^2}}}$

T_A Time read on A's clock by A

T_B Time read on B's clock by A

V   Velocity of B's ship as measured by A (A assumes he is standing still).

C   Speed of light (taken as 186,282 miles/second)

At 99.999999999625 % of the speed of light, B's clock only moves 24 hours in 1,000 years of A's time.

That is at 186,281.999999302 miles per second.

Or .000000698 miles per second less than the speed of light.

$$= .0025 \text{ miles/hour}$$

$$= 13. \text{ feet/hour}$$

SELECTED BIBLIOGRAPHY

Bernhard Anderson, *Rediscovering the Bible* (New York: Association Press, 1951)

Isaac Asimov, *Is Anyone There?* (New York: Ace Books, 1967).

Bernard J. Bamberger, *The Story of Judaism* (New York: Schocken, 1957).

J. B. Billings, *Your God Is Too Small* (New York: Macmillan, 1955).

Joseph H. Blumrich, *Spaceship of Ezekiel*, (Bantam Publishers, N.Y., 1974)

D. Bohm, *Quantum Theory*. Quoted in Koestler, *Roots of Coincidence*. 1973

C. L. Brace and Ashley Montagu, *Man's Evolution* (New York: Macmillan, 1965).

Raymond E. Brown, *An Introduction to the New Testament* (Doubleday, N.Y. 1987)

Rudolf Bultmann, *Kerygma and Myth* (Guildford and London: Billing and Sons, 1964) .

Rudolf Bultmann, *Jesus and the Word* (New York: Scribner, 1958).

Sir Cyril Burt, quoted in *The Country of the Blind*, in Arthur Koestler, *The Roots of Coincidence* (New York: Random House, 1972).

Joseph Campbell, *The Masks of God Vol. I: Primitive Mythology* (New York: Viking, 1959).

Fritjof Capra, *The Tao of Physics* (New York: Bantam, 1977).

Pierre Tielhard de Chardin, *Hymn of the Universe* (New York: Harper and Row, 1960).

The Book of Jubilees or the Little Genesis, tr. R. H. Charles (London: Adam and Charles Black, 1902).

Maurice Chatelain, *Our Ancestors Came from Outer Space* (Garden City, N.Y.: Doubleday, 1978).

Arthur C. Clarke, *Profiles of the Future* (New York: Harper and Row, 1973).

Richard Dawkins, *The God Delusion*, (Houghton Mifflin Co., N.Y., 2006)

Max Dimont, *Jews, God and History* (New York: Simon and Schuster, 1962).

Adrian Dobbs, *The Feasibility of a Physical Theory of ESP.* Quoted in Koestler, Roots of Coincidence. 1972

Theodosius Dobzhansky, *Mankind Evolving* (New York: Bantam, 1969).

Stephen Dole, *Habitable Planets for Man* (New York: Elsevier Publishing Co., 1975).

Bart D. Ehrman, *How Jesus Became God*, Harper One, (N.Y., 2014)

K. A. Ericke, "The Extraterrestrial Imperative," Bulletin of Atomic Scientists. Quoted in Berry, *Next Ten Thousand Years.*

Lori Ann Ferrill, *The Bible and the People* (Yale University Press, New Haven and London, 2008)

Arthur Ford, *The Life Beyond Death* (New York: Putnam, 1971).

Sigmund Freud, *Moses and Monotheism* (New York: Vintage, 1939).

Mohandas K. Gandhi, *Satyagraha* (Ahmedabad: Navajwan, 1951).

Amit Goswami, with Richard E. Reel and Maggie Goswami, *The Self Aware Universe*, (Penguin Putman, Inc., New York, 1995.)

William K. Hartman, Mars, The Mysterious Landscape of the Red Planet, (Workman publishing, N.Y., 2003)

Steven Hawking, *A Brief History of Time*, (Amazon Kindle, 1998).

Gerald S. Hawkins, *Stonehenge Decoded* (Garden City, N.Y.: Doubleday, 1965).

Allen J. Hynek, *The UFO Experience: A Scientific Enquiry* (New York: Ballantine, 1972) .

Journal of Astronautics and Aeronautics, quoted in Allen J, Hynek, The UFO Experience, 1972.

Sir James Jeans, *The Mysterious Universe* (Cambridge, England: The Macmillan Co., 1937).

Shafica Karagulla, *Energy Fields and Medical Diagnosis.* Quoted in Nicholas Ragush, The Human Aura (New York: Berkeley, 1974).

Jacob Katzman, *The Jewish Influence on Civilization* (New York: Block, 1974).

Michio Kaku, *Physics of the Impossible*, Doubleday, (Random House, N.Y. 2008)

Soren Kierkegaard, *Purity of Heart* (New York: Harper Torch, 1956).

Martin Luther King, Jr., *Why We Can't Wait* (New York: Harper and Row, 1963).

Lawerence M. Krauss, *A Universe From Nothing*, (Free Press, N.Y., 2014)

Bjorn Kurten, *Not from the Apes*, (New York: Pantheon, 1972).

Arthur Koestler, *The Roots of Coincidence* (New York: Random House, 1972).

William Johnson, *Silent Music* (New York: Harper and Row, 1974).

Desmond Morris, *The Naked Ape* (New York: McGraw Hill, 1967).

On the Biological Essence of the Kirlian Effect: quoted in Thelma Moss, *The Probability of the Impossible* (New York: J.P. Tarcher, 1975).

Richard A. Muller, *Now, The Physics of Time*, (W.W. Norton, & Co., N.Y., 2016)

Edward Murray, *Enoch Restitutus* (London: J. G. and F. Rivington, 1836).

Adam Nicolson, *God's Secretaries*, Harper Collins Publishing, N.Y., 2003

Gerald K. O'Neill, "The Colonization of Space" *Physics Today* Quoted in Adrian Berry, *The Next Ten Thousand Years* (New York: New American Library, 1975).

Sheila Ostrander and Lynn Schroeder, *Psychic Discoveries Behind the Iron Curtain* (Englewood Cliffs, N.J.: Prentice-Hall, 1970).

Jaroslav Pelican, *Whose Bible Is It*, (Penguin Inc. NY, NY. 2005)
H. St. J. B. Philby, *Arabia* (New York: Scribner, 1930).

Lisa Randall, *Warped Passages* (Harper Collins, N.Y., 2003)

J. B. Rhine and J. G. Pratt, *Parapsychology, Frontier Science of the Mind* (Springfield, Ill: Charles C Thomas, 1957).

Bertrand Russell, *Mysticism and Logic* (New York: Anchor, 1951).

Carl Sagan, *The Cosmic Connection* (Garden City, N.Y.: Doubleday, 1973)

Carl Sagan, *Other Worlds* (New York: Bantam, 1975).

Albert Schweitzer, *The Quest of the Historical Jesus* (London: A. C. Black, 1910) .

John L. Sherill, *They Speak With Other Tongues* (New York: McGraw-Hill Inc., 1964)

I. Shklovskii and Carl Sagan, *Intelligent Life in the Universe* (San Francisco: Holden-Day, 1966).

Morton Smith, *Jesus the Magician* (New York: Harper and Row, 1977).

William Smith, *Smith's Bible Dictionary* (Old Tappan, N.J.: Revell, 1967).

James Strong, *Exhaustive Concordance of the Bible*, (Thomas Nelson Publishing, N.Y. 1990)

V. A. *Firsoff, Life, Mind and Galaxies,* Oliver and Boyd, (Edinburgh and London: 1967).

Williston Walker, Richard N. Harrison, David W. Lotz, Robert T. Handy A *History of the Christian Church,* (Scribner and Sons, Manchester Publishing, N.Y., 1985)

Joseph Weiner and Bernard Campbell, *Climbing Man's Family Tree*, eds. T. McCown and H. Kennedy (Englewood Cliffs, N.J.: Prentice-Hall, 1972).

E.O. Wilson, *Evolution*, (Belkins Press of Harvard University Press, Cambridge, M.A., 2009)

E.O. Wilson, *The Social Conquest of Earth*, (Harper Collins, Whiskers, N.Y., 2012)

Herman Wouk, *This Is My God* (Garden City, N.Y.: Doubleday, 1961).

The Secrets of Enoch, in *Lost Books of the Bible and the Forgotten Books of Eden* (Cleveland: Collins and World, 1948) .

Made in the USA
San Bernardino, CA
12 March 2020